Leisureguy's
Guide to Gourmet Shaving

the Double-Edge Way

By
Michael Ham
'Leisureguy'

POGONOTOMY PRESS
MONTEREY CALIFORNIA

EDITION 7.0 – MAY 2015
ISBN-13: 978-1511515832
ISBN-10: 151151583X

To EH, WHO HAS FOUND IT USEFUL
To GM, CM, BH, CH, AND JH, WHO SOMEDAY WILL READ IT
To KV, FOR THE PHRASE "GOURMET SHAVING"
To K★, FOR TAKING UP WETSHAVING
AND, OF COURSE, TO THE WIFE, FOR LISTENING TO ALL THESE
DISCOVERIES WITH EXEMPLARY FORBEARANCE.

Contents

Preface to the Seventh Edition

YOU are reading a book written through iterative refinement, this being the seventh iteration, greatly expanded and improved compared to the modest first edition. I first encountered iterative refinement (aka iterative development) as an explicit technique when I began programming in Forth, a programming language that encourages rapid iteration: create a new command, execute it, modify it as needed, and execute it again. (In Forth, you program by adding commands to the language, each command built from those previously defined.) As you use each new command, you continue polishing and improving it as experience dictates. As I wrote at the time, "Hindsight is powerful. Use it early and often." This book has benefited from iterative hindsight based on many trials and much experimentation. I trust it will serve you well.

One example of hindsight in action: this edition is titled as a guide to shaving with a double-edge razor. "Gourmet" is used to emphasize that shaving can provide enjoyment, but it was also unfortunately vague and some bought the book in hopes of learning how to shave with a straight razor, which I do not cover. My hope is that the new and more explicit title will help potential readers better understand the focus of the book.

I've seen considerable change over the years of writing and revising the book: more vendors, more forums, more new razors, more men using a double-edge (DE) razor and true lather. The remarkable growth in traditional shaving with a DE razor gets its energy and impetus from a promise fulfilled: DE shaves really *are* better, and cheaper, and actually enjoyable.

The rapid growth of the wet-shaving movement, using single-blade razors—double-edge (DE) safety razors, the focus of this book, and also straight razors (SR) and single-edge (SE) safety razors—is due to several factors:

- Increasing awareness by men of their skin's health and health issues.
- Increasing visibility and availability of traditional shaving tools: more vendors and more products, including razors.
- Increasing prices of multiblade cartridges and canned foam, coupled with an economy that has required many to find cheaper lifestyles.

Over the past couple of years the third reason has come into high relief as the global economy stuttered and faltered, and in this edition I identify many good low-cost options for razors, brushes, soaps, and shaving creams.

I've observed that men who have shaved only with cartridge razors and canned foam frequently express a fairly firm conviction that traditional shaving would be "too much hassle." However, that conviction is based on their expectations rather than any actual experience, and we find that experience very often contradicts expectations—which is why the scientific method is invaluable.

Aristotle, for example, expected that, given two objects, the heavier will fall faster than the lighter. That makes perfect sense: if you're holding a bowling ball and a golf ball, one in each hand, it is obvious that the bowling ball will fall faster: it's *heavier*. Duh.

Galileo's demonstration that unequal weights fall at the same rate shows how experience can contradict even those expectations that make sense. Aristotle was reasonable in his expectation, and since the outcome he predicted made sense, the idea of subjecting it to an actual test did not occur to him or (for almost 2000 years) to anyone else. Indeed, we all carry around many ideas and notions that make sense to us, so we don't test them. (For a clear example of an expectation that makes sense but fails utterly when subjected to experience, consider the double-slit experiment in physics.)

We all tend to make judgments about events we have yet to experience (that is, we all tend to jump to conclusions) despite often[1] having had the experience of dreading an event that turns out to be not so bad and perhaps even enjoyable, or of eagerly anticipating an event that falls flat or turns out even worse (blind dates, for a notorious example). Young children often provide clear examples of the error of not testing expectations: they *know*—even without tasting it—that a particular food tastes awful and often are unwilling to compare the expected taste with the *actual* taste.

So we make decisions based on our expectations even though numerous psychological studies have demonstrated that we are extremely poor at predicting what future experiences will be like for us, and in particular, we are poor at predicting what will make us happy. Given the evidence, we should know that we should always test expectations because they often prove false. But gut feelings are difficult to ignore even when we know they're frequently wrong.

Moreover, our expectations are subject to a strong confirmation bias: we can quickly think of reasons and examples that suggest that a (preconceived) expectation is correct, but—since we have already embraced the expectation—it's much harder to think of reasons or examples that indicate that it's wrong. However, once experience or experiment has proved the expectation false, then hindsight, that powerful tool, immediately uncovers *many* reasons and examples that show why the expectation was wrong.

The phenomenon is familiar to any DE shaver who discusses shaving with someone still using multiblade cartridges and canned foam. Quite often, a man who has yet to try traditional DE shaving has much "knowledge" about what DE shaving is like, which is why he's not interested in trying it. For example, he already knows that a multiblade cartridge gives a smoother result, that traditional shaving is tedious, that in using a DE razor you cut yourself all the time, that using a brush to make lather from a shaving soap or shaving cream is a time-consuming chore, that he would hate traditional shaving, that multiblade cartridges are better for his skin, and so on. (Experience has repeatedly demonstrated that, for almost all men, each of those suppositions is false.)

Men arrive at those conclusions much as Aristotle did: the conclusions make sense (to them). They *know* they won't like traditional shaving, just as the toddler *knows* that a food will have a bad taste. Since a Fusion cartridge costs 40 times what a DE blade can cost ($3.60 vs. 9¢), they believe the Fusion cartridge must be *much* better—perhaps not 40 times better, but certainly significantly and noticeably better. Moreover, the Fusion is a newer design, and it's commonly believed that "newer" equals "better" (thus advertising's great love for the word "New," second only to its love for "Free"). And canned foam is more modern, easier (the only skill required is the ability to push a button), and more expensive than dopey old shaving soap and a brush. That means, to some, that using canned foam must be better than the alternative: brushing a shaving soap to make a (warm, fragrant, skin-friendly) lather in 10 seconds or so—though in return for the 10 seconds of work you gain the tactile and olfactory pleasures of brushing your face with a soft, warm, lather-filled brush, enjoying the fragrance that wafts from it. It may seem quicker to squirt foam from a can and smear it on your beard with your hand, but you save only a few seconds and you lose a lot.

Learning occurs when you *try* things, to see what they are *really* like. The cartridge shaver's opinions about traditional wetshaving are often *extremely* clear, but the productive step is to test those expectations through gaining some actual experience: buying a starter kit and trying it out. (Dan Gilbert gave a couple of interesting TED talks[2], one on happiness and one on why we make bad decisions. Both talks describe the unreliability of expectations.)

The direction of commercial innovation is always to reduce—and ideally to remove—skill requirements. As with canned foam and cartridge razors, businesses always seek ways to make it easier to use their products—for example, heat-and-serve meals allow one to avoid learning how to cook.

Making things easy to accomplish does have advantages. As Roger Fisher and William Ury point out in their extremely useful book *Getting to Yes: How to Negotiate Agreement without Giving In*[3], if you want a horse to jump a fence, you make the fence as low as possible. Stated generally: if you want someone to do something, remove all possible obstacles, thus making it easier to do. Vending machines went from requiring exact change to making change, then to accepting paper currency, and now even accepting credit cards.

Another example they give is a "yessable" proposition: a proposition in which all implementation details have been worked out so that the person whose approval is required has only to say yes to make it happen. Many do not grasp this principle. I recall, for example, a person I managed who wanted a new computer—but expected me to do all the work of filling out the appropriate forms, writing the justification, and so on. As William Oncken puts it in his useful book *Managing Management Time*[4], he tried to put the monkey on my back. I helped him learn how to offer a yessable proposition by having him complete all the preliminary work himself so my contribution was simply to sign the finished requisition. He did the work, I signed it, and he got his new computer.

But easy accomplishment can have a high cost. A person who too frequently finds ways to avoid learning new skills eventually will lose the skill of learning skills. Carol Dweck, a research psychologist at Stanford University, describes this outcome in the book *Mindset*[5], her account of her research about learning and what her experiments revealed. People who have not learned the skill of learning skills (or who through disuse have lost it) often feel that they *cannot* learn, that mastery comes from an in-born talent, and if they try something and fail awkwardly, then that means they lack that talent and thus cannot learn it. I highly recommend the book for its fascinating and invaluable insights, and I particularly recommend it to parents and to students.

By always going for a canned solution and turnkey approach, one becomes less a participant and more an observer. The heat-and-serve meal may provide physical nourishment, but one's spirit (and self-esteem) are undernourished by relying on such approaches. By demanding nothing from you, making something easy also tends to make it boring, tedious, and ultimately a chore. In contrast, things that requires focused attention and skill—particularly skill involving our hands, because of our primate nature—capture our interest, and the more skill we acquire, the more interesting they become. We derive on-going satisfaction from increasing our mastery of a skill, and daily pleasure in exercising the skill: almost everyone enjoys doing something he or she can do skillfully. Those pleasures are completely lost to those who avoid the skill altogether. So it is with shaving.

I continue to find great satisfaction and enjoyment in using products made by small businesses: soaps, shaving creams, razors, brushes, and aftershaves made from excellent materials on a small scale. Often, the quality of these products exceeds that of products from mainline commercial manufacturers, while the prices are often much less. (Those listed in this book I've used and found good.)

4

That's the appeal of artisanal products: a better product made with better ingredients at a lower price *and* a backstory of its development and creation, together with some degree of personal connection to the artisan who made it. Commercial products just can't compete—not on price, not on performance, and certainly not on emotional satisfaction. It's also pleasant to use a product that isn't advertised everywhere and indeed is unknown to most people. It's like knowing a secret shared by few. (For more on this sort of pleasure, read Robert Louis Stevenson's wonderful essay *The Lantern Bearers*[6].)

One problem that can arise when helping someone learn traditional shaving is that sometimes—and, I gather, not infrequently—a man is uncomfortable in being instructed by his brother (or his father or his son). If that's the case, presenting him a copy of this book can smooth the learning process. It's easier to accept information and advice from a third party uninvolved in the relationship because relationship issues don't arise.

Once he has learned the basics, however, he and his more expert family member(s) generally enjoy sharing information and new discoveries—for example, things they learn about various blades, brushes, razors, and soaps. Since each can contribute, none feel instructed. Still, a competitive aspect may still be present: who gets the best shave, for example. ☺

I've added quite a bit to this edition. As I've finished each previous edition, I've thought, "Well, that does it. Complete at last." And then, of course, I learn more, new vendors and products appear, and a new edition begins. But at this point, perhaps it's time to end the revisions and leave the book alone. Some link-rot is inevitable over time and new products will emerge, but search engines and forums can keep you updated. I turn that responsibility over to them and to you.

Michael Ham
Pacific Grove, California
gourmetshaving@gmail.com

Preface to the Sixth Edition

I REALIZED recently that this book might have been more accurately titled *The Epicure's Guide to Shaving*, for Epicurus[7] would surely approve making necessary tasks enjoyable. He thought that chance encounters of atoms falling through the void, randomly interacting, produced—after much time—us and the world in which we live. In his view we cease to exist when we die, while the atoms of our body continue to tumble along through time and space.

Because Epicurus believed that life is a one-shot deal, he made enjoying life a high priority. A dissolute lifestyle tends to have highly unpleasant consequences, so it makes sense to seek enjoyment first in the small things of life, which is what we mostly encounter day to day. Learning new ideas and mastering new skills are examples of activities that provide enjoyment without harm.

Take, as a random example, the morning shave: an Epicurean who shaves will seek a way to derive enjoyment from the task: to spend his (limited) time doing things he doesn't enjoy makes no sense when he could instead do them enjoyably. Moreover, an enjoyable task requires little willpower: you are drawn to the task rather than having to push yourself. Indeed, a task can even be restorative and energizing; rather than draining you, a task approached properly can provide both enjoyment and a satisfying sense of fulfillment.

The psychologist Mihály Csíkszentmihályi wrote several books on a mental state he termed "flow": a focused, absorbing, satisfying involvement in what is happening in the moment[8]. So another way to state the Epicurean position is that one should arrange his or her life to maximize the opportunities for flow to occur. Flow is a mental experience, so introspection combined with an attitude that encourages the enjoyment of small things—to *look* for joy, and to think about how to find more occasions of joy—is an obvious step.

This book is my contribution to an Epicurean lifestyle: the book offers a way to make a necessary chore enjoyable. But don't stop just at shaving.

I note that traditional wetshaving continues to grow rapidly:

- New on-line vendors of traditional shaving products continue to appear. The vendor list now has more than ~~120~~ [now 150] entries.

- On-line forums devoted to shaving continue to increase in number and in membership. Reddit's Wicked_Edge grew from 3,000 members six months ago to 16,000 as I write [and is well over 70,000 today, two years later]—and continues to grow rapidly.
- Not only are established manufacturers introducing new safety razors, we're also seeing *new* manufacturers: Above the Tie, iKon, Los Angeles Shaving Company, Maggard, Western Razors, and Wolfman Razors, for example, offer top-quality razors. Some time back I wrote an article in Sharpologist about the implications of this phenomenon[9].
- The price of vintage safety razors on eBay continues to increase, which shows that demand continues to increase (supply being fixed).

All this is evidence that the number of men who have decided to abandon expensive, heavily advertised shaving tools for the pleasure, comfort, and economy of traditional shaving is growing rapidly. I hope you'll join us.

Although the total number of traditional wetshaving vendors has increased, some vendors have closed their doors since the previous edition. Many of the vendors mentioned in the Appendix are small operations that depend totally on one or two people. Naturally enough, such businesses are vulnerable to disruption or sudden shutdown from any number of causes: health problems or the passing of the proprietor or a family member, or financial exigencies (or the opposite: the fine on-line store Razor and Brush had to close when its owner, who ran the business as a sideline, was promoted to a more demanding job), or for other reasons.

These businesses, which often offer exceptional handcrafted products of high quality, thus have a certain cherry-blossom quality: they bloom briefly and their products may be available only for a relatively short time. I now treasure irreplaceable soaps, creams, and equipment that I purchased only a few years ago from businesses now gone, never to return.

If you like any products offered by these artisans and small-business owners, buy promptly. You will get something that you can use and enjoy, possibly long after the business is gone. Shop early and often and stock up for your future needs—and when you're thinking about gifts, consider how a good brush and a shaving soap or shaving cream can improve anyone's shave.

I thank the shavers who have suggested ideas and improvements for the book. Special thanks to betelgeux, cathartica, greyzer, HeyRememberThatTime, mpperry, Dirty Texan, Hyzerflip, NoHelmet, Papander, psywiped, wicked_VD, do_not_follow, Release-the-Kraken, JustHereForTheTips, and others of the Wicked_Edge community for their insights and interest. They have increased my understanding with their questions (especially those from newbies) and their discoveries.

Preface

FOR most men, shaving is a daily yet unappealing task: a routine at best, and more often a tedious, boring, hateful chore. A surprising number of men believe that they have "sensitive skin" on their face (but nowhere else) because the tug-and-cut action of the common multiblade shaving cartridge and the pressure these men exert on the razor trying to get a close shave, together with inadequate beard preparation from a pressurized can of dry, foamy shaving mix and a tendency to use the cartridge well beyond its useful life[10] (because of the cost of replacing it), produces skin irritation, razor burn, razor bumps, and in-grown hairs.

You can avoid all that: the daily shaving task can easily be transformed into a pleasurable ritual that leaves the shaver feeling renewed and pampered and his skin healthy. All it takes are the right tools and a little practice.

This book introduces the shaver to the world of traditional wetshaving: the shaving brush, exquisitely formulated shaving soaps and creams, and well-designed safety razors—readily available and still being manufactured—that use a double-edged blade to provide a smooth (and enjoyable) shave.

Moreover, the blades (which usually last around a week) are much cheaper than cartridges—even if the shaver continues to use his cartridges beyond their effective lifespan (to postpone the expense of replacing them).

The learning curve is short and the enjoyment immense, so start today. You can jump to the section on the recommended beginner's kit, but I suggest you first read through the book: as always is the case, your choices require balancing various tradeoffs, and you may be unfamiliar with those involved in wetshaving.

A shave, like Gaul, is divided into three parts:

1. **Prep** – Preparation is everything you do before picking up the razor. Prep usually involves first a shower, and then at the sink at least a shaving brush along with a shaving cream or shaving soap.
2. **Shave** – Once prep is complete, you pick up the razor and shave; this step involves only the razor and the blade (which is not so simple as you think, as you'll learn later) with the focus on pressure and angle.

3. **Aftershave** – Once you rinse and put away the razor, you do the final steps, generally involving an alum block and an aftershave and occasionally, should you get a nick, a styptic. Aftershaves come in many forms (splashes, balms, creams, gels, etc.), and your choice of aftershave may vary with the season if you live where winter's cold.

In explaining how to shave I shall follow the above sequence, discussing the tools and techniques appropriate to each step. (You'll also find a chapter on skin issues—acne, razor bumps, in-growns, dry skin, and so on.) Before beginning the shave, however, I'll provide some background to establish the context.

Note that you might want to move to traditional wetshaving in two steps. In Step 1 you master prep, as described above, but continue to use your cartridge razor. You learn the grain of your beard and how to prepare it for a good shave—this in itself will greatly improve your shave. Then later, once that is in hand, you take Step 2: get double-edged blades and a safety razor and learn to use those. (Some readers may even want to take a third step: to get a straight razor and master that kind of shave. I include a brief section on taking that step, but straight-razor shaving is not treated in this book.)

Men on a student budget will immediately see that this two-step approach splits the cost into two small purchases instead of one larger one: Step 1 can come from one month's paycheck and Step 2 from the following month's. Moreover, the two-step approach allows the novice shaver to learn only one set of skills at a time: first prep, then shaving. The chapter "Recommendations for a beginner" thus uses this two-step approach.

This book is the culmination of much experimentation and trial-and-error, along with many suggestions and contributions from others. All quotations are, of course, used with the permission of the authors, and I hope their insights help you as they have helped me.

ONE

What this is

THIS book is for men whose shaves fail to provide enjoyment or who are just learning to shave. It describes a method of shaving that transforms a daily chore into a pleasurable ritual. It's a beginner's guide to wetshaving: how to shave with a safety razor and double-edged blade and not hurt yourself. (A safety razor that uses a double-edged blade is often called a "DE razor.")

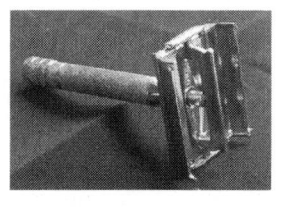

Shaving with a safety razor and using a shaving brush and high-quality shaving cream or soap for lather has several benefits:

- The shave itself is enjoyable and satisfying. (It's a strange sensation to be actually eager for your next shave.)
- Your skin feels better because a double-edged blade cuts the whiskers easily and cleanly, unlike electric razors and the "tug-and-cut" action of the multiblade disposable cartridge[11] (which encourages in-growns).
- The cost of shaving is substantially less. Double-edged blades cost pennies and are normally good for 4-6 shaves; a puck of shaving soap or tub of shaving cream lasts for months.
- You get a smoother, closer shave without irritating your skin.

This guide takes you step by step through the process. It discusses in detail the equipment and supplies you need and where to get them and, for the do-it-yourselfer, how to make some items for yourself. It describes how to prepare your beard for a shave and the basic techniques in building a good lather and using the razor. It provides guidance for dealing with common problems like acne and razor bumps. And it points to on-line sources of more information that can help you address particular problems you might encounter.

My goal is to provide the novice safety-razor shaver with a useful and comprehensive reference that answers both the questions he has and also questions he doesn't know to ask. Based on what readers have reported, that goal has been achieved.

I should note that I am a "shave critic," and my recommendations, like those of a movie critic or restaurant critic, are based on my own direct experience. I buy products as a regular customer, at retail, and I receive no remuneration, kickbacks, discounts, or other consideration from manufacturers or dealers. I retain my independence and maintain an arm's-length relationship with vendors (whom I like, admire, and respect) so that I will not feel I have to tailor my opinions to curry favor or repay special treatment. What you read in this book is simply what it appears to be: an independent assessment from a man who enjoys a good shave with proper tools and fine products.

Companion web page

The Web is home to a vast profusion of information about any topic, including shaving. In no way could I include in this book all the information—or even that fraction that is accurate and useful—that you can find on the Web. But, I realized, I can provide *links* to some of that information.

So my approach to writing the book was to include in the book all the essential information to take you into the pleasures of shaving with brush and soap and safety razor—and also to provide links to ancillary information that you may find interesting and/or useful. I suggest that you simply read the book, reserving the links for later, and only for those things that you want to explore further.

To make the text easier to read—and since I hope you'll read the links later—I've placed the links in endnotes following the Appendix. And, to make the links even easier to use, I've also provided them on the Web as hyperlinks so that you can simply click each to go to the site of interest. In time, the Rockies may crumble, Gibraltar may tumble, and some links will go away. Resourceful use of search engines can help you find the information if the link doesn't work, and in any case the book itself does provide complete basic information.

The companion Web page listing the links is especially worth checking since I update it as new information becomes available—for example, price changes that affect recommendations, or the appearance of new vendors or products. See **tinyurl.com/leisureguyfe** for the list of clickable links. I recommend that you bookmark that page.

You can review shaving posts on leisureguy.wordpress.com (my blog) by clicking "shaving" in Category Search. That will present all shaving entries in abbreviated form—click on the title of any post to see the whole thing. If you comment on a post, I will normally reply. Links to some specific shaving posts can be found on the "Useful Posts" page of the blog (see the list of links at the right when viewing the blog).

TWO

Who I am and why this book

I BEGAN shaving (with a Gillette DE safety razor) around 1955. A couple of years later I switched to a Schick Injector, a safety razor that uses a single-edged blade. But that was in the dark age of isolated shavers, when each shaver was on his own except for what knowledge he could pick up from his family and friends.

The only sources of information I had, for example, were my step-dad (who knew no more than I about shaving, though he had more skill than I because he had more experience) and ads and commercials, whose general content was "Buy this product." I used a badger brush, Old Spice shaving soap, and Gillette Blue Blades, and my shave consisted of two complete passes: one down and one up, the second pass without lather. I used little pieces of toilet paper on the resulting nicks and over the course of my high-school career must have gone through several rolls. As soon as I got to college, I grew a beard.

I still remember reading in high school a near-future science-fiction novel about a guy getting ready for a big night. He lathers up and shaves with the grain, then he lathers up *again* and shaves against the grain. I thought, "That's odd—he lathered a *second* time." It never occurred to me that lathering before each pass might be the right way to shave.

Today—now—is truly the golden age of shaving. Only with the Internet has it been possible for the far-flung band of safety-razor shavers to pool the knowledge gained from their experience and experiments and provide all shavers, new or old, with so much information, and to gain easy access to vendors of wet-shaving products all over the globe.

This book grew out of my own experience and experiments, augmented and illuminated by questions other shavers posted in the on-line shaving forums. I thank the guys on the shaving forums. I also am grateful to the vendors listed in the appendix for the fine array of products they offer, essential to the practice of traditional shaving. And in particular I want to thank shaving novices, whose questions and desire for a reliable and organized introduction to wetshaving first stimulated this book.

I am not a dermatologist or a cosmetologist and have no professional background in skin care or shaving. I am a retired guy who found a way to make shaving enjoyable, and I wrote this book as a report of my own experience and observations, not as specific recommendations for you, whom I don't know. In it you will find information about tools and techniques you can adapt to your own situation, at your own pleasure and risk. I certainly cannot guarantee the results, since I don't know what your shaving issues might be, but I do consistently point out ways you can safely experiment to find what works best for you. So read, enjoy, be judicious in your experimentation, and observe outcomes closely.

With the existence of the Internet and active shaving forums, is a book like this even needed? I believe it is. For one thing, a book, unlike a collection of Internet links, can serve as a gift for men who currently hate to shave, and I hope that this volume will often be among presents such men receive for graduation, Father's Day, bar mitzvahs, birthdays, and other gift occasions—most especially those men for whom shaving is still an unrewarding chore.

Some who receive the book will not have previously considered traditional wetshaving. One of their friends or family members knew that they found shaving a tedious, hateful task and gave them the book so they could *enjoy* the morning shave. Thus the next chapter makes the case for traditional wetshaving—just in case you're now considering the idea for the first time.

Although the Internet does provide access to much information, that information is disorganized, so a beginning shaver must spend considerable time wading through esoteric minutiae discussed at length while searching for basic guidance—fundamental information that may be hidden, glossed over, misstated, or omitted altogether (because "everyone already knows that"). Of course, beginners can ask questions in shaving forums, but newbies often don't know what questions to ask and sometimes fear to expose their ignorance—and in any event the answer provided may simply be wrong or based on a single trial. This book was written for a beginning shaver who values his time and wants an organized and consistent presentation of reliable information.

Information in online shaving forums also is volatile: new threads constantly push old threads out of sight, and occasionally entire threads are deleted, erasing all the information and photos they once contained. The information in this book will still be here when you return.

The shaving forums are nonetheless valuable, and I encourage you to participate. For one thing, you can ask questions about specific problems that you encounter (and the final chapter includes a useful template for asking questions effectively). For another, forums provide information and discussions concerning new products and new ideas. Also, questions asked on a forum can stir your thinking and lead to new approaches. I learned much by subjecting ideas I learned from forums to my own judgment, tests, and interpretation, and have even contributed some discoveries of my own.

THREE

Why to do it

BEFORE we start, I should answer the question, "Why bother?" Why put aside all the modern technology of pressurized cans of shaving foams and gels and the modern multiblade razor cartridge that allows you to shave while still half asleep? Why pick up tools and techniques from a generation (or two) ago? Isn't it obvious that we have seen real progress[12] in our shaving tools? Traditional shavers offer several answers to such questions.

Care of skin

Some reasons to switch to traditional wetshaving are pragmatic and down-to-earth: the multiblade cartridge uses a tug-and-cut technique that, combined with the dry chemical foam squirted from a can and the pressure required to pull 3, 4, 5, 6, or 7 blades at a time through stubble, leads to ingrown whiskers, razor bumps, and skin breakouts and irritation.

Many shavers who experience these problems think that they have "sensitive skin." They continue to suffer, buying loads of products promoted as protective pre-shaves or as soothing and healing aftershaves in hopes of repairing the damage. Some, however, switch to the double-edged blade and safety razor and find that, after mastering the techniques and skills of traditional shaving, their skin problems disappear. (Of course, some men do in fact have sensitive skin. But if your skin is sensitive only where you shave, that should arouse suspicion that something else might be at work.)

That older methods work better seems counterintuitive. Shaving has been a part of human culture from very early in our development—even some stone-age humans had razors of obsidian, which can be substantially sharper than a modern steel razor[13] as modern anthropologists (and straight-razor shavers) who have tried shaving with obsidian blades have found[14]. With such a long period for developing refinements, you would think that the most modern and recently designed shaving tools would be the best, but experience proves that is not in fact the case. Why do so many believe that it is? The answer is superb marketing, which has the power to cloud men's minds (and, alas, has never pledged to use its power only for good). The marketing of today's shaving tools is much better and more effective than the shaving tools themselves[15].

I repeatedly see shaving-forum posts by guys with bad skin conditions—acne, for example, or in-growns or razor bumps—that clear up shortly after they begin shaving with a DE razor. It's so noticeable a trend that an experiment is in order. If you're a cartridge shaver and have skin problems, try switching to traditional wetshaving with a DE razor and see whether the problem clears. You can get a basic kit for very little. Recommended starter kits at several price levels are listed in chapter 13, "Recommendations for a Beginner." Often you can find a vintage DE safety razor for free (from a family member who once used it) or for a pittance at a garage sale, thrift shop, flea market, or the like.

One reason so many cartridge shavers believe the skin on their face is sensitive is that cartridges now use 3-7 blades, which means the shaver must force the razor to cut through 3-7 blades' worth of stubble at a time. It requires noticeable effort to pull that many blades simultaneously through stubble even when the blades are sharp—and because cartridges are so expensive, many shavers continue using them long after the edges have been worn dull. Stropping cartridges on denim to eke out a few more shaves is a common practice. (Cartridge blades are made from the same steel as DE blades, and DE blades generally last at most a week before the edge dulls, tugging as it cuts, and so the blade is replaced. Some blades provide only one or two good shaves for some men with particularly tough beards before the blade must be replaced—but a DE blade costs pennies, not dollars.)

The effort needed to pull multiple blades through the stubble explains why cartridge shavers, after their first shave with a DE safety razor, often comment on how *easy* it is: "It's no effort at all! It just *glides* along!" That makes sense: they are now using a razor that cuts only *one* blade's worth of stubble at a time: much less resistance from stubble, resulting in a much easier shave with little pressure required—generally no more than the weight of the razor.

To keep the blade in contact with the skin when pulling a cartridge with so much force results in a lot of pressure *against* the skin. So the cartridge shaver presses hard, scraping his skin with 3-7 blades at a time, and most of the time using blades dull from (over)use. Often their problems are not due to "sensitive skin" but to how they are treating normal skin.

Force and pressure mash stubble, foam, and flakes of skin into the crevices, nooks, and crannies of the cartridge's moist, dark interior. Result: a microbe incubator. Often the shaver finds his face breaking out after a shave. A DE safety razor has fewer places for microbes to linger and easily rinses clean, so such skin problem often vanish as soon as a shaver makes the switch to DE.

If pimples appear after you shave with a multiblade cartridge, try this: after finishing the shave, first rinse your cartridge razor head well under hot water and then rinse it in high-proof (70% or higher) rubbing alcohol. And before starting your shave, rinse the razor head again in the rubbing alcohol. Also try using a fresh shaving towel daily—thin, lint-free barber towels (also known as bar towels) cost about $11/dozen[16] and are easy to launder. Or just switch to a DE razor. Once you switch to traditional wetshaving tools and methods, most men notice that their skin becomes clearer and healthier.

A man in one of the shaving forums commented that he started traditional shaving and, after a few months, returned home from college to see his mom. She felt his cheek and commented that it was the smoothest and softest it had been since he was 5. He said he had been aware that traditional shaving had improved his skin, but the improvement was so gradual he really didn't understand how dramatic the change was.[17]

Quality of shave

A "good shave" is of course smooth and without razor burn, irritation, nicks, or cuts—but that's merely the absolute minimum, and any shave that doesn't rise to that level is not worth considering. Beyond that, a good shave is *enjoyable*: it certainly results in a good outcome, but in addition the experience itself is a pleasure. Otherwise, what's the point? To toe the line to satisfy grooming conventions, getting nothing out of it for yourself? That's the sad lot of too many.

Men who choose a safety razor with a double-edged blade find both enjoyment and a better result: a shave that's smoother, closer, and longer-lasting. This contradicts ads about the latest disposable multiblade cartridges, but ads—brace yourself—frequently stretch the truth. Men who have switched from cartridge to DE safety razors often comment that their kids or grandkids tell them that their face is not so scratchy as it used to be. They discover that a traditional shave has a smoother result than a cartridge shave while also being more enjoyable.

Such close shaves are also possible with a skillfully wielded straight razor, but using a straight razor demands a substantial investment and learning various skills, including honing and stropping. This book focuses on the DE razor, which uses an inexpensive, disposable, double-edged blade.

A shave with a DE razor initially takes more time than a cartridge shave but with practice and experience, the time required drops steadily: perhaps 20-25 minutes initially, but within weeks, you'll find that the shave is down to 15 minutes, even though it will not seem to you that you are shaving any faster: you simply become more efficient over time. A few months or a year later, you'll find your shaves take around eight minutes. Today, my own shaves take five minutes from start to finish, and I have no sense that I am rushing or in a hurry. I take my time, enjoy the process, and discover, five minutes later, that I'm done. Subjectively, it feels as though I'm taking the same amount of time and care I always have.

Occasionally some will poke fun at the pleasure a traditional shaver derives from his face having absolutely no trace of stubble. After all, they say, the BBS (baby-bottom smooth) result lasts only a few hours, after which the stubble has grown enough so that some roughness is detectable.

But that same objection applies to a fine dinner in a four-star restaurant—they presumably would see no point in having a meal of great food, wonderful tastes, and mouth-watering aromas because, after all, in a few hours you'll be hungry again. In fact, the same logic results in not seeing the point of many activities—for example, pleasurable sex: it doesn't permanently satisfy the desire for sex, so what's the point? And so with all pleasurable activities.

It's the nature of pleasure to be fleeting, but most still enjoy the pleasure in the moment rather than rejecting a pleasure because it is impermanent.

Cost of shave

As I write this, one Gillette Fusion ProGlide Power disposable multiblade cartridge costs $4.12 (Amazon discount price for pack of 8). One double-edged blade, which will normally last a week (depending on brand of blade and nature of beard), generally costs around 15¢-20¢ but better prices are available with bulk purchases. As I write, Derby blades are available for $12.93/200 (6.5¢/blade), so that a shaver who likes Derbies can shave for a *year* and spend a total of $3.37 for blades, assuming one blade per week. (Derby blades don't work for everyone—see the chapter on blades.) I like Astra Superior Platinum blades, which cost 9¢ per blade: a total of $4.68 per year, using one blade per week.

Gillette claims that a cartridge lasts for five weeks of shaving[18] (although cartridge shavers agree that after the first week or two the comfort level drops significantly), so in the course of a year the ~~poor sap~~ cartridge shaver will buy 10 cartridges, for a total cost of $36.40—more than **ten** times what Derbys cost for a year—*if* the five-week cartridge lifespan is not some advertising fantasy.

Given the price of cartridges, many cartridge shavers gamely continue to use the same cartridge for three months (sometimes more—the worst I've seen is eight months). Using four cartridges a year, the suffering shaver will pay $14.56, about four times the cost of using Derby DE blades for the same period.

For lather, a puck of a hard (triple milled) shaving soap can easily last a year or more. The razor and the brush last a lifetime—indeed, even longer: some shavers enjoy using double-edge razors from 90 or more years ago.

18

Quality of life

"Quality of life" refers both to the quality of one's own personal life and also to the quality of the environment in which we all live.

Environmental benefits

The environmental benefits of traditional wetshaving are obvious: the landfill impact is negligible, and soap and shaving cream are made of benign ingredients. A year of shaving with a DE safety razor generally uses about 50 double-edged blades and their paper wrappers and a puck or two of shaving soap. In contrast, using a cartridge system means discarding a dozen (or more) plastic and metal cartridges, the plastic packaging in which they come, and several cans that once contained pressurized shaving foam. For my discarded DE blades—which, being steel, are recyclable—I use a small can that once held evaporated milk. It holds six years' worth of blades.

In terms of environmental impact, traditional shaving is *much* better than shaving with a cartridge razor and canned foam. Indeed, even a comparison of ingredients between a can of shaving foam and a puck of good shaving soap will show that the soap is more environment-friendly (and skin-friendly as well).

Personal benefits

I didn't have skin problems and wasn't all that unhappy with the result of a Mach 3 or Schick Quattro or Fusion shave in terms of smoothness. I turned to safety-razor shaving for the sheer pleasure the morning shave now provides. Shaving has changed from a routine at best, a chore more often, to a wonderful ritual from which I emerge feeling truly pampered. I now *look forward* to shaving each day. That feeling more than repays the little bit of equipment required. The daily shave: a daily pleasure. How many men can say that?

Very few. I suspect that the current fashion of young men wearing a stubble of 4 or 5 days' growth originated because shaving is unpleasant for most men who use today's shaving paraphernalia. Fashion photographers, seeing many young men with visible stubble, decided it was a "look," and put such men in ads, trying to appeal to that demographic. In fact, many of these young men simply dislike shaving but for whatever reason may not grow a full beard. So they put off shaving, and the look becomes a fashion statement which gives their Significant Other a sandpaper experience with every kiss.

Those who use traditional equipment, in sharp contrast, *enjoy* shaving. Indeed, the focused attention and meditative mindset of shaving with a safety razor can provide a morning ritual not unlike the Zen tea ceremony. Take a look at the similarities:

Special room – check
Special mode of dress – check
Contemplative, unrushed mindset – check
Cleanliness and order – check
Practice of technique requires focused attention (aka flow) – check
Use of special tools, often old – check
Tools both functional and aesthetically pleasing – check
Suspension of mind chatter, critical judgments – check
Senses—sight, hearing, touch, smell—fully engaged – check
Physical enjoyment of sources of warmth – check
Awareness & enjoyment of aromas arising from hot water – check
Reassuring familiarity of quiet, soft sounds – check
Definite sequence of steps – check
Structure of the entire experience repeated each time – check
Feeling of pleasure, fulfillment, and satisfaction at end - check

In the preface I mentioned the mental state of "flow," in which one loses consciousness of self and of time, becoming totally focused on a task whose intricacy and difficulty require about 85% of one's capacity. (Attention wanders when a task is too easy; if a task is too difficult, anxiety disrupts flow.)

Most people know from their own experience that a state of happiness is usually recognized only after the fact—at the time, one is unaware of it *per se*, but simply enjoys each moment. Flow seems to exactly describe the state of experiencing happiness, so the more flow one can arrange, the happier one's life. Shaving, with the right approach and mindset and attention, can promote flow.

The contemplative aspect of a satisfying shaving ritual is revitalizing. Most of us live busy lives, multitasking and rushing about, harried by time demands. The morning shave with a safety razor offers a small oasis of unhurried calm and single-minded attention to remind you what it feels like to be unrushed and focused only on what you are doing at the moment, rather than doing one thing while thinking of other things you must get to.

Joanna Field was the pseudonym used by Marion Milner, a psychotherapist who wrote several books. I particularly recommend her first two: *A Life of One's Own* (1934) and *On Not Being Able to Paint* (1937). These I found both insightful and practical. Among other things, she discusses how we sometimes find ourselves not feeling the immediacy of what we experience, responding more as an observer from a distance than a participant in the moment. We might be taking a walk, unmoved by our natural surroundings, or at a concert, removed from the music, or physically close to a loved one but involuntarily disengaged and feeling remote. She describes what she terms "gestures of the mind" that help re-engage us in the experience at hand.

She does not talk about shaving, since for her that would not have been a daily activity, but I think shaving helps us achieve what she discusses: locating ourselves in, and focusing our awareness on, what is happening in the moment instead of being immersed in our thoughts, hopes, worries, and plans. Perhaps this is because moving a razor-sharp blade over your face is in itself enough to engage your full attention: mindless shaving generally produces a sharp correction in the form of a nick or cut. I highly recommend her two books (secondhand copies are plentiful[19]). See what you think.

Shaving thus promotes mindfulness—nonjudgmental awareness of the content of the present moment of experience. Mindfulness has been shown to reduce emotional stress and to heal damage that emotional stress does to the body[20]. Once someone has learned what that state of mind feels like and has experience in achieving it, he can find it at other times of the day and in other situations (cf. the tea ceremony mentioned above). In other words, mindfulness is a skill, and a skill is learned through practice.

I advocate shaving in a silent bathroom: no fan, no running water, no music, and no radio talk. One reason is purely functional: the cutting blade makes a quiet sound that guides one in optimizing blade angle. But another reason for silence is the meditative aspect of shaving: a time in the day when you closely focus on one task only (with the focus probably even closer for men who shave with a straight razor) with full awareness of what you're directly experiencing at the moment. Distraction dilutes the experience.

And yet some seem curiously attached (addicted?) to distraction. I think one reason is that focusing on a task without distractions is a skill and thus must be acquired through practice. A person with little experience in being free of distractions while closely focusing on what he is experiencing in the moment will suffer the negative feelings common to beginners in any skill: feeling awkward, unsure how best to do it, uneasy about its unfamiliarity, being hyper-conscious of "mistakes," and so on. I can understand how such feelings would make anyone look for a distraction. But with practice it becomes easier to enjoy a mindful awareness without distractions and even, once you've learned the skill, something one will seek.

It's quite clear that feeling comfortable in the absence of distractions is something one must learn. Most people will give themselves an electric shock (severe enough that they would pay to avoid it) rather than sit quietly alone with their thoughts[21]. Lacking meditative skills, they find being in the moment is more painful than a shock.

A scene in Brian De Palma's The Untouchables, for which David Mamet wrote the screenplay, describes in another context a mindset useful for shaving.

Jim Malone (Sean Connery) is an old-time, experienced cop, and Eliot Ness (Kevin Costner) is a young, up-and-coming Treasury agent. They are waiting to ambush a Capone whisky shipment coming over the Canadian border, and Ness is antsy—pacing back and forth, repeatedly looking out the window. Malone tells him, "Take it easy. It'll all happen in time. This is the job. Don't wait for it to happen. Don't even want it to happen. Just watch what *does* happen." And in shaving, you should be watching what is happening, not thinking about something else or distracting yourself with music. Be present for the shave.

In addition to being restorative in itself, the daily shave provides a foundation of structure for the morning. Men who once leapt from bed, quickly ran a cartridge razor over their beard (or decided to postpone shaving for another day), then grabbed a quick bite of breakfast[22] and dashed out the door, lurching into the day's events off-balance, find that their shave leads them to develop an entire morning sequence, ordered and satisfying, that provides a stable platform from which to launch the day. The morning shave becomes a ritual of preparation, and rituals, psychologists have found, do indeed work[23].

Moreover, psychology suggests that the ritual of shaving can increase your self-respect: Cognitive dissonance[24] posits that a person holding contradictory beliefs (or observing himself acting in contradiction to his beliefs) will add to or modify his beliefs to resolve or reduce the contradiction[25]. Recent experiments show that people who feel pride in themselves and have a sense of self-respect are more cooperative in promoting the common good[26].

Naturally, I thought of this with respect to shaving. By acquiring shaving's specialized tools and supplies and taking the time and care to create a shaving ritual, the shaver presents himself with a behavior that leads to increased self-respect and a sense of pride: "If I'm taking this much time to pamper myself, I must be worth it." Not a bad feeling at all. And the cumulative effect of having the feeling reinforced every weekday morning can be substantial, as described by one shaver[27]:

> Throughout my life I have been saddled with responsibility and plunged knee deep into competition, whether it was through my parents' or my own volition. From a very young age competition enveloped me. From my school work, with ever-critical parents pushing me to do better, to whatever sport I was playing at the time, competition was an active and dominating force for me.
>
> During my undergraduate studies, my hobbies eventually focused themselves due to a minimum of time available. My life was consumed with essentially two main activities: schoolwork and my sport at the time, fencing. My parents' critical nature had worked itself into my persona by this point, and therefore every practice, every competition I went to was filled with self-

judgment, stress, and just dwelling on how I screwed up and why I lost. It was not something I could easily just forget about after the fact, but something that constantly lingered.

My studies eventually led me to graduate school, where the competition and stress rose further. As the only white person in my research group, it was made fully aware to me from the beginning that my being white (in a group of Chinese/Taiwanese students) meant that I had all eyes on me, as I was told that because I was white I was automatically assumed as being lazy. Pressure to surpass expectations was high. While I had stopped fencing, I picked up cycling, which led to racing, which led to more intense training and competition. It seems that no matter what I chose, it centered on competition. Eventually, I lost the joy of my hobbies, and everything had become a chore, a task, an obstacle to overcome. There was less enjoyment, just stress to do better.

I tried finding some new hobbies, something I could enjoy just for fun. I tried throwing darts again with my buddy, but that led to a weekly darts tournament. I tried picking up golf to play with my girlfriend, but the self-critical nature keeps creeping in with every slice, every topped ball, every trek through the rough, every goddamn water hazard.

After graduate school there was work, which continued to bury me under mountains of stress and anxiety. Combined with hobbies that also seem to promote stress in me, I noticed a complete lack of any outlet for my stress that didn't just generate more. It was bad.

Then I found traditional wetshaving. "What an odd thing," I thought. How could shaving have this many devotees? How could such a chore have so much enthusiasm behind it? Is there a similar group of people who love folding laundry? *What the hell is wrong with these people?* I'd had straight razor shaves before, and they were very nice, but this? This just seemed like too much.

I did my research, I trudged through the volumes of information present here, and eventually picked up my own kit and began the process. Leisureguy really does make an apt analogy in that it's almost like a Japanese tea ceremony and is very Zen-like. Psychologists worldwide will agree that self-reflection, meditation, and general "quiet time" are all needed in order to be healthy, happy, and sane. Up until this point, I never had the ability, or had a reason, to make this time available to me. Suddenly I had the time. The concentration needed for shaving helped me focus, but at the same time I was able to approach it differently than every other hobby. It was not a competition, it was not a race, it was not going to be graded or judged, it was an activity, an action with definite steps to follow, a procedure. I like procedures.

The methodical nature of shaving made for a much-needed routine and regularity in my hectic schedule. A definite time set aside for me. Not for my friends, nor my coworkers, nor my boss, nor my family, nor my lovely and patient girlfriend, but for me. To be able to shut everything and everyone away once a day for a short amount of time and not be questioned as to why I was being withdrawn or reclusive is extremely relaxing. The result? More confidence from learning a new skill and looking better; less stress due to a set schedule, routine, and procedure; enjoyment of a new hobby because I can still tinker (new soaps, blades, etc.); and an overall better outlook on things due to all of the above.

Somehow I have found a hobby, as silly as it might seem to some outside this group, which quite literally makes me feel better about life in general. While it may only be a small part of a bigger picture, it's *my* small part.

I believe that shaving's freedom from stress and competition stems in part from the gradual realization that discovering what works best for you doesn't put you ahead or behind any other shaver—he, too, is engaged in figuring out his own optimal combination, which may be quite different from yours, just as he is different from you. Thus there's no external measure or standard to meet or beat. When shaving, a man is totally engaged in achieving the best shave he can for himself: he is very much involved in the particularities of the moment and removed from other worries and concerns that plague us. Our lives indeed consist of an on-going stream of particularities, a string of present moments. When we pay attention to the present moments, rather than worrying about the future, obsessing about the past, and measuring ourselves against others, we find ourselves re-centered and renewed and feeling a sense of peace. Even joy is perhaps involved.

The role that traditional wetshaving can play in personal renewal is something on which others have commented[28]. Even though it works at an unconscious level, cognitive dissonance is powerful, and starting each day taking time and care to do something that is clearly for yourself, treating yourself nicely, gradually results in feeling that you must be worth this effort. If you don't feel that, cognitive dissonance results, and the simplest way to resolve it, given that you continue the self-care, is to accept that you deserve it. That means you start to view yourself in a better light, and thus you begin acting in ways consistent with that view—that is, you unconsciously start living up to how you now view yourself, which results in observing yourself doing things that such a person would do, thus reconfirming to yourself that you are indeed this better person, which leads to still more good actions consistent with your self-image as a person you respect, and so on: a virtuous circle.

In any situation or circumstance, most people already know what actions they should undertake or what decisions they should make. (This becomes evident when people say that they don't know what to do in a situation, but when asked what a counselor, therapist, coach, teacher, or minister (or rabbi or priest or imam) would advise, they usually find it easy to state the advice they would get.) Starting each day with a ritual of personal grooming adds just enough push so that you will do some actions or make some decisions that you already know you *should* do or make, and those steps are enough to start the cycle of positive feedback, which can grow quickly (cf. regenerative feedback).

This process works because the force driving it is (1) *unobtrusive* (that is, it comes from doing a routine and necessary task, not something out of you ordinary routine, which would require some deliberate commitment) and (2) *enjoyable* (in attracting flies, honey works better than vinegar: people learn faster from seeking pleasure than from avoiding pain) and (3) (quite important) *daily*: the push may be small, but it's steady and on-going, and once the effects start to become evident, the process picks up speed because of its self-reinforcing (regenerative) nature.

It's also worth noting that people are often drawn to products that require effort or skill because using such products helps one feel a sense of control[29]. Several have commented on how shaving has helped them when facing bad situations in which they felt a lack of control over their lives: when a family member has a serious illness, for example, or when they've lost their job or a relationship has ended. They often mention that shaving in such situations feels calming and restorative, and I think that feeling results from increasing their sense of control, thus regaining the locus of control[30].

Some call the shaving ritual a hobby, but that's a misnomer. Most of us have attended a party or event at which we want to look our best, so that the process of getting ready is important. Your preparation includes grooming, selecting what to wear, getting dressed, and then inspecting yourself in a full-length mirror when you're ready to go: looking good and feeling at the top of your game[31]. This sort of preparation for a fine party, though enjoyable, is hardly a hobby. That pleasure of preparation is what the morning ritual of grooming offers: the feeling of taking care of yourself, preparing yourself for the day. A good shave is a pleasure, not a hobby, unless you consider getting ready for a splendid party to be a hobby.

Collecting shaving paraphernalia, however, is indeed a hobby that some take up, and I discuss that later in this book. But shaving in itself is not, in my view, a hobby but simply grooming, albeit a grooming ritual that provides pleasure.

One source of the pleasure of the traditional shave, using a razor that you yourself control and a true lather you yourself made from shaving cream or shaving soap with a brush, is that you are more involved in the shave. It's said that the first cake mixes required the cook to add only water, but manufacturers found that many cooks were adding eggs and milk, even though those were not needed. The cooks, however, wanted to feel that the cake was something that *they* had made, and adding water was not enough to produce a feeling of accomplishment. So the mixes were reformulated to require the cook to use an egg and milk, and even though the cake tasted the same as the add-water mix, the cook was much more satisfied with the result.

A shave with canned foam (just press the button and pseudo-lather is produced for you) and a cartridge razor (you have no control of blade angle, which adjusts automatically) is pretty much a cake-mix shave, whereas the traditional shave, using a razor you learn to wield correctly and a lather you make from shaving soap or shaving cream, requires your active and mindful participation to achieve a good result—and that's much more satisfying, just as baking things from scratch can be[32]. The phenomenon of user involvement resulting in increased satisfaction even has a name: the Ikea effect[33].

Moving to a more mundane consideration: men who suffer from hay fever and other such allergies can improve their quality of life by shaving during allergy season. Pollen and other allergens get trapped in mustaches and beards, exacerbating the sneezing and sniffling. To minimize symptoms, men with facial hair should wash it frequently during the day, particularly after being outside— or (easier and simpler) stay clean-shaven during allergy season.

An important quality-of-life consideration for most men is their sex life. Stiff, abrasive stubble is poorly suited to the tender intimacies of lovemaking compared to skin that's smooth-shaven and fragrant. Barbed wire conveys a clear message: "Keep Away."

Perhaps for the reasons cited above, daily shaving is associated with better health and a longer life[34].

A summary of reasons men enjoy traditional shaving:

- **Sensual enjoyment**: hot lather, the soft feel of a resilient shaving brush loaded with lather, the razor making a nice sound as it mows through the stubble, feeling your smooth face after the shave, the fragrances of the lather and the aftershave, etc., as well as the pleasures of making love without abrasive stubble.
- **Flow**, as described above: focused attention on a task that requires around 85% of your capabilities, with a clear goal and immediate feedback as you work at it. Flow clears the mind and reconnects you with your body.

- **Gadget appeal**: brush styles, razor mechanisms, blade characteristics, soap varieties, etc.
- The great feeling of **transforming a daily chore into a pleasurable daily ritual**: conquering, in a small way, drudgery itself.
- The **psychological benefits** from taking care of yourself, including a sense of control and self-respect.
- **Frugality**: the satisfaction of knowing that soap and blade cost just pennies, rather than the high-priced products of marketing that other men typically use—plus the environmental benefits that result.
- Finally, **getting the best (smoothest, closest) shaves** of your life with zero skin irritation.

The YMMV factor

A common saying in traditional wetshaving is "YMMV": "Your mileage may vary." The proverb of the same sentiment is "One man's meat is another's poison." In shaving, *nothing* works for everyone. (And this principle—like others I shall point out—applies with greater generality than just in shaving.)

Although something—a razor, a blade, a soap, an aftershave—may work extremely well for me, it may not work at all for you. An obvious example: some men's skin reacts to sandalwood. Although I may love my sandalwood soap or aftershave, some men find it makes their face turn red and feel hot for five or ten minutes. Another example: men with chrome contact dermatitis find that chrome-coated blades do not work well for them. Such issues are not a matter of "right" and "wrong"; rather, it's simply that what works for me may not for you, and vice versa: YMMV—nothing in shaving works for everyone.

One can readily understand how fragrances are YMMV, but surprisingly, the YMMV phenomenon particularly affects razor blades. One would expect that objective standards of sharpness would rule, but in fact shavers vary tremendously in their experience with any brand of blade: a blade that was a "best blade" for me was termed "a tragic waste of metal" by another shaver. Who was right? We both were: blades can perform very differently for different men (and in different razors), and we each were describing our own experience.

When you consider how beards vary in toughness and density, from light and fine to thick and coarse, and how skins vary from highly sensitive to tough as leather, how prep routines and technique vary, and how water varies in hardness—it's really not so surprising that a blade that works well for one may not for another. The brand of blade may be the same, but perhaps that's the *only* similarity between the two situations. (And, true to YMMV, some men are unable to detect any difference at all among different brands of blades.)

The great variation in individual responses to every aspect of shaving means that every traditional wetshaver must willy-nilly experiment. To determine whether a product or technique will work *for you*, you must try it. It may work, it may not, but you have no way to know without trying. Judicious experimentation combined with close observation of outcomes is the most efficient route to learning. Some, of course, will attempt to shorten the process by making decisions based on their expectations, but actual experience trumps expectations, and expectations (as I've mentioned) quite often prove to be wrong. The man who likes his badger brush and avoids trying a boar brush because he doesn't think he would like it is basing his decision on (mere) expectation. He is trying to compare an experience he's had with an experience he's not had, and that turns out not to work very well at all.

The three-week test protocol – I recommend trying a new product or procedure for a week (assuming you shave daily, thus in this context "a week" means "6-7 shaves," thus it's 6-7 weeks for a man who shaves weekly), then reverting to the old way for a week, then another week the new way. After that, decide (based on your experience) whether the innovation is in fact an improvement.

If the product or technique being tested is truly awful, you don't need to spend an entire week on it, but do give it a fair chance. For example, some brands of blades are much better on the second shave than the first. And something that feels awkward on the first try may feel much more natural after you've done it a few times and figured out the best approach.

When you first try it, any new product or practice is likely to feel odd or different or unsettling—in a word, "wrong"—but by using the innovation over two full weeks (with a week off in the middle to allow the learning to settle and be assimilated), you become enough accustomed to the innovation that it loses enough of its novelty and strangeness so that you can better evaluate it for what it is without being distracted by its novelty.

The week-long break from the innovation is important. In the chapter on Habit[35] in *The Principles of Psychology*, William James wrote, "We learn to swim during the winter and to [ice-]skate during the summer." (That chapter on Habit had quite an impact on me. It's well worth reading and study. Although James may be wrong on some of the underlying mechanisms, he was a keen observer of phenomena.)

The YMMV factor means that the optimal combination for one shaver may well differ in various ways from another's best set-up—thus the lack of competition. He likes boar brushes, you like badger, I prefer horsehair, and that's that: these choices cannot be sorted into the categories "right" and "wrong". They fall under "personal preference," and I will again add that such a preference can be validly established only through actually trying the alternatives. You cannot know which you in fact prefer until you've tried them. You discover, more than decide, your preferences.

It follows that if someone recommends a product highly—a razor, a blade, a shaving soap, or whatever—and you discover it's awful when you try it, you were not tricked or betrayed and he's not guilty of "hyping" it. You simply came out on the wrong side of YMMV. The guy recommended the product because *for him* it worked great—but that does not mean it will work great for you, though it does suggest that it might be worth a try. Samples—of shaving soaps and creams, aftershaves, and blades—are extremely useful in seeing how the products will work for you.

Surprisingly often in the forums you'll see a particular product or practice strongly recommended by someone who has tried no alternatives—the recommendation is based on a positive experience with a product or practice and no experience with any alternative product/practice. (Settlers, described below, are particularly prone to this.) For example, Escali badger brushes— mediocre at best—get many glowing 5-star reviews on Amazon because that brush, being quite inexpensive, is often the first shaving brush for men whose only experience previously was with canned foam; they are comparing their experience in using a brush and true lather to their experience with the canned foam they previously used, and impressed by the improvement, they praise the brush. However, never having tried another brush, they have no knowledge of the brush's quality *as a brush*—only as an alternative to canned foam.

Beware of recommendations from the inexperienced. Look for recommendations from men who have used a *range* of brushes, or razors, or whatever—and recognize that, even with good recommendations, you still must experiment to find what works best for you.

The idea that someone else's experience can be so different from one's own is hard to internalize, especially for those who believe that their own responses are not only "typical" but universal. Yet the idea should be familiar from our experiences with food: we know that a food we love might taste terrible to someone else, and vice versa. (Even here, some have trouble believing that their own preferences are not universal—reject fried liver as too awful to touch, and you will at some point encounter a liver lover who will say, "You just never had it cooked right." No, people do in fact have different preferences, and one must recognize that.)

I will frequently mention something works "for me" as a signal that I think it's worth trying but am aware that some others will find that it's not for them. In some cases I can offer an estimate of the breakdown, based on (totally unscientific) polls on shaving forums, but that doesn't help you to know in advance into which group you will fall.

One common instance of YMMV is whether something is "worth" a given amount—for example, is the iKon Shavecraft #102 slant, which currently sells for $75, worth $30 more than the Merkur 37C slant? The #102 performs better (for me), but is the improvement worth $30?

The problem is that "worth" (measured in dollars) is very much YMMV because it depends on how many dollars a person has: the more dollars you have, the less value a dollar has for you and the more willing you will be to spend it[36]. A Purdy shotgun can cost six figures and is clearly better than a Wal-Mart shotgun, but is the improvement worth so much more? Quite obviously, some think it is, but for most it's not. "Worth," like taste, is subjective, so each must decide for himself whether something is "worth" its price, just as each must decide for himself whether a food tastes good.

One also frequently encounters a phenomenon I call "YMMV even in the same car": a product that doesn't work for you when you begin shaving may, after six months or a year of practice and experience, turn out to be quite good when you retry it. This is particularly true of blades but applies to razors as well.

Over time you will work out the set-up, procedure, and technique that works best for you. It's nice that it fits you like a glove, not so nice that you have to make the glove yourself. The key is to enjoy the exploration and the experimentation, to delight in discoveries, to develop and test theories, and to increase your knowledge and skill along the way.

It follows that, while almost all men will find DE shaving an enjoyable way to get a fine shave, the YMMV factor means that DE shaving doesn't work for some. For example, some men choose not to shave at all and wear a beard. Some who do shave find that a straight razor works best for them. Starting with a double-edge razor is one standard route to straight-razor shaving: using a DE razor to prep techniques and become acquainted with the importance of pressure and blade angle, and then moving to a straight razor and developing the skills that straights require (stropping, shaving, and honing), while perhaps continuing to use a DE razor when traveling or for a fast shave when running late. Some use a DE razor during the week, a straight razor on the weekends.

Some men, however, cannot use a blade for shaving at all because of skin issues, physical disabilities, or water scarcity. In such situations, an electric razor may be the best solution. (Of course, some men use an electric razor because they don't realize that shaving can be enjoyable, so they want to shave with minimal attention while doing something else at the same time—reading the paper, eating breakfast, driving to work, or whatever.) True to YMMV, though, others find that using an electric razor is hard on their skin.

30

The following two sections on straight and electric razors are simply to introduce those alternative: they are not the focus of this book.

Straight razors

Before King Camp Gillette developed the double-edged blade that propelled the safety razor to popularity, the common shaving tool was a straight razor: a razor-sharp blade with a tang by which to hold it, protected by scales when not in use. (However, Japanese kamisori straight razors[37] do not use scales.) Although Gillette did not invent the safety razor itself[38], he perfected the disposable blade and ingeniously promoted the Gillette razor and blades.

New straight razors from a manufacturer such as Dovo, Hart Steel, Boker, and others are generally not sold in "shave-ready" condition. Almost always it is necessary to send a new straight razor to a honemeister for a professional honing before you can comfortably shave with it. Some dealers (e.g., Straight Razor Designs, Maggard Razors, Vintage Blades LLC , and Whipped Dog, all listed in the Appendix) offer professional honing on the straight razors they sell so that a straight razor from them will indeed be "shave-ready"—but always ask whether the razor has been honed.

One common introductory route has been to buy a restored straight razor that's shave-ready and an inexpensive strop, like the "poor-man's" strop from Whipped Dog. (Novice straight-razor shavers seem inevitably to mar their first strop in learning how to use it.) The razor, being secondhand, may have cosmetic flaws, but in quality of steel and sharpness of blade, you get a good razor that shaves well: a cost-effective way to test the straight-razor waters.

The consensus of straight-razor shavers is that a beginner's best course is to learn with equipment he can replace as his knowledge and skills improve and his preferences emerge (e.g., for a wider or narrower blade, for a hollow-ground or wedge shape, and so on). And if the razor doesn't work well for you, let the vendor know. Most vendors will make good if the product's defective.

Good sources[39] of used razors:

- Edson Razors
- Gemstar Customs
- Maggard Razors
- Straight Razor Place classifieds (look for "shave-ready" razors)
- Strazors.com (in Israel)
- Whipped Dog

Two useful basic guides to straight-razor shaving are available for free download as PDF files: *The Art of the Straight-Razor Shave*[40], by Chris Moss, and *Straight Razor Shaving*[41], by Larry Andreassen.

In addition to straight razors, which do require honing and stropping (and thus learning to strop and perhaps also to hone) and acquiring the tools needed, some prefer to use a *shavette*[42]. A shavette is shaped like a straight razor, but it uses a disposable blade, either a specialized blade or a regular double-edged blade broken in half. Shavettes have quite a different feel from a straight razor, but they are cheaper than a straight razor and do not require stropping or honing. Often, for hygienic reasons, they are used by barbers.

Sometimes a novice will refer to a straight razor as a "straight edge" (the unmarked ruler of Euclidean geometry). It's a natural mistake: he gets the "straight" part right but then, conscious of the razor's sharp edge, he uses "edge" instead of "razor." Of course, the cutting edges of double-edged and single-edged blades are also straight. The proper term is "straight razor," not "straight edge." "SR" refers to straight razors, "SE" to single-edge razors.

Electric razors

As noted above, some men find that an electric razor works best for their situation—for example, because they have rosacea or contact dermatitis or Parkinson's disease or some other condition incompatible with using a blade to shave, or for some reason they must shave without water, or they wish to do something else while they're shaving.

The consensus is that electric razors are something one is forced by circumstances to use. It seldom seems to be a first choice, perhaps because for many men an electric razor is unsatisfactory both in shave result and skin health.

If DE razors are so great, why are cartridges so popular?

Some men are skeptical about DE shaving because "everyone" uses cartridges. So why was the double-edged blade abandoned? The answer will shock you: money.

In the 1950's Personna (GEM/EverReady etc) invented the Stainless Steel Blade and marketed them for their single-edge razors. The blades were sharper but they found that the edge deteriorated quickly and became quite rough to shave with.

Wilkinson Sword was in the forefront with the technology to coat the edge with Platinum, Chromium, PTFE (Teflon), etc., for a smoother shave. Wilkinson held many of the patents and grabbed a considerable proportion of Gillette's market share ever so quickly in the late 50's early 60's — basically, WS blades were noticeably better. And so Gillette made a deal for them to use Wilkinson technology. All of this helped in the demise of the DE as Gillette's patents were coming to an end and they were no longer in the controlling seat. Gillette decided to take a new direction in the early 1960's and cartridge systems would be the end result.[43]

The double-edged blade, now a commodity, is still widely available at low cost, a situation that presents a challenge for companies like Procter & Gamble, which must strive to increase profits continually. The solution, as companies see it, is to exploit intellectual-property law[44]. As a result, P&G is working hard in India to offer a single-blade cartridge, the Guard, to drive the double-edged blade out of existence. The Guard is currently quite inexpensive (in contrast to the Fusion 5, for example), but once double-edged blades are gone, price escalation will begin[45]. (In fairness, the safety razors commonly used in India are generally of poor quality and do not shave well—and the Guard can serve well as one's razor when traveling by air with carry-on luggage.)

The Change Barrier

Resistance to change is common for an obvious reason: change involves risk, and risk means the possibility of failure of one sort or another, whereas continuing the status quo entails no risk of failure: we get what we already have. ("Better the devil you know...") So our default setting is "Don't change." But changes do occur, and the interesting book *Changing for Good*[46], by James O. Prochaska, John Norcross, and Carlo DiClemente, describes their research into why some people succeed in making a big change (for example, quitting smoking). They found that successful change is done in six stages, the first stage being that one becomes aware that a change is possible. By considering how you might change your shave routine you've already begun the process of change: you realize that it's possible, and now you're figuring out the route you'll take if you make the change. So, although the change barrier is real, that you've gotten this far means you've made it through the toughest part.

Still: recognize that a change in your shave routine is indeed a change, and be patient with yourself through a period of adjustment and learning. The decision to change is generally a conscious decision, but a lot of unconscious work is also required—see *Strangers to Ourselves: Discovering the Adaptive Unconscious*, by Timothy Wilson, a fascinating book on the adaptive unconscious, how we study it, and what we've learned about how it works. Getting all one's internal furniture rearranged, as it were, takes a while. Pay attention to what you're doing and the results you get and you'll quickly pick up the new skill of shaving with a DE razor—that is, your adaptive unconscious will learn it so that in time little conscious attention is required for the mechanics.

The transition from having to pay close attention to the details of each step to paying attention at a higher level is common to many areas: the novice chess player must focus on remembering the rules and how the pieces move; the more experienced player no longer (consciously) thinks about those and thinks instead about his strategy for the game and tactical combinations to realize the strategy. The novice fencer thinks about keeping good form; an experienced fencer thinks more about his opponent and a strategy for his attacks, paying no conscious attention to form, which the adaptive unconscious manages.

For some, the transition to traditional shaving will go smoothly, and in most cases the novice will see clear signs of progress from shave to shave and from week to week. My own transition went fairly smoothly, though there's a reason I think so highly of My Nik Is Sealed, a liquid styptic I found quite useful when I began but now require only a few times a month. So if your first few shaves don't go so well as you hoped, remember that you are making a change, that a learning period must be allowed, and pay attention to the basics: prep, pressure, blade angle, and blade brand, as explained in the following pages.

Focus on *progress* rather than *result*. Try to treat the result (the experience and outcome) merely as a means of measuring progress. This helps, because in the early stages of learning anything, your results are generally not so good as your progress. If you focus your attention on the latter, learning becomes much more enjoyable.

Practice being patient (an extremely useful skill to acquire) and don't expect to gain six months' experience in a week: give yourself time. One important lesson in shaving is learning not to press too hard, a lesson that has a more general application: in general, not merely in shaving, it's best to press (down, forward, up, or back, depending on the context) just enough to achieve your goal and not more. A subordinate quickly learns not to press his boss too hard, and a wise boss knows not to press his subordinates too hard. In learning to shave, don't press yourself too hard—in both senses: razor against cheek, or yourself to improve more quickly. Being patient and paying attention produce the best progress.

The psychologist Carol Dweck wrote an interesting and useful book based on her research, which describes the mindset—the set of attitudes—that best supports rapid learning of new knowledge and skills. The book applies generally, and if you're interested in improving your efficiency and effectiveness in learning new things, it's definitely worth reading.

The basic finding is that a person who views his (or her) capabilities (intelligence, skill, talent, whatever) as fixed and having definite limits will see a failure as a sign he has hit such a limit. In contrast, a person who views his capabilities as essentially unlimited will view a failure as a sign he's found an area in which he can improve—and the worse the failure, the greater the possible improvement. Indeed, this sort of person views a failure as a source of learning, the failure itself suggesting ways to improve. With such a mindset, a big failure is *good* because it reveals an area with great growth potential. (If you

34

easily succeed at a task, you have less potential for growth and improvement in that area.)[47]

Another aspect of human nature that affects change-tolerance is the difference between "explorers" and "settlers". Explorers look for any excuse to try something new, settlers seek any excuse to stick with the status quo. Most of us are a mix: explorers in some areas (physical sports, for example, eager to try any new sport or physical challenge) while being settlers in another (sticking with familiar foods and not venturing beyond meat, potato, and a vegetable).

Settlers tend to rely heavily on expectations, ruling out new things based on pessimistic expectations of what would result (risk-averse), while explorers, always eager for novelty, tend to be optimistic in their expectations (risk-tolerant). Final judgment should always be based on experience, and the settlers' problem is that they frequently fail to get the experience required for a sound decision. Explorers may be disappointed from time to time, but their choices are more apt to be based on a range of actual experiences rather than supposition.

The settler/explorer distinction is also observed in studies of animal behavior, sometimes called shy/bold[48]. A species benefits from having individuals of both types, the bold to try new foods and new environments, the shy to keep the species going when those experiments have disastrous consequences. A willingness to explore, however, does benefit brain development[49]. The different attitudes apparently stem from small differences in brain chemistry, which also seem to influence one's political outlook[50].

The extreme settler in shaving would be a man who sticks with the first razor, brush, soap, and brand of blades he tries, figuring that the results he gets are "what DE shaving is like." Settlers generally resist making any changes; "If it ain't broke, don't fix it" is their identifying call. That view fails to see that one often cannot know whether something's "broke" until he's tried a few alternatives. Any improvement necessarily involves a change, by definition.

The Fear Barrier

Some have expressed a fear of the safety razor, but it's called a *safety* razor for a reason: the only damage you might encounter are some few nicks while you're learning (in contrast to years of skin irritation and other problems from using multiblade cartridges). With daily practice, your technique quickly improves so that any start-up problems quickly vanish.

Indeed, one option is to continue to use your multiblade cartridge razor, just substituting a fragrant lather you create with a shaving brush and a high-quality shaving cream or shaving soap for the canned foam or gel you previously used. I discuss this approach in the chapter "Recommendation for a Beginner

Kit." It's perhaps worth noting that the strong consensus among experienced shavers is that the quality (and enjoyability) of a shave is ranked like this:

Worst:	cartridge razor + canned foam
Better:	DE razor + canned foam
Better yet:	cartridge razor + true lather
Best:	DE razor + true lather

Thus sooner or later you should try using a DE razor: a great shave using a blade that can cost as little as 2% of what you pay for one Gillette Fusion disposable cartridge.

If you want, you can use a practice blade to perfect your technique before using a real blade: cut a piece of thin, stiff plastic to blade size and use it in your razor to practice using very light pressure and the correct blade angle (shallow, the blade almost parallel to the skin being shaved).

In a way, the fear that precedes your first shave with a safety razor resembles the similar fear that precedes your first kiss with someone on whom you have a great crush. Your mind is filled with everything that can go wrong, but you decide to try it anyway, and you get a kiss in return—and suddenly everything is okay. The fears are revealed to be but phantasms, and they vanish in the pleasure of the experience.

Don't just take my word for it: give DE shaving a go. I suggest you take special notice of this fear, because it's like a flower that blooms ever so briefly and only once in your life: in that instant after you lather, as you hold the razor before the first downstroke, you may (like many new shavers) feel an odd little thrill of fear, but once you make that first downstroke, that fear is gone forever.

One safety-razor shaver pointed out that, if you were to describe a cartridge razor to someone in the old days, it would sound quite scary: *"Five blades at a time?! Won't you cut yourself a lot?"* Fear of the safety razor is often merely the fear of a new experience, a distaste for feeling awkward when you first begin to learn a new skill. But if you focus on your *progress*, you can always look forward to the next shave to see how much you've improved.

You also might want to read the following report[51] from someone who's grown accustomed to the safety razor:

Last weekend I went home. My uncertainty about whether to check or carry on was solved by forgetting to pack my Futur [razor]. (I was going to decide when I left work whether to leave it in the bag.) So my only real shaving option were the things that I had left at home. I wasn't about to drag out the old Norelco, so that meant the Mach 3 that I left there as a spare.

I have not tried a Mach 3 a single time since picking up a DE, so I was actually very curious how it would go. I had often wondered if it was really that much different. After all, unlike some, I remember getting decent shaves with it. But then, I never went against the grain, so my shaves were not that smooth. I did use shaving soap and a brush.

First impression is that this thing does not sit well in the hand. I remembered the metal handle having decent weight, but, well, by comparison [with the Futur] the Mach 3 felt dinky. Also much too light in the head.

With the grain. Ugh. Maybe good soap is not as compatible/does not protect as well when using a cartridge? It felt REALLY scratchy. Not tearing up my face or anything, just not pleasant. Much to my surprise, I realized that even with three blades, the one-pass N-S result was not as good as I can get with many DE combinations. So I decided to keep going, and see if my improved technique and good soap would allow a good multipass shave.

I did three passes, but never fully against the grain because I was getting too much irritation going across. With a Feather DE blade in any decent razor, this would have left me with a near BBS [baby-bottom smooth] shave. With the M3 it was good, but not great. But the real problem was irritation. My skin simply did not look happy. And sure enough, there came the red bumps.

I had to back down to a one pass with the grain the next day, and the third day just did not shave at all.

So, the conclusion is that a DE really does get me a MUCH better result, both in closeness and comfort. What is interesting about this, though, is that this is coming from someone who was perfectly happy with his Mach3 and saw no need to change. I only tried a DE because of the price of stupid cartridges, and the guy love of gadgets.

And, more recently, this note appeared under the title "What was I thinking?"[52]:

I've just returned from a week in DC. Given that I have a few Mach 3 blades lying around, I decided to take these instead of my DE. Not only that, but I used a can of Nivea shaving foam. It's been some time since I used a combo like this, and my face didn't thank me one little bit!! It's taken a week of using my usual combo (Progress [razor], Trumper [shaving cream], and Rooney [brush]) to calm my face down and get rid of the ingrown hairs. Needless to say, none of the offending items accompanied me on the flight home and all my remaining Mach 3 blades have been sent off to a good home. Don't think I'll make that mistake again...

On a positive note, it has made me appreciate more the whole shaving 'experience'.

The experience of returning to a multiblade cartridge and canned foam after becoming accustomed to a DE razor and true lather seems to be universally disappointing[53].

Beyond the beard

Traditional wetshaving can also be used to remove hair from the body beyond the beard, and it offers advantages over other approaches such as waxing (painful), permanent laser hair removal (costly), or using depilatory creams or lotions (applying to your skin caustic chemicals strong enough to dissolve hair). Many women find shaving with a DE razor works extremely well[54], and many men shave their heads using a DE razor (or a single-edge razor—the GEM razor discussed later uses a single-edged blade, and the correct angle is achieved when the razor's flat head is held directly against the skin—easy to feel even if you can't see the razor, a feature especially helpful to head shavers). Women often comment that their legs are noticeably smoother and softer when shaved with a DE razor and true lather than with a multiblade cartridge and canned foam.

Whenever you use shaving to remove hair, the same basic rules apply:

- Use good prep so the hair is easy to cut.
- Make sure you use light pressure with the razor.
- Maintain the correct blade angle.
- Use an aftershave to soothe your skin.

Some differences will be noted. For example, the scalp seems less sensitive than the face, and beard hair is generally stiffer and tougher than hair on the head, so blade selection is less an issue for head shavers than for beard shavers. Head shavers generally have found that a regular double-edge razor works quite well, but as noted above some prefer a single-edge razor like the GEM, whose shaving position is easy to maintain by feel.

In shaving the farther reaches of the body—the legs, for example—a long-handled razor, like a Lady Gillette (a vintage razor found often on eBay), can be helpful—though many prefer a long-handled razor even for shaving the face or head. Some positions help—for example, in shaving the back of the knee, lock your leg straight and turn your knee outward so the back is easier to reach.

The key is to understand the importance of prep and to use a good shaving soap or shaving cream and a brush, working up a good lather wherever the shaving is to occur—beard, upper lip, legs, armpits, head, arms, chest, or crotch[55]. The lather makes the hair easier to cut, producing a better shave (and a more pleasant shaving experience) even if you use a multiblade-cartridge razor. Not only do good soaps and creams produce a lather that makes the stubble easy to cut, thus improving the experience, they also come in a wide variety of fragrances that make the entire task more pleasant. (Shave sticks, described later in this book, are a convenient form of shaving soap for the legs.)

When you use a DE safety razor in place of a multiblade cartridge razor, the experience becomes (as skill improves) even more pleasant and effective. It's probably best to practice the moves using a razor without the blade to get an idea of angle and position. If you make a little fake blade as described above, you can feel the (dull) edge, which helps to judge the angle.

Aftershave care is also important. One woman noted that she liked shaving her legs with a DE safety razor except that afterwards her legs itched. I suggested that she try an aftershave balm, such as Neutrogena Post-Shave balm, and that solved the problem.

What to expect

BASED on what many shavers have experienced, you can expect something like the following.

You initially feel skeptical of the idea of making lather from soap and using a DE razor, but that's followed by the thought that you *really* do not like shaving the way you shave now, and your skin is in terrible shape. So, you think, why not give it a go?

You order a razor, either from an on-line vendor (see Appendix) or on eBay[56] or through the Buy/Sell/Trade section of one of the shaving forums or via Reddit's Shave_Bazaar. (You may even get one from some family member.) You go to the drugstore and get a cheap brush and shaving soap. You buy any convenient double-edged blade—because the blade is so cheap, it doesn't seem all that important.

You lather up and—very carefully—pull the razor down your cheek. You try to remember what you've read about the correct angle, and you try to exert very little pressure. (Light pressure is hard to learn for cartridge shavers who have been using firm pressure to try to get a close shave—and to make that expensive cartridge last just a little longer.)

You finish, perhaps with a nick (but maybe not: the first shave is done *very* carefully) and—on the whole—not bad. In fact, it was sort of interesting.

You decide to check in at the shaving forums—to read more and also perhaps to brag a little. So you go to one of the forums listed in the Appendix. You post the results of your experience, and you start reading.

You suddenly realize you've spent more than an hour reading messages in the forum, and you now understand quite a bit more about the process, including some ways you can improve your technique.

You order a blade sampler pack so that you have a large number of different brands of blades to try in addition to all the brands you can find locally in the drugstore, and you order a better brush and a shaving cream or soap.

Within a week of your first shave with the DE razor, your shaves have gotten progressively better and the nicks are not so frequent. When you do get a nick, you check pressure and blade angle and resume.

When you encounter a problem or difficulty, you post a question on Reddit's Wicked_Edge or one of the shaving forums. You usually get advice from someone who had the identical problem and figured out a solution.

You start to really get the hang of it. You've spent some time reading the forum and eyeing the various choices of razors, brushes, soaps, creams, and aftershaves. You've found in the sampler pack a blade that seems to work well for you, and already you can tell that this blade does a better job—or maybe your technique is improving—or both.

You are learning so much, and it's so interesting—fascinating, really—that you eagerly tell your significant other all about it. You observe a certain amount of rolling of the eyes, whatever that means.

Now, as you read the forums, you occasionally find a question from a newbie that you can answer.

One day, after a few weeks, you feel your face after shaving and realize that it's smooth—and not just "smooth," but baby-butt smooth! In every direction! You rub your chin and cheek and feel no sign of whiskers or stubble—you can't even tell when you're rubbing against the grain.

And there's no razor burn! Your face is totally comfortable as well as being totally smooth. All through the morning you surreptitiously feel your face, and you find yourself thinking of tomorrow's shave—which soap or cream to use, which aftershave...

You're hooked[57]. And the learning process continues for quite a while—often taking the form of a gradual awareness. When I first started using horsehair brushes, for example, I thought they were okay, but over time, I began to awaken to their particular virtues, distinct from those of boar or badger brushes, and now I'm quite fond of them. Or when I first got an Edwin Jagger DE razors with the new head design after using Merkur razors, at first I barely noticed the difference, but as I continued to use the EJ razor, I gradually became aware that for me the shave was easier and better: the EJ head fit my shaving style better, though at first I didn't realize it[58]. Another example was in using J.M. Fraser shaving cream: at first it was just another cream, but over time I began to realize it was curiously effective for my beard, a tad better than most other shaving creams for me.

So take your time and give yourself a chance to find the particular virtues of whatever products you're using. And remember the YMMV principle: another's experience with the product may not match your own. Another person will have a different sort of skin, a beard of a different type, his prep and technique will not be same. Give yourself time to discover your own style and what fits best with it. And to learn your own preferences, explore and test alternatives. And expect some surprises along the way[59].

FIVE

Where to buy & when to make

AS traditional wetshaving grows more popular, large corporations arrive, drawn by the fragrance of money. Procter & Gamble's Art of Shaving stores represent one approach: sell wetshaving products (at prices substantially higher than from other vendors—possibly to create the illusion that cartridge razors and canned foam are economical) while continuing to promote their most profitable shaving item (multiblade cartridges). But in addition to that wolf in sheep's clothing you can find many excellent on-line vendors that specialize in traditional wetshaving (see Appendix for a list). Some vendors also have a brick-and-mortar store.

Nowadays many new shavers turn to Amazon: one-stop shopping and, with Amazon Prime, "free" two-day shipping. But I strongly encourage you to look beyond Amazon, whose offerings are limited in range and sometimes of indifferent quality even when the reviews are overwhelmingly 5-stars. (Wetshaving novices generally rate the new brush or whatever by comparing it to their previous cartridge razor + canned foam shaves, rather than to the range of wetshaving products available, which they have yet to try.)

Let me suggest some ways to shop wisely using non-Amazon on-line vendors. First, look for free shipping offers from other vendors. For example, every few months The English Shaving Company (home of the Edwin Jagger line of products, but with many other brands as well) offers free shipping worldwide. Also, many on-line shaving vendors offer free shipping year-round for orders that total more than $25 or $50 or some other minimum.

In addition, look closely at prices. Shipping must be paid by someone, and frequently items on Amazon are priced higher than on a site that charges for shipping, the higher price being roughly the same as the lower price plus the shipping cost—perhaps merely a coincidence, but it happens surprisingly often, particularly with vendors selling through Amazon as a portal and eager for the "Prime" designation. In such cases "Prime" saves nothing. For example, recently Amazon listed Musgo Real Glyce Lime Oil soap, a pre-shave soap I like and will discuss later, for $12/bar with free shipping. BullGoose Shaving sells it for $8/bar and you pay shipping. If you order two bars (one to use and a spare), using Amazon Prime would cost you money: around $24 with free shipping versus $16 plus about $4 shipping.

If you must pay shipping, or if you're trying to order enough to qualify for free shipping, look at adding to the order some consumables that you eventually will need and use up in any event—aftershaves or shaving soaps or creams. Even if you still must pay shipping, by adding a few items to the order you can greatly reduce the shipping cost per item when the increase in shipping is small: every item you add drives down the per-item shipping cost.

Another good way to reduce shipping cost is to get together with some friends and place a single order that includes items for each of you. The shipping cost, split among the group, will be small—indeed, the combined order may qualify for free shipping. Doing a combined order would be a pain if you ordered every week, but orders for shaving supplies tend to be infrequent. (Shaving soap or aftershave lasts for months; a razor lasts a lifetime.)

Also, step back and look at the actual cost of shipping. Consider that a product from an independent vendor (for example, one of the artisanal soapmakers) may simply be unavailable elsewhere, so if you're going to get it, you have to pay shipping. But how much is the shipping cost compared to, say, a Starbucks coffee confection? Is getting a special soap or aftershave unavailable on Amazon worth foregoing one or two coffees?—especially since your order will help an independent vendor who offers special items. I just placed an order with an Irish vendor, Shaving.ie, and the shipping cost (for a brush and tub of shaving cream) came to $6.04 for airmail delivery to California: perfectly reasonable, in my view.

Also look for local retail stores that carry traditional shaving equipment. Procter & Gamble's Art of Shaving stores are appearing in more malls and other locations, but their stock is limited and more costly than when purchased from other sources, and the staff often know little about DE razors and wetshaving (though this varies widely from store to store, with some boasting true experts).

For shaving hardware—razors, mugs, and brushes—your best bets locally are independent knife/cutlery stores (the kind with crowded displays) and some pipe/cigar/tobacco stores of the traditional sort. Department stores, particularly high-end department stores, often offer a good range of shaving soaps, shaving creams, aftershaves, and sometimes shaving brushes. Razors are less likely to be found, and razor selection in such stores is generally limited.

For razors, mugs, and brushes, also check the Buy/Sell/Trade threads in the various forums (listed in the Appendix), Reddit's Shave_Bazaar, and eBay.

Double-edged blades can be found at some drugstores as well as at discount stores like Wal-Mart, but selection is limited and blades are costly, so most shavers buy their blades on-line. *After* a shaver knows for sure which brand works best for him, it's wise to lay in a large stock: brands can abruptly be discontinued, and stainless, coated blades last indefinitely if stored in a dry place.

(Some shavers buy 100 or so blades before they know whether that brand is a good for them. That works about as well as you'd expect.)

Occasionally you can find an independent drugstore with a selection of traditional shaving equipment and supplies, and the selection may be excellent if the drugstore is located in a large city. For example, Pasteur Pharmacy in New York City is good, and Leavitt & Peirce on Harvard Square and Stoddard's Cutlery nearby in Newtown have friendly and knowledgeable staff and good stock. Q Brothers, the wetshaving store spun off from Merz Apothecary in Chicago, is another fine store. If you're near Adrian, MI, look in at Maggard Razors. In Calgary, AB, a store called Knifewear has good stock. Look around your city, or inquire in shaving forums to find local stores.

For soap and brushes, check out Bodyshop (they give out free samples if you ask), Bath & Bodyworks, Whole Foods, Target, large drugstores, and beauty-supply houses. You probably will not find really good brushes, but you might find something with which to start.

Whenever you look for traditional wetshaving equipment and supplies in any brick-and-mortar store, be sure to *ask* about the items you want. For one thing, they may be stored in a drawer because counter space is valuable and few now buy such things. For another, retail-store operators are nowadays a desperate lot, and you can be sure that they will be pay close attention to your request—and if they hear something similar a few times, who knows? You may return to find a display case filled with razors and shaving brushes.

For vintage razors, you can occasionally make a lucky find at flea markets, thrift stores, antique stores, and the like—and, of course, you should ask your relatives about old family razors, used by your grandfathers or your uncles or great-uncles—such requests will often turn up a treasure: a vintage razor in excellent condition that comes with a history and family connection.

Think also about what's outside the frame. J. Edward Russo and Paul Schoemaker, in their excellent and invaluable book *Decision Traps: Ten Barriers to Brilliant Decision-Making and How to Overcome Them*[60], describe how decision "frames" work and how sellers often use them: the seller learns what the buyer values and includes "in the frame" (that is, focuses attention on) the benefit the buyer seeks, while putting "outside the frame" compensating charges so the buyer doesn't notice them, allowing the seller to achieve his profit goals—in a way, a win-win situation, though only the seller's win is actual, the buyer's "win" being but a perception.

For example, if you're buying a car, as soon as you ask about the trade-in value of your current car, the seller knows that if he maximizes the trade-in allowance (visible in the buyer's frame), he can readily jack up interest rates and/or stretch out the loan period, minimize the discount and freebies on the new car, and charge full price for options. Since the buyer's frame focuses on trade-in value, he will accept a deal that costs him more than if he had a different frame: the big trade-in becomes mesmerizing.

Amazon Prime uses this technique by putting "free shipping" in the frame, focusing your attention on that benefit. As noted above, quite often the "free shipping" is accompanied by a higher price. And it works: if you point out to a friend an independent vendor's lower price, the response often is, "Yeah, but then you have to pay shipping," without even bothering to compute the total amount or thinking how to minimize shipping costs. Because Amazon Prime's framing emphasizes "free shipping," many fail to look at the full picture. Indeed, you might not notice that the range of products available on Amazon is *much* less than what's available from independent vendors—and many wonderful specialty items are not offered on Amazon at all.

The entire field of behavioral economics draws heavily on discoveries by Daniel Kahneman and Amos Tversky on how people *actually* make decisions (which turns out to be very different from the rational maximizers on whom economists had based their theories). Dan Arley, in his intriguing book *Predictably Irrational: The Hidden Forces That Shape Our Decisions*[61], offers a wonderful example: the use of decoy choices. The book itself is worth reading (if only to become aware of how your choice is manipulated by cunning marketers), but take just the example of the decoy choice.

The Economist offered three subscription options:

a. Internet-only subscription for $59
b. Print-only subscription for $125
c. Both print and Internet subscription for $125

Pretty easy choice, eh? His MBA students at MIT's Sloan School of Management chose as follows: option a: 16; option b: 0; option c: 84. Because no one chose option b, Arley dropped that option and offered only two choices:

a. Internet-only subscription for $59
b. Both print and Internet subscription for $125

With these two choices the distribution changed significantly: option a: 68 (up from 16 previously); option b: 32 (down from 84). Weird, eh? In the book Arley explains why this happens, how decoy choices (such as "print-only for $125") work, and how this technique is often used to make people choose as the seller wants. (Realtors use it a lot.) It's a book that repays reading.

For the do-it-yourselfer

One option is to make rather than buy, and quite a few shavers enjoy making their own equipment and supplies. Silvertip knots, for example, are available from various sources, and it's not difficult for those with a lathe to turn a nice handle and then use a dab of 3M™ Marine Adhesive to glue the knot in place: a shaving brush you made yourself[62]. (You can use other glues or epoxies, but marine sealant is totally waterproof.)

BadgerBrush.net, Blankety-Blanks, The Golden Nib, Penchetta, and Whipped Dog sell badger knots and handle blanks, and a Google search will find more. BadgerBrush.net also sells horsehair knots. Another option is to restore an old brush[63], and it's satisfying to use a brush whose handle has a history.

Many new shavers want a stand for their brush and razor (though a stand is certainly unnecessary: shavers with a collection of brushes and razors normally do not bother with stands). Homemade stands can be made of wood or plastic, but coat-hanger wire is a popular choice, and for that a wire-bending tool[64] is handy. Home Depot sells heavy-gauge copper wire, which bends easily (especially with the tool) and looks attractive.

Recipes for other homemade supplies (aftershave, shave oil, pre-shave beard wash) will be presented in the course of the book.

SIX

Shaving step by step

IN the following chapters I explain in detail the process of shaving, following the sequence of the shave. Each chapter focuses on a single part of the shave or a single tool. Optional steps are indicated. YouTube videos made by Mantic59[65], geofatboy[66], Michael Freedberg[67], and betelgeux[68] are an excellent complement to the information in this book.

Grain of your beard

Before you begin to shave, determine the grain of your beard—that is, the direction it grows. You must know grain direction because your first pass is to shave *with* the grain (WTG), your second pass *across* the grain (XTG), and later, once you're comfortable using the razor, a final pass *against* the grain (ATG), except you do not shave ATG in areas in which you tend to get in-grown whiskers. You'll probably find that your beard's grain has different directions on different parts of your face and neck. Part of learning to shave is learning the lineaments of your own face.

When you shave with a single blade (rather than a multiblade cartridge), you make 2, 3, or even 4 passes—though when you begin, stick with doing just 2 passes. Multiple passes are made to get a close shave while using minimal pressure: instead of trying to achieve a close shave by pressing hard while making one pass, you make multiple passes using **light** pressure.

Too much pressure causes nicks, cuts, and razor burn (caused by scraping away the top layer of your skin). In shaving with a safety razor and a good blade, the weight of the razor is generally as much pressure as you need. Using a bad blade angle causes cuts and nicks.

To determine the direction of your beard's grain, wait 12-24 hours after you've shaved, then rub your fingertip (or the edge of a credit card or a cotton ball) on your beard. The roughest direction at each point is against the grain at that point.

For most men, the beard grows downward on the cheeks, so that part of the beard feels roughest if you're rubbing upward. But your beard may have anomalies. For example, I discovered that at the corner of my right jaw, my beard grows horizontally toward my chin: at that point, against the grain is horizontally toward my ear (which happened to be the opposite direction that I shaved in my XTG pass, so the slight roughness I felt there after each shave was because I never shaved ATG at that spot). And at another spot, the grain tilts.

The grain on your neck may well grow in some odd directions. It's not unusual, for example, for the beard on part or all of the neck to grow upward, so that shaving downward is against the grain. One reason the neck is so often a shaving challenge is that the beard's grain is often irregular on the neck. Other reasons are that the razor position can feel awkward and that the skin on the neck is sometimes softer and more flexible and thus harder to shave—stretching the skin by (for example) jutting your chin out will help. If the grain's irregular, good prep is particularly important.

For really gnarly patterns of growth (usually on the neck, but they can occur elsewhere) such as a whorl, where at least some against-the-grain shaving occurs even on the first pass, excellent prep is vital: washing the beard at the sink following the shower, a hot, moist towel laid over lather or Coral Skin Food—the works.

A slant razor, discussed later, can be an enormous help, especially on the neck[69] because irregular neck grain can result in irritation, apparently due to the way a regular razor pushes directly against the stubble, which then pushes against the skin (particularly the softer skin of the neck). Because of its slanted blade, a slant razor cuts thick stubble more easily, and since the blade doesn't push so hard against the stubble, the stubble does not push so hard against the skin. With a regular razor, useful techniques are the Gillette Slide and the J-hook that Mantic59 demonstrates in his video on Advanced Shaving Techniques[70].

Before your first shave, make a small sketch of your face and indicate the grain directions with arrows as a memory aid. You can use an interactive diagram[71] to prepare a printable map of your beard's grain. Making the map shows you the grain, and once the map is made, you will probably have to refer to it only a few times before you know your beard's grain quite well.

The winter bathroom

In colder climes the bathroom mirror may show a tendency to fog up in the winter. You can prevent that by applying lather to the mirror, then wiping it off with a towel. Or use liquid hand soap: apply a little to a paper towel and wipe it over the mirror, then take a clean paper towel and wipe the mirror until it's clear once more. It will then be fog-proof, though ultimately the treatment must be repeated.

Commercial compounds like Aquapel Anti-Fog treatment are available, but lather's right at hand and liquid hand soap is cheap.

Another wintertime problem in very cold climates is dry air: cold air holds little moisture, and when cold outside air is heated indoors, relative humidity plummets. If the problem is serious, vaporizers can help, but if the outside temperature is cold enough, the inside air will still be too dry, which affects the quality of the shave (among other things).

If humidity is very low, lather will quickly dry on the face—instead of providing lubrication, the lather seems to grab the razor. To avoid this, try making a wetter lather and/or adding a little water to the brush during the shave and working that into the lather on your beard. You can also experiment with adding a few drops of glycerin to your lather. (You can get glycerin at the cosmetics section of a healthfood store; glycerin from plant sources is readily available if you wish to avoid animal products.)

If you use a shave stick, you may have to dip it in water—the water on your face following the beard wash at the sink (or after simply wetting your beard if you find your shave goes better without a wash) will dry so quickly that the shave stick starts to feel tacky. When relative humidity is so low, dipping the shave stick makes sense. With normal humidity, that step is unnecessary since the water on the beard is sufficient to wet the stick.

With extremely dry air, you probably will want to look for shaving products that will help moisturize your skin: shaving soaps with lanolin or shea butter or avocado oil or other moisturizing content, and aftershave balms or milks, discussed in the section on aftershaves.

Skin sensitivities

Many men erroneously believe that they have "sensitive skin" because their skin's health has been damaged by using dry chemical foam instead of lather and by scraping their face with multiblade cartridges applied with pressure. But some men do in fact have sensitive skin, which reddens and/or breaks out easily when exposed to common products, sweat, sunlight, or the like. (As noted earlier, if your skin is sensitive only in the areas you shave, the sensitivity may simply be due to skin damage.)

If your skin reacts strongly when you use particular products (a soap or an aftershave or the like), the product probably includes ingredients to which you are allergic to some degree. Some men, for example, find that their face turns red and hot—even a burning sensation—for some minutes after using a soap or aftershave that includes (say) sandalwood, or rose, or lime (or other citrus). Proraso's (quite good) menthol and eucalyptus shaving cream will trigger a skin reaction for some men. In contrast, Taylor of Old Bond Street Avocado or Speick shaving creams seem rarely to cause any reaction.

If you know or suspect your skin might be sensitive to some ingredients, take advantage of samples as much as you can to test the product. Rather than testing on your face, smear a little in the crease of your elbow and wait for half an hour to see if your skin reacts. A sensitivity will usually show itself within minutes. Artisanal soapmakers generally sell samples of their soaps and aftershaves and several sites (see Appendix) offers samples of a wide range of commercial shaving products. Trumper and Taylor of Old Bond Street sell sampler kits. To make lather from a soap sample, you can use it like a shave stick, rubbing it on your beard, or hold it in the palm of one hand, brushing briskly to load the brush, or grate it coarsely and mash the gratings into a bowl. Once the gratings are dampened, they will fuse into a solid puck.

If you know that you have skin sensitivities—for example, you cannot wear wool against your skin—keep that in mind when you buy shaving products. If you're allergic to wool, you might find that animal-hair brushes (badger, boar, and horse) are less pleasing than a synthetic brushes—and fortunately synthetic brushes nowadays are excellent and perform as well as their natural counterparts. You might also find that products containing lanolin, such as Mitchell's Wool Fat Soap, don't work for you; at the least, try a sample before buying a puck, and always read the list of ingredients in the products you buy.

I find Musgo Real Glyce Lime Oil soap (MR GLO) a superb pre-shave soap, but some men have skin that reacts badly with the lime oil. Several reported some burning sensation with MR GLO but found when they used less—for example, when they washed their beard with the soap using just their hands rather than a washcloth and/or brush—they had no further problem and their shaves were still improved. Again, there are good alternatives, which I'll discuss later, but a person with this sensitivity should test carefully any shaving product using lime, a popular fragrance, or any other citrusy products.

Hard water reacts with soap to form a sticky scum, which can also cause skin problems. I later describe workarounds to avoid soap scum, but keep that issue in mind if your tap water is very hard. Extremely dry air, as noted above, can also affect the skin's health, and using a good moisturizer can help there.

Some fragrances seem more apt to trigger reactions—sandalwood, for example. Some men have reported that their initial use triggered a reaction, a second use less of a reaction, and by the third or fourth use, their skin no longer reacted at all. Other men see no diminution of the reaction—YMMV in action.

The alum block, a post-shave skin treatment, makes the skin red and hot for a few minutes for some, though most experience no problems. Again, you can test an alum block on the crease of your elbow joint before using it on your face.

Most shavers do not experience any skin sensitivities or reactions at all. Those who do have skin sensitivities learn quickly what ingredients to avoid.

In addition to sensitivities, consider insensitivities as well. If you use a cologne daily, your nose in time becomes habituated to the fragrance so that you yourself no longer smell it. But if you apply enough so that you can clearly smell it even though your nose is habituated, and the resulting fragrance overload allows others to smell you coming from twenty paces away. Be aware of the problem and avoid gradually increasing the amount over time.

Fragrances add a lot to the shaving experience, and are worth some exploration. Few have the nose of a Luca Turin[72], but most can learn to appreciate good, complex fragrances in much the same way one learns to appreciate fine foods (often loved because of their aromas): through experience.

Because some are quite sensitive to fragrances—to the point of allergies—it's good to avoid fragrances if you will be cheek-by-jowl with strangers, as in airline travel, elevator travel, crowded parties, and the like. Modesty in fragrances is becoming. When I travel, I use an aftershave having no fragrance or only a short-lived fragrance, like the Thayers witch hazels.

Beyond skin sensitivities—which are allergy reactions—the skin can also be damaged in time by some ingredients—menthol, for example, is generally regarded as damaging to the skin. Sometimes the ingredient itself may be harmful, sometimes the ingredient is harmful only in combination with other factors (for example, direct sunlight—citrus ingredients such bergamot, bitter orange, grapefruit, lemon, lemon verbena, lime, mandarin, neroli, orange, or tangerine can cause photosensitivity[73]). My skin seems robust and moreover I'm an indoorsy guy, but it's worth checking lists of potentially harmful substances[74] and to favor products whose ingredients do not include those substances at all, or if they're used, they appear only near the end of the list of ingredients.

Still, I must admit that I frequently ignore these issues, which seem to affect only some people. Sodium lauryl sulfate (SLS), for example, is a surfactant and foaming agent often used in shampoos, toothpastes, and soaps. My wife is quite sensitive to SLS and must search for shampoos and toothpastes that do not include it, but it has no effect whatsoever on me so far as I can tell, despite the dire warnings one can find on the Internet. My lack of reaction to SLS seems to be true for many, given its ubiquity in products and the FDA's willingness to accept it as an ingredient. So the rule I suggest is to exercise reasonable caution and care, recognizing that the meaning of "reasonable" varies from person to person. Do not be *too* cautious and keep in mind that YMMV.

Animal issues

Some shavers—vegan or not—may wish to avoid products *tested on* animals. But first consider ingredients *derived from* animals and used in shaving products.

Brushes rather obviously use animal ingredients, as it were. Badgers in China—the source of the hairs used in badger brushes—are vermin and are killed in any event, but still some will wish to find alternatives. Boar brushes use bristles that are a by-product of animal slaughter—as with badgers, the animal will die in any case, if that makes a difference. (It never does.)

Horsehair brushes, however, are a by-product of grooming, and horses not only are unharmed by grooming, they actually benefit from it. Still, if you wish to avoid animal products entirely, synthetic brushes are the way to go, and excellent synthetic brushes are now available. Mühle synthetics have led the way, but now excellent synthetics are available from Omega (specifically the S-Series brushes), Plisson, Kent, and others.

Many good shaving soaps are tallow-based, but those are easily avoided in favor of plant-based soaps that use vegetable oils such as coconut or palm oil. However, palm plantations are terribly destructive of animal habitat and a case can be made that, overall, tallow-based soaps are more benign environmentally than soaps that use palm oil. Trade-offs must be made.

Many glycerin-based soaps use glycerin derived from plant rather than animal sources. You can check with the vendor for individual products if the information is not published.

Testing products on animals has been a common practice in the cosmetics industry. Many companies now state that they do no animal testing, and artisanal soaps, shaving creams, and aftershaves are rarely if ever tested on animals. However, cosmetic manufacturers and soap artisans generally don't say (probably because they don't know) whether their *suppliers* do any animal testing. Companies in general *really* do not want their products to hurt people, who are prone to hire lawyers and start class action lawsuits. Animals, on the other hand, seldom sue and thus testing on animals, to ensure that products will not harm humans, continues to some degree. One can exercise diligence, but supply chains now are long and global in scope and to learn exactly what happens along the way is difficult and sometimes impossible.

Prep

THE quality of your shave depends largely on how well you prepare your beard for the shave. A dry whisker, according to Gillette, is as tough as a copper wire of the same diameter—but a whisker, unlike a copper wire, can soak up water and become easier to cut. Good prep ensures that your whiskers are ready for the razor and will offer little resistance to being cut. Inadequate prep leaves your whiskers tough, so the blade tugs, catches, and skips, giving you an uncomfortable and scraggly shave, complete with nicks and cuts, and a blade that's now dull. In fact, shaving with poor prep and shaving with a dull blade feel exactly the same.

Shaving resembles painting in that you spend a good amount of time preparing the surface before actually picking up the paintbrush (or razor). The actual painting/shaving occurs only toward the end of the process and goes more or less easily (and works more or less well) depending on the quality and thoroughness of your prep as well as on your skill and the quality of your tools and supplies. Good-quality paint works better than poor-quality paint, pretty much by definition, and the same performance difference holds for many products, such as shaving soap—not a great surprise, though the difference still can be impressive[75].

A thorough prep, however, does not mean using every possible pre-shave product you can find. Just as in shaving you apply to the razor the least pressure that works, and on an adjustable you use the lowest setting that gets a good shave (rather than the highest you can stand), so in prep the ideal is to find the minimal set of products and procedures that produce a superb shave: efficiency and a smooth flow are goals just as much as is effectiveness. Some go at their skin with hammer and tongs, as it were, almost as though they carry a grudge against their skin.

Their frustration and search for solutions is understandable if they are coming from shaving with cartridges: having healthy skin is a challenge if you're using a high-count cartridge razor (high count both in number of blades in the cartridge and, because of price, in number of shaves demanded from each cartridge). In this scenario the skin suffers horribly, and the shaver uses all sorts of unguents and nostrums in an effort to repair the damage. But since the damage is repeated daily, it's a losing battle. In contrast, a single-blade razor correctly wielded is kind to the skin, and you'll quickly discover that you can get an excellent shave from the smallest number of blades possible: one. In the same way, you should use only the products you actually need to get a good prep.

Start by using just a shaving brush and shaving soap or shaving cream: lather is your prep. Add a pre-shave soap later, and see whether it improves the shave, using the three-week test protocol. (MR GLO definitely improved my own shaves, and other glycerin soaps also work.) That may well be enough, but experimentation is good. Test each new addition to the routine, as well as testing different shaving soaps and creams. Your two goals are (1) to get the best possible shave and (2) to do that using as few products as possible: the products that are both necessary and sufficient.

Step 1: Shower – but this varies by shaver

For a majority of men, it's a good idea to shave after showering: the hot water and steam of the shower start preparing the beard for the shave. Some men, however, find that showering just before a shave makes their skin sensitive and prone to irritation; if you find that's true for you, shave *before* you shower. I did an informal poll and found that about 60% of those responding shave immediately after their shower and 40% shave without a preceding shower—they shower after shaving or at some other time.

A moisturizing hair conditioner used on your beard in the shower may help and is worth a try. Look for a hair conditioner that claims to soften hair—conditioners come in different types[76]. And *always* test any pre-shave procedure. In this case, do *not* automatically make using a conditioner a standard part of your routine, but first do a test: shave a week using a conditioner, then a week without, then another week using it. Or if a week's too long, try doing the same test, for three days with, three without, and then with again for three days. See whether it makes a difference for *you*. Use only what works for you—and only as much as you need.

If you shower in the evening, consider shaving then as well. For a novice, an evening shave works well: in the evening, unrushed, he can take his time as he masters technique. And since the ritual of wetshaving is relaxing, as noted above, it's a fine prelude to a date night.

Some guys use a facial scrub as part of their routine. If you're switching to DE shaving, ditch the scrub for now: the shave itself is exfoliating, and your skin can profitably do without additional agitation. If you believe you must use a facial scrub, use it on the unshaved parts of your face—forehead and nose—

and/or skip shaving one day a week and use the facial scrub on that day. Too much care can be as hard on the skin as too little.

If your water contains things that irritate your skin (for example, highly chlorinated water), a shower filter might prove helpful[77]. My experience with plastic-cased shower filters is that they tend to split, so I got one made of plated brass[78] (like vintage Gillette razors ☺). And I very much like my high-velocity low-flow aerating shower head[79] that, despite its invigoratingly brisk spray, uses only 1.5 gallons of water per minute. As I've moved from place to place over the years, I always remove and take along my shower filter and showerhead, reinstalling the original showerhead that I replaced when I moved in.

Step 2: Wash your beard

Even though I've just showered, I still wash my beard at the sink with soap and water before lathering. Some get a better shave if they don't do this step but instead simply rinse their face with water. (Experiment to find what works best for you.) Note that hard water combines with soap to form a sticky scum, so if your tap water is hard, use distilled or softened water for this step or skip it. (See the section below on water.)

I generally wash my beard using a high-glycerin soap. One that I've used for several years is Musgo Real Glyce Lime Oil soap (MR GLO), specifically designed as a pre-shave soap. The identical soap is available also as Ach. Brito Glyce Lime Glycerin soap[80] at a lower price. (Both Musgo Real and Ach. Brito are owned by Claus Porto; the only difference I can tell between the soaps is the label— sometimes literally: I have unwrapped soaps labeled "Musgo Real" and find the bar stamped "Ach. Brito.") I tested these  soaps using the three-week test protocol, and they passed with flying colors, noticeably improving the shave. Given YMMV, some will notice no improvement, and sometimes that's due to having hard water. (Soap plus hard water equals sticky soap scum.) Note that MR GLO is **not** a shaving soap and doesn't create a lather: it's a *pre-shave* soap.

Some find that their skin reacts to MR GLO's lime (or another ingredient) and becomes red and hot for a few minutes after using the soap. If you think lime may prove to be a problem, try a sample (from one of the sources listed in the appendix under "Samples") and test it as noted earlier, in the crease of your elbow joint. If you do have a reaction, try another high-glycerin soap.

I wrote a brief article on several alternative pre-shave soaps[81], all high-glycerin soaps. The glycerin soaps sold by Whole Foods under its 365 brand work particularly well, and those currently cost less than $2/bar and come in a wide range of fragrances. Dr. Bronner's bar soap works well; Clearly Natural glycerin soap is widely available and works well. Several artisanal soapmakers make their own high-glycerin pre-shave soaps.

One caution regarding glycerin soap: it melts easily, and in a hot car in the summer, the soap can become more than soft.

Wash your beard with the soap, using your hands, *partially* rinse with a splash, and then apply lather (from a shaving soap/cream) for a fine shave.

I also occasionally use a formula I developed based on an idea from jlocke98. He puts a small amount of Dr. Bronner's liquid Castile soap in his palm, adds a couple of drops of lanolin oil, and washes his beard with that. In order to maintain a smooth flow in the shave, I premix the components. After some experimentation, I bought an 8-oz. (250 ml) pump bottle. Into it I pour in 3/4 cup (180 ml) of Dr. Bronner's liquid soap and 2 tablespoons (30 ml) of oil. Before each shave, I shake the bottle well and use about 1/2 teaspoon (3 ml) to wash my beard. (The ratio to observe if you're mixing batches of another size: use 1 fluid ounce (30 ml) of soap to 1 teaspoon (5 ml) of oil.)

Lanolin oil has two drawbacks: first, some men find that lanolin triggers a skin reaction (and cannot, for example, use Mitchell's Wool Fat shaving soap); second, after sitting on the soap for a few days lanolin oil clots into a solid mass and doesn't mix well—and the same is true for olive oil. I also tried jojoba oil, almond oil (often used in therapeutic massage), and grapeseed oil, and they all worked fine; hempseed oil is favored by some.

Of all the oils I tried, emu oil has worked best: it's a light oil and mixes readily with the soap—and it even seems to have some therapeutic benefits[82]. After washing the beard with a little of the mix, rinse partially with a splash and then apply lather. I tried using Clearly Natural Vitamin E glycerin hand soap instead of Dr. Bronner's, but the mix with Dr. Bronner's worked much better.

Dr. Bronner's soap, like other MR GLO and other soaps, is somewhat alkaline (pH > 7) and since the skin is protected by a acidic mantle, some have expressed a concern that using soap (Dr. Bronner's or, indeed, shaving soap) will damage the skin. I have not found it to be so, but I wanted to mention the possibility. If you do find problems from using this pre-shave beard wash and/or shaving soap, discontinue use. (Obvious advice, I know.) The three-week test should help determine whether problems arise. Based on reports in the forums, problems are in fact extremely rare.

Some shavers have experimented using a scrubby shaving brush with their pre-shave soap, **not** to work up a lather but to do a better job of scrubbing skin and beard than when just using their hands. Others find the brush too rough and get a skin reaction and that using their hands works better. You can also try washing your beard using pre-shave soap with a washcloth, but don't scrub hard—and do rinse only partially: the glycerin contributes lubricity.

I recommend against shaving in the shower, but some men prefer that, so if they use a high-glycerin pre-shave soap, they will use it in the shower. However, the soap must **not** be *stored* in the shower: glycerin is hydrophilic, and a high-glycerin soap will not long survive a high-humidity environment like a steamy shower. The soap will first show beads of water on its surface and soon turn to mush. A bar of MR GLO lasts me exactly three months, shaving six days a week; if kept in the shower, a bar lasts a fortnight.

Obviously, since you're running a razor-sharp blade (no exaggeration) over your face, your face should *definitely* be clean. No grime, if you please.

Step 3: Apply a pre-shave [optional]

Before you lather, you can apply a pre-shave—oil, cream, gel, or lotion (or even CVS Electric Pre-Shave)—to your wet beard. With any pre-shave, be sure to try the three-week test to see whether the pre-shave actually helps your shave. Some find a pre-shave helpful, others do not. I never found a pre-shave that helped (except for the pre-shave beard wash described above).

Compare the shave that you get when using your pre-shave only before lathering for the first pass and the result when using it before lathering for each pass. (Some do find their pre-shaves work best if used before each pass.)

Another technique is to apply the pre-shave and then let it sit—some leave it on as they shower, others apply it and then apply a hot, moist towel (though then it may be that the perceived benefits are from the hot towel, not the pre-shave: when you wonder whether something works, experiment to find out).

My only pre-shave is to wash my beard with MR GLO or the jlocke98 pre-shave mix and to take my time brushing a good lather into my beard before the first pass. The shave results are excellent. I did, however, experiment with all the pre-shave options.

Pre-shave creams/gels

Proraso, an Italian company, makes Proraso Pre- and Post-Shave, a cream that can be used both as a pre-shave and an aftershave. Most apply it only once, before lathering for the first pass, and then leave it on for about five minutes before lathering. Some apply it before showering, and leave it on in the shower. As the name says, it can also be used as an aftershave.

Crema 3P and PREP Classic Cream are Italian pre-shave creams similar to Proraso's. Another Italian pre-shave is a gel: Floïd Sandolor Preshave Gel. Taylor of Old Bond Street (aka TOBS) makes a pre-shave herbal gel that some men with tough beards have found effective. After the beard is washed and rinsed, rub the gel into the wet beard and then let it sit for a minute or two. You could do this step before the shower, for example. Then lather on top of the gel and shave as you normally do.

The Shave Den's pre-shave balm is perhaps more related to a pre-shave oil, though it is a thick paste. The ingredients are shea butter, lanolin, jojoba oil, avocado oil, sweet almond oil, vitamin E, and fragrance (sandalwood and oakmoss). Rub it into your beard before showering and perhaps also apply a hot towel, then lather. Samples are available if you wish to experiment.

Although not intended as a pre-shave, some have found that Noxema Facial Cleansing cream works well as a pre-shave, and some use a thin layer of Neutrogena Skin Saving Latherless shaving cream as a pre-shave, applying lather (made with a brush and a shaving soap or a (lathering) shaving cream) on top.

Trumper Skin Food

Geo. F. Trumper's Coral Skin Food, available also in Lime or Sandalwood, is normally used as an aftershave balm and skin treatment. Dr. Chris Moss, mentioned earlier, discovered that Coral Skin Food makes a very good every-pass pre-shave, applied to the wet beard just before lathering for each pass. At Trumper's barber shop, Coral Skin Food is applied to the beard and then covered by a hot towel (as described below). Coral seems to work better than Lime or Sandalwood. Note also that a few drops of Skin Food atop puck or brush seems to alleviate lathering problems with some soaps, such as Mitchell's Wool Fat.

100% glycerin

Dr. Moss noticed that Skin Food uses glycerin, so he tried a few drops of glycerin as an every-pass pre-shave. It had much the same effect as Coral Skin Food, but at a much lower price. Healthfood and drug stores carry 100% glycerin[83].

Pre-shave oils

I've never liked oils as a pre-shave (though later I discuss their use in a final polishing pass), so I don't have much to say about them save that they exist. It's not clear to me that they're compatible with a good lather. When I've tried them, I have found that the lather has suffered and the shave was not improved. Your experience may differ—some guys love them—so you may want to experiment with using them.

If you do want to try a pre-shave oil, try using a few drops of jojoba oil or olive oil or coconut oil, recommended by various shavers. Grapeseed oil also gets high praise: it is high in linoleic acid, which is anti-inflammatory, anti-acne, and moisturizing.

Pacific Shaving Company's All-Natural Shaving Oil seems to include some emulsifier so that it doesn't feel so oily as other shaving oils. The fragrance of Nancy Boy Pre-Shave oil is good. Truefitt & Hill make a highly regarded (and expensive) pre-shave oil. The Art of Shaving pre-shave oil is generally disliked as being too gummy, but since this is shaving, YMMV applies: some guys like it a lot.

Pre-shave oil is one of the items for which you can find many recipes on-line[84]. On reddit's Wicked_Edge sub-reddit, indiexsunrise offers one recipe[85]:

1 part jojoba oil

1 part vitamin E oil

1 part castor oil

2 parts glycerin

1 drop of your favorite essential oil for fragrance

Later in the book I discuss a variety of pre-shave oils that can be used for a final polishing pass, after all lather work is done.

Step 4: Apply hot towel [required if you get in-growns]

If you get a shave in a good barber shop—shavers often report that the Trumper and Truefitt & Hill shops in London are excellent—part of the prep by the barber consists of placing moist hot towels over your beard and often your entire face. Sometimes a hot towel is used after applying a layer of lather, or rubbing the beard with Coral Skin Food or with a shaving oil. (Choose one, not all three—or experiment with trying various combinations to see how they work for you.)

The warmth and moisture from the towel helps ready the beard for an easy shave. The basic technique is to wash and lather your beard (or apply Coral Skin Food or a pre-shave oil or other pre-shave preparation), then lay a moist hot towel over your prepared beard (including your neck), lean back, and meditate quietly for 1-3 minutes. The towel's moist heat combined with the lather, Skin Food, or oil softens the beard remarkably[86]. Then remove the towel, apply lather, and shave. You can also tie the towel around your face and neck to hold it in place. If your neck's grain is irregular, you may want to focus the towel's action on your neck.

If you have a microwave, you can heat the towel by dampening it and putting it into the microwave for 45 seconds. Otherwise, soak a hand towel or a dishtowel under the hot-water tap and wring it "dry." A hand towel is large enough to remain hot for the 2-3 minutes; a washcloth is too small and will cool too quickly. Sybarites can spritz a little hydrosol[87] or other fragrance on the damp towel before heating it.

Using a hot towel before shaving is *not* optional if you suffer from razor bumps or in-growns. In that case, the treatment is particularly important.

Prep Step 5: Apply lather

THE quality of your lather is a key factor in the quality of your shave. Canned foam (or gel) is the source of lather for most men, and even traditional shavers use it on occasion—Barbasol[88] is most often mentioned as a reasonably satisfactory canned foam. But the almost universal consensus is that a true lather, created from either shaving soap or shaving cream by using a shaving brush and hot water, is better than any canned foam, including Barbasol. As mentioned earlier, if you change only one—the razor or the lather—change the lather: switch from canned foam to true lather, and your shave will improve noticeably and immediately and provide more enjoyment to boot.

With experience you can create a true lather from scratch in 40 seconds or so (loading the brush for 10 seconds, then working up the lather on your beard[89]), so it makes sense to get a lot of experience quickly—that is, to make a series of test lathers each day until you can reliably and quickly create an excellent shaving lather. Be patient and observe carefully as you go, thus helping the adaptive unconscious learn the process. A good lather is dense, thick, and heavy, with microscopic bubbles. (Larger bubbles indicate too much water or water added too fast to be worked into the lather.) Your whiskers are easily cut after absorbing water; a thick, heavy lather holds water against the stubble, plus it lubricates the skin so the razor glides easily.

A good lather may be somewhat drier[90] and thicker than you expect—or it may be wetter. Experiment to find the best lather for you. Judicious experimentation is always encouraged—to some extent you teach yourself how to make lather, just as you teach yourself to make free throws: frequent practice and paying close attention to what you do and what results. Let's look at the components of the process, beginning with the lathering tools.

"Wetshaving" extends beyond using a true lather (a lather made with a shaving brush from shaving soap or shaving cream and water) to include more broadly any prep that uses shaving soap/cream and water, whether or not a brush is involved. However, even though some brushless shave creams are excellent[91], I recommend using a shaving brush simply because most find that using a brush is effective—and enjoyable to boot, providing a more pleasurable shave. Consider: you're going to have to spread stuff over your beard, and you can use your hand or a brush. Most prefer a brush (once they've actually tried it, and are not merely speculating) because it does a better job, it's not so messy, and it's more enjoyable, increasing the pleasure they get from the shave.

Lather provides pleasure is in part because the making of the lather is a skill, and a skill once learned is enjoyable to practice—and, to be honest, making lather is a skill you can easily learn. So that's part of the pleasure: observing how skillfully you whip up a really fine lather—and while you're doing that, you get additional enjoyment from the fragrance the lather releases. (The enjoyment of one's skill—taking pleasure simply in observing how skillfully one does a task—also provides substantial enjoyment in straight razor shaving: honing, stropping, and shaving are all skills whose exercise provides enjoyment once they are mastered.)

After making the lather, you bring the brush to your beard, and that also is truly enjoyable if you have a brush of any decent quality at all—and if touching your face with the warm, lather-filled, fragrant brush is not a pure pleasure, then you don't have the right brush for you.

Tools for true lather

To create lather from shaving cream or soap, one uses a shaving brush and (optionally) a lathering bowl or warming scuttle. Some shaving creams are "brushless," generally meaning that they do not require a brush and using them with a brush does not produce lather. The idea is to smear those creams on your beard using your hand, but this has some drawbacks, the most obvious being that it's messy and requires rinsing your hand after applying the cream for each pass. Moreover, using your hand also wastes shaving cream: if you use a damp brush instead, you avoid the mess and the brush holds enough cream from the first pass to do the later passes as well.

Moreover, most brushless shaving creams compare poorly to lathering shaving creams. Nancy Boy shaving cream is a notable exception. In this section, however, I will discuss only lathering shaving creams and shaving soaps.

Shaving brush

The bristles in a shaving brush are synthetic, horse, boar, or badger—generally bristles of just one type, but brushes are also available that combine badger and boar, badger and horse, and boar and horse. The collection of bristles is called the "knot," and the length of the knot is the "loft." Brushes with synthetic bristles[92] are favored by those who have allergies, who wish to avoid the use of

64

animal products, and/or who travel (since synthetics dry quickly)—or, nowadays, just because the brush is so good. Horsehair brushes and boar brushes have been around for centuries and are popular still. Badger has long been the standard for expensive shaving brushes, with silvertip badger brushes (the tips of the bristles being white or off-white) as the top of the line.

Knots range from dense, short, and fairly stiff/scrubby to fluffy, soft knots. Even dense and stiff knots can have soft velvety tips, but the knots themselves are not soft—the "softness" of those knots is like the softness of a velvet-covered golf ball, a softness that is, in effect, skin-deep. These brushes are said to have lots of "backbone." A fluffy knot is soft all the way through, though still resilient—it's like a soft fluffy pillow that mashes easily but springs back to its original shape when the pressure's released. I suggest the following nomenclature for the feel of the brush:

"Scrubby": these brushes generally have dense knots and short lofts so they are quite firm on the face and you can feel the scrubbing action. A thick boar knot with short loft would fall here, and short, dense badger knots such as the Chubby Super or the knots used currently by Brushguy.com.

"Stiff": a step removed from scrubby. This brush generally has a dense knot with a somewhat longer loft than a scrubby brush, so the knot bends more readily when brushing your face. Some boar brushes fall here, along with some horsehair brushes.

"Resilient": a step removed from stiff: these brushes have more give than stiff brushes and feel somewhat lively and willing to bend. Most badger brushes, some boar brushes (with long lofts), horsehair, and synthetics like the Omega Hi-Performance synthetic.

"Soft": no boar or horsehair brushes in this category. These brushes have a soft and fluffy knot. The individual bristles still have resilience, but also a lot of give. For example the Plisson synthetic and Omega S-Series belong to this category, as do a couple of large Omega silvertip badger brushes I have. A soft knot, set somewhat deeper, will act as a resilient knot instead.

Knot capacity (and lather generosity) generally increases as you move from scrubby to soft. The fluffier the knot, the more room for lather.

It's important to note that brushes in **all** of those categories can make good lather quite efficiently and with no problem, even from hard soaps. The notion that one requires a stiff brush to get a good lather from a hard soap is simply false (based on my own direct experience). With hard water, a stiff brush may scrape up more soap, needed when using hard water, but the problem in that case is the water, not the brush. With reasonably soft water, any brush will quickly generate good lather, and the brush can be loaded in 10 seconds or so[93].

I would like to drive a stake through the heart of "floppy" as a brush category. This is clearly a pejorative term (few say that they like a "floppy" brush) and it is also inaccurate: I've never seen a brush knot flop over when wet or loaded with lather. Some, naturally enough, do not like soft brushes, but that doesn't mean that they should denigrate the category. Quite a few of use enjoy the feeling of a soft brush loaded with lather as we brush it over our face. My hope is that "soft" (or "fluffy") will replace "floppy" as a brush description.

The main basis for choice of brush thus is not lathering efficiency (any brush can make good lather if the water's soft and your technique is good) but personal preference: how well you like the feel of the brush on your face. And to discover your preferences, you must use a variety of brushes. Choose based on experience, not expectations, because expectations have proven unreliability.

Some novices use the brush with some delicacy, as in using a paint brush on a smooth surface. That does not work well. Use reasonable firmness in loading the brush and working the lather into the stubble—not scrubbing hard, nor gently brushing the surface, but between those: a gentle firmness.

Some users find that their new animal-hair brush (horse, boar, or badger) has a distinct animal odor. That odor goes away after using the brush a few times. Its departure can be hastened by shampooing the brush (some use dog shampoo) and/or making practice lathers. In my experience, brushes with strong odors are relatively rare, and the odor may even strike those who enjoy the company of large animals as being pleasantly rustic.

Synthetic-bristle brushes

In the past few years, much progress has been made in synthetic knots for shaving brushes[94], driven in part by rumors that the EU may ban the use of badger hair. I expect research and improvement in synthetic shaving brushes will continue, so check for the most recent information when you buy.

Most brushmakers— Edwin Jagger, Frank Shaving, G.B. Kent, Mühle, Omega, Simpson, Taylor of Old Bond Street—now include excellent synthetic brushes in their line-up. Mühle in particular seems to have invested heavily in R&D regarding synthetic brushes, and their black synthetic and silverfiber knots are particularly good, though Plisson also offers an excellent synthetic knot, and the same fibers are used in The Grooming Co. brushes. However, Plisson and TGC knots are noticeably different. Plisson's knot is soft and pleasant, but the TGC knot is stiffer and more resilient—*too* resilient for my taste—probably because the knot is set deeper.

The HJM line, made by Mühle is also good. The best bang for the buck is Omega's S-Series "synthetic boar" brushes. Those brushes perform superbly, feel good, and sell at a very low price (currently under $10). I recommend an Omega S-Series (*not* the Omega Syntex) as an excellent brush for a beginner.

The cheapest synthetic brushes (like Omega Syntex brushes) use relatively thick white nylon bristles (like those found in a plastic whiskbroom) and might serve as a brush you keep in your gym locker: they can generate a good lather, and though quite sturdy are not particularly comfortable. But the best new synthetic bristles are thinner than the white nylon, though still resilient, and are treated so that the tips are fine, soft, and bushy.

These new synthetic-bristle brushes are completely satisfactory as shaving brushes, with bristles designed and engineered specifically for the purpose. Moreover, synthetic bristles offer some advantages over natural bristles, including drying fast and being hypoallergenic and nonabsorbent.

Because synthetic bristles are non-absorbent, synthetic brushes make efficient use of water. Indeed, give synthetic brushes a couple of good shakes before lathering to remove excess water, since otherwise it can spill out of the brush and make loading more difficult. This is important, so please take note.

In Chapter 11 of *The Selfish Gene*, Richard Dawkins describes "memes," the basic units of cultural inheritance. The same laws that drives genetic evolution in lifeforms will drive the evolution of memes, so that cultural phenomena and objects evolve. Memes, however, evolve *much* faster than genes.

A brush, for example, is an example of a meme: it is a cultural artifact, made initially by one person, and then imitated (and modified) by others. Brushes constitute a genus in the family "tools" of the order "physical artifacts" (other orders might be "musical artifacts," "language artifacts," and so on). Brushes have evolved into a great many species to suit many different purposes; they now are found in all shapes and sizes, with the shaving brushes species having many varieties.

Brushes using natural fibers—badger hair, for example—have some natural limits: if demand grows rapidly, as it is doing now, the supply of badger hair will not be able to keep up, and thus badger hair of high quality becomes more expensive as demand outstrips supply. Moreover, badger hair itself changes only at the rate of the evolution of lifeforms: *very* slowly.

A meme (cultural artifact) such as synthetic brush fiber can evolve *much* more rapidly—as you can see by comparing Omega's Syntex brushes of a few years ago with their S-Series brushes of today. Moreover, synthetic processes scale: once you have it figured out, you can ramp up production and pump out thousands relatively easily, something impossible with natural-fiber brushes.

We can expect the evolution of synthetic brushes to continue (quickly) and prices to drop as supply and competition increase. The shaver benefits, and it's a nice example of the evolution of memes that Dawkins discusses.

You can see the same kind of evolution of memes, by looking at the various genera and species of razors.

Horsehair brushes

Horsehair brushes have enjoyed a renascence among traditional wetshavers, with a rapidly growing number of fans. Horsehair brushes seem to be favored particularly in
Spain and are available in a range of designs, including some made of a mix: horsehair and badger, or white horsehair and boar. Horsehair brushes have good flow-through with none of the tendency to hog the lather one sometimes finds in boar or badger, and horsehair brushes also dry faster than boar or badger.

The best source of horsehair brushes I've found is GiftsAndCare.com, located in Spain: a benefit for those ordering within the EU. I've ordered from them many times with no problems at all, and I found that shipping charges to the US are modest. Some US vendors (BullGoose Shaving, for one) also sell horsehair brushes.

The Spanish company Vie-Long makes a wide variety of shaving brushes, including most of the horsehair brushes now made. Horsehair is finer and softer than boar and slightly stiffer than badger, and horsehair brushes do a particularly good lathering job. Mane hair is softer, tail hair stiffer and more resilient, and the two are mixed to make a shaving brush. Common ratios are 50/50 and 35 mane/65 tail. Gifts and Care will do custom mixes and customs lofts on request: tell them with your order.

A few users have reported tangles developing. I've not encountered the problem, but those who have report that combing the knot will undo the tangle. The problem seems to be relatively rare and caused by using too much pressure on a brush—for example, using the same amount of pressure on a horsehair brush that would be used on a boar brush—while brushing in a circular motion, especially on the chin. Use back-and-forth strokes and the problem is unlikely to arise even with gentle firm pressure. (Longer lofts may tangle more easily.)

Some horsehair brushes have a dyed stripe, and in the first few lathers some dye bleeds, so the lather is slightly grey, but after that all is well. I prefer my own brushes without the dyed stripe: the solid color looks good and the knot feels better and sturdier than those processed to produce the stripe. The knots come in various colors (as do horses). Some chestnut brushes are particularly beautiful in good sunlight, which brings out highlights.

Though horsehair brushes fell in popularity around the time of the Great War (because of an anthrax scare[95]), they have new popularity because of their solid performance in the lather department and their modest price compared to badger. Right now, horsehair brushes are my favorite, and they routinely produce exceptionally good lather. It took me multiple shaves to awaken to this.

Vie-Long also makes brushes of horsehair and badger combined, and these brushes have a very nice and vigorous action. They feel quite dense, and the knot color tends toward gray. I find, however, that I much prefer pure horsehair to the horsehair+badger mix.

Horses are unharmed in the harvesting of the hair—and indeed grooming seems much less traumatic for a horse than shearing is for a sheep.

Horsehair brushes do become softer after soaking (as does boar). Soaking is easily done by wetting the knot well under the hot-water tap and then letting brush sit for a few moments—while you shower, for example. You do not have to submerge the brush. But, as always, experiment: a week with soaking, a week without, another week with, then decide.

Boar-bristle brushes

Boar brushes have been used for generations and continue to be popular, in part because of price (boar bristles are plentiful and easily obtained) but also because of their excellent performance. Although the boar brush you find in your local drugstore may not amount to much, a well-made boar brush, once broken in, has a pleasant feel and makes a superb lather. Italians especially favor boar brushes.

Unlike synthetic, horsehair, or badger brushes, boar brushes do require a break-in period. Because it's often mentioned that the ends of boar bristles split with use, imparting a softer feel, I at first thought that was the entirety of the break-in. But a new boar brush can be lathercidal: when you pick up the brush for your second or third pass, you find that the lather has completely decayed and you must reload to continue. This property quickly fades as you use the brush (and thus is accelerated by making practice lathers). After a week of daily use you'll see a big difference, and break-in continues for some weeks thereafter as the bristles split at the ends, becoming finer and softer.

Boar bristles, like other natural bristles and unlike synthetic bristles, absorb water (and boar bristles absorb much more than badger or horsehair bristles), so you "soak" the bristles before use. This is most easily done by wetting the brush knot well under the hot-water tap and let the brush sit dripping wet while you shower.

Developing a good lather from soap with a boar brush requires practice and rather more vigorous and extended loading than with other brushes.

The major players in the boar-brush market are Omega (Italy) and Semogue (Portugal). Omega brushes are excellent and generally inexpensive, though the 21762 with a solid resin handle (in the colors of the Italian flag) with unclipped boar bristles costs a little more—but it has a wonderfully soft, thick knot, the only boar brush I've tried that could be called "soft." The Omega 20102 is a very nice brush with a wooden handle, which I prefer to the plastic handle 10048 (the "Pro 48"), also a popular brush. Those two cost the same. Some find the Omega Pro 48 somewhat large for face lathering (though it works well for me), but the Omega family is large with many options available[96].

Semogue makes a wide variety of boar brushes (and badger as well), and you can find a good selection at VintageScents.com. I find the quality of Semogue is not quite so good as Omega. I had one Semogue 2000 that worked reasonably well (though the knot seemed higgledy-piggledy), the next Semogue 2000 I got had a splayed knot that would never close when in use. Some men do like Semogue boar brushes—perhaps I have been unlucky in getting brushes with bad knots, and certainly many shavers praise Semogue brushes highly. Still, I have used at least a dozen Omega brushes and have yet to encounter a bad knot

The Omega 11047 boar/badger brush is excellent and a favorite of mine (and many others). Soak it for the boar, and it performs like a badger. Its small size makes it a good travel brush and does not affect its (ample) capacity.

Many new shavers will start with a badger, horsehair, or synthetic brush: it's easier to create a good lather at the outset (no break-in required). But boar brushes remain popular, and the quality/price ratio is quite high. An enthusiast named Zach wrote a detailed and comprehensive guide to boar brushes[97] that is well worth reading. At one time boar brushes were considered inferior (due to those drugstore brushes), but now they are more esteemed.

Be warned, though, that some boar brushes never work well, so don't assume that problems you may encounter with a boar brush are necessarily your fault. If you do start with a boar brush, I recommend you try one made by Omega.

When I first began using boar brushes, I got the impression that they lacked good capacity for lather, as compared to the alternatives. I have since learned—been taught, in fact—that proper loading of a boar brush (brushing the soap vigorously for perhaps 30 seconds) shows that a good boar brush (the Omega 20102 or 48 or 49, for example) has ample capacity once broken in. More and more men are finding that they really *like* boar brushes: they don't "settle" for them, they *prefer* them.

Badger-bristle brushes

Most shavers will sooner or later acquire a brush made from bristles taken from the Asian badger. These bristles are available in several grades[98].

Badger brushes are made by hand[99]. There are clear differences[100] between pure, best, and silvertip badger brushes, though the meaning of the categories vary by manufacturer. Here are photos of three badger brushes: from left to right: an Omega "pure badger," a Simpson "best badger," and a Rooney "finest badger." Badger brushes with the lighter-colored tips are softer (and more expensive).

Besides the type of bristle, you should also consider the overall shape of the brush. English shaving brushes tend toward a fan shape, with a more or less flattish top (though slightly domed), but German brushes (the Shavemac, for example) and French brushes (Plisson) often use a domed or light-bulb shape. As with everything in shaving, preferences vary. I like the fan shape but lately have come to enjoy the (domed) H.L. Thäter brushes. In the photo of the four brushes, from L to R: a domed Edwin Jagger brush, a domed Plisson HMW 12 brush, a fan-shaped Rooney Style 3 Size 1, and a fan-shaped Sabini brush.

Below are four German brushes, showing the dome shape Germans

seem to prefer: from the left, two H. L. Thäter brushes, a Mühle, and a Shavemac. These are all excellent brushes, though I find the Shavemac too large for my taste.

Another difference among brushes: the knot may be very tightly packed, or it might be more loosely packed. I find that a tightly packed brush with a short loft just doesn't work for me: such a brush (often said to possess "backbone") is scrubby and holds less lather than a looser brush with more loft. A slightly looser, longer-loft brush is "fluffy": it feels softer on the face, and it holds a lot of lather. You can efficiently make a good lather with either type if you load the brush properly (and if the water is soft enough: see the section on hard water).

As noted above, "soft," when applied to a brush, is ambiguous. It may refer only to the tips or to the entire knot: a silvertip scrubby brush may have soft tips, but a fluffy knot is soft all the way through.

Some brush makers (for example, WhippedDog.com) offer the option to mount the knot a bit deeper than the standard depth. The standard (shallower) depth allows the knot to "bloom" more, so that the same number of bristles occupy a larger volume, thus making the brush fluffier with the advantages pointed out above: softer feel and greater lather capacity. A deeper mounting makes a denser knot (and, some report, a tendency to hoard lather). As in all things shaving related, personal preferences vary. The ideal would be to get two brushes identical except for the mounting depth and see which you actually prefer in practice—one's expectations are often contradicted by experience.

Brush knots are described by two measurements: the diameter of the knot at the handle and the loft, the height of the knot from where it emerges from the handle to the tip. For face lathering a badger knot diameter around 20mm-22mm seems good to me, but naturally men's preferences vary and some like knots of larger diameter. Note that knots of smaller diameter (the Simpson Wee Scot or the Omega 11047 badger+boar, for example) can have excellent capacity for lather. HeyRememberThatTime refers to the Wee Scot as "the Tardis of Lather."

Simpson brushes[101] are made now as a subsidiary of Vulfix. Both Simpson and Vulfix brushes came in a variety of handles and knots, and the choice of brush will depend on what you like. Simpson makes a series of sizes with a given handle style. Some styles that I like are the Emperor (at right), the Duke, the Commander, and the Persian Jar. Those who prefer dense knots with a shorter loft like the Chubby brushes.

Simpson's Wee Scot is surprisingly good. Though diminutive in size, it performs as well as (if not better than) a brush of larger dimension. The Wee Scot is made of the very finest badger bristles, tightly packed, so the number of bristles in a Wee Scot exceeds that of most brushes made with regular bristles, and this enormous wettable surface no doubt accounts for its surprising capacity. The small size is obviously a benefit when hiking or traveling, but it's also a benefit at home because it offers unparalleled precision in lather placement: a shaver using the Wee Scot no longer risks filling his nostrils when lathering his upper lip. The Simpson Case is the Wee Scot's big brother. I wondered why only the Wee Scot bears Simpson's signature, and Gary Young, of the Simpson family, answered[102]:

> I am lucky to have the honour of having Alex Simpson as my Great Uncle so I can answer this quite easily.
>
> The Wee Scot was the brush that Uncle Alex believed optimised a Simpson brush. Yes, it bears all the hallmarks of a Simpson brush. The Wee Scot was the final part of the apprenticeship. This was the hardest brush to make by hand because of its diminutive proportions. You really had to be confident in all aspects of brushmaking, from turning the handle to forming the knot, to be able to put the Wee Scot together. All of us who were taught to make Simpson brushes had to make one and have it scrutinised before being allowed to run riot with all the other brushes in the range. Funnily enough it wasn't the current Wee Scot (actually the Wee Scot 2) which we had to make - it was its smaller brother the Wee Scot 1.
>
> This is why Uncle Alex signed the brush because in his eyes, and in ours, the Wee Scot was THE brush that could be held and inspected in chemists, barbers and shops around the world and the holder could see the craft that was used in its making. It was the perfect 'model brush'.

A line of artisanal shaving brushes, some of exceptional beauty, are made by Rod Neep and shown on his Web site Pens of the Forest[103]. Neep offers the option of embedding a coin in the handle, minted in the year you specify. He has handles in a variety of materials, including stone. New Forest Brushes, reviewed by Bruce Everiss[104], makes shaving brushes of traditional design.

Elite Razor also makes interesting brushes (and razors and razor handles). Some handles are made of semiprecious stones. Wiborg is a German company that makes superb brushes.

Rooney[105] makes superb brushes, including a regular line (styles 1, 2, and 3, my favorite being Style 2), shown in the photo at the right.

In addition to their regular line, Rooney makes the "Heritage" line. I have two Rooney Heritage brushes, an Emilion and a Victorian, and I noticed that they, like my H.L. Thäter brushes, showed the phenomenon of "hooked tips," and I posted photos in the forum ShaveNook.com[106] to get more information. Badger brushes with slightly hooked tips present a "spiky" appearance when the brush dries. Brushing the dry brush across your hand restores the usual look, and in use the only difference is that the brush feels extra soft on the face, and if you gently rub the wet tips with your finger, the brush feels "tacky."

At first I shied away from hooked tips, but now I consider them an indication of a very good brush. Gary Young, quoted earlier, notes[107] in the same Shave Nook thread:

> 'Hooked' filaments can be created way back at the sterilising stage of the hair's 'life'. If the hair has naturally very fine tapered filaments sterilising can cause slight splitting of the hair. Until the hair is used to form a knot and then used by the shaver in the completed brush the 'hooking' doesn't occur. We used to find that some batches of the finer super hair reacted this way, it was something that did create a different feel to the brush - not a bad feel, just a different feel than normal.

That Shave Nook thread includes several close-ups of hooked-tip badger brushes from forum members—Andrew posts some excellent photos[108].

Simpson brushes (measurements here[109]), Rooney brushes, and Omega brushes[110] (measurements here[111]) are all excellent. Both Rooney and Omega Silvertip brushes are amazingly soft and thick—quite a luxurious feel.

G.B. Kent brushes[112] are quite nice and soft and do an excellent job building a lather from shaving soap. The BK4, pictured with its box, is the best all-round size. One shaver commented that the BK4 can work up a good lather from a pot roast. ☺ If you like a larger brush, the BK8 or even the BK12 would be good. These brushes are also available with black handles. The presentation in the red cylindrical box makes this a nice gift brush.

Wet Shaving Products is a relatively new vendor whose brushes all are excellent: very good knots, attractive designs, and well made. WSP brushes are among the best now available. The WSP Monarch's handle is similar to the Kent's, and the brush is just slightly firmer and more resilient than the Kent.

Plisson, a French manufacturer, makes high-end brushes with handles made of horn, ebony, briarwood, rosewood, and other natural sources, as well as handles of brass and acrylic. Some consider the Plisson High Mountain White the best of all badger brushes, but their Chinese Grey—not a silvertip—has a wonderful coarse feel on the face and is a great brush for daily use.

Morris & Forndran is a British line of shaving brushes that Bruce Everiss mentions with approval[113]. When I used my Morris & Forndran "Blonde Badger," my immediate impression that this is the brush the Simpson Stubby wished it could be. Morris & Forndran brushes are quite high-quality, sort of the English equivalent of the German Wiborg brushes.

For a first badger brush, your best bet and the biggest bang for the buck is a Whipped Dog silvertip brush with your choice of resin handle. It's has an unprepossessing appearance, but it's highly serviceable and does an excellent job. Like most new brushes, it will shed some bristles in the first few uses, perhaps a few more than a very expensive brush, but bristle loss quickly stops. (If it does not stop within a week, seek a replacement.) As noted, my preference is for a knot diameter of 20mm or 22mm; experience will show you how the size suits you. I like the knots set to the standard depth; a knot set deeper will be somewhat more dense and scrubby. I highly recommend the Whipped Dog brushes for a first badger brush, to determine whether you like the type.

The Frank Shaving brush, typically found at Ian Tang's Shaving Workshop on eBay but also from some vendors, is a good badger brush at moderate prices. Another source of inexpensive but serviceable brushes is Lijun Brushes, again sold via eBay.

Tweezerman and Escali are popular brushes on Amazon, but they are at best mediocre and too frequently the knot falls out after some weeks of use. I would not recommend getting either brush. The high ratings these brushes receive on Amazon are from first-time users who have not tried any other brush; the ratings seem to be comparing using a brush and soap to using canned foam rather than comparing the brush to other brushes on the market.

Some brush handles are made of natural substances such as wood or horn, which would be vulnerable to water damage if you soaked the handle for long periods, though in practice such brushes do just fine[114]—many boats and paddles are made of wood. Normal use and care will not harm the handles.

You may also be interested in Mantic59's video of various innovations in shaving brushes[115], even though some designs are not now available.

You can even make your own badger brush with supplies from vendors mentioned earlier: BadgerBrush.net, Blankety-Blanks, The Golden Nib, Penchetta, and Whipped Dog. A search on the Web will turn up other suppliers. Look for "badger knots".

Since excellent knots are readily available, some artisans create the handles and affix the knot to make excellent brushes. Take a look at Brent Brushes, Brushguy.com, and Wolf Whiskers, all of whom offer fine brushes.

Soap brush vs. Shaving-cream brush

Lather is produced from a shaving cream or shaving soap (as discussed below), and sometimes the question arises, "Which brushes are best for shaving cream, and which are best for soap?" In fact, any brush can do a fine job with both soaps and creams provided that the water is adequately soft. You learn how to use the brush to create lather (described later in this chapter), and that's it.

So the distinction between "soap brushes" and "shaving cream brushes" is a red herring. Just pick a brush that *you* like. For me, that's a softer brush with a good loft; for others, it's a stiffer brush with a short loft. I made a video[116] showing a soft brush (an Omega S-Series synthetics) making an excellent lather from a dried-out puck of Mitchell's Wool Fat hard soap in about 40 seconds.

You will notice in the video that it takes only about 10 seconds to load the brush with soap, the first step in making lather: brushing the surface of the soap briskly and firmly to fill the knot with enough soap for a good lather. Once the brush was loaded, I moved to my beard and brushed it briskly and firmly for about 30 seconds to work up the lather. (In this demonstration, I had omitted the pre-shave beard wash, and I discovered that lathering a dry beard is harder and less efficient than lathering a wet, washed beard.) It's good to spend more time working the lather into the beard before the first pass. Experiment.

Loading the brush is a crucial step that I discuss later in this chapter. For soaps in a mug or tub (as opposed to a soap in stick form: a shave stick), loading requires a bit of practice to perfect. The usual error is to spend too little time and/or too little pressure when brushing the soap to fully load the brush. Although I generally load my brushes in 10-15 seconds, I've had a fair amount of practice and also have relatively soft water. You might want to spend as long as 25-30 seconds loading the brush when you first start. Again: experiment.

Travel brushes

A travel brush typically allows the user to unscrew the knot (the bristles) and then store it inside the hollow brush handle, thus protecting it during travel.

The best travel brush design (in my opinion) is the Mühle travel brush[117]. It is compact and its design expedites drying by putting a large hole just above the stored knot. The aluminum version is the best design and comes in various colors. Aluminum is lightweight but also relatively soft, so you must exercise care with the threads in the handle. The knot can be badger or Mühle's synthetic silvertip fibre, a good idea for travel.

Another form of travel brush is a small brush that will fit inside (for example) a plastic prescription pill bottle. The most well-known in this line is the Wee Scot; its big brother, the Simpson Case, is quite good as well. (Shave Place in fact sells the Case with the option of a matching travel tube.)

The Omega 11047 badger/boar combination brush works quite well as a travel brush, and Omega also makes a small badger brush and a couple of small boar brushes (the 50068 and the slightly larger 40033). Despite their size, all these brushes have ample capacity: I regularly enjoy using them even at home.

When you travel, a good shaving bag is a big help. Shaving bags are available in various designs from many vendors. I like very small shaving bags, like the Eagle Creek Quick Trip, but there is a wide range of possibilities[118].

Which brush(es) should you get?

Obviously, you should get a brush or brushes you like, preferably that you like a lot. Equally obviously, you cannot know whether or not you like a brush until you've tried it: expectations are an unreliable guide, as shown repeatedly by experience.

I suggest you start with a synthetic, with one of the Omega S-Series being an obvious choice: excellent performance, low price. Then at some point add an Omega boar brush—say, the 20102—to see what you think of boar. At this point your total cost is well under $30. Then later—and there's no need to rush—get a good horsehair brush. These are not costly, and they perform extremely well. And top it off with a badger brush.

As you add each new type, work to discover its peculiar virtues and how to best exploit those virtues. Try to avoid simple (and dull) comparisons and value judgments (this brush is "better" than that). It's rarely so simple: each type of brush, once you figure out its unique properties, can do an excellent (albeit different) job from the other brushes you have.

After accumulating one brush of each type, you have a good range of brush experience, probably have learned what you want from a brush, and possess a stable of brushes that can undoubtedly satisfy you for years to come. If you do decide to buy other brushes, you can have each new brush replace one you already have so that the flock doesn't grow too large.

I have a lot of favorite brushes of each type. For synthetics, the S-Series, the Plisson, and the Mühle Silverfiber are quite nice. In boar, the Omega 20102 and the 21762 are my favorites, along with the 10047 mixed badger/boar. I have a Vie-Long chestnut horsehair with red and translucent white handle that I dote on, and quite a few badger brushes I like—mostly Rooney, Wet Shaving Products, Rod Neep, G.B. Kent, H.L. Thäter, Mühle, and Simpson.

Care of your brush

If you soak your brush prior to shaving and you do a hot-water (rather than a cold-water) shave, use hot water from the tap, *not* boiling-hot water. Boiling-hot water will ruin the bristles. I don't soak a badger brush—I simply hold it under the hot-water tap until it's full of water—but I do wet a boar brush or a horsehair under the hot-water tap and let it sit, dripping wet, while I shower: both types of knot absorb water and soften considerably.

However, in this as in all things, experiment: try wetting your badger brush before you shower and compare how it performs when left wet during your shower and how it performs if you simply wet it under the tap just before lathering. Use the 3-week test protocol to decide.

Lather is generally alkaline, which acts to assist in wetting the hair shaft. This alkalinity presents no problem to the brush knot during the shave: the lather's water dilutes the action, and the lather's rinsed out at the end. But some, thinking not to "waste" the lather, let it dry in the brush, and the alkalinity becomes concentrated as the water evaporates. This will over time can destroy your brush. Thus it is vital to clean the brush before putting it away. When you complete your shave, rinse all the lather out of your brush with warm or hot water, and then do a final rinse of the clean brush using cold water. (The hot water should not be so hot that you cannot keep your hands in the stream.)

The reason for the cold-water rinse is that the hair shaft is covered with cuticle—overlapping scales somewhat like roofing shingles[119]. In hot water, these scales stand out from the hair shaft; in cold water, the scales hug the shaft tightly. This is one reason shaving with hot water is more comfortable than shaving with cold: hot water (along with the soap's alkalinity) opens the cuticle and the whisker absorbs water more readily. And this is why beauticians do a final shampoo rinse with cool water: so the cuticle lies flat and the hair will look shiny instead of dull. (Thus synthetic brushes do not need a cold-water rinse.)

You may want a stand for the brush, but stands that grip the brush at the base of the knot (bristles downward) can damage the outer bristles. It's better if the stand holds the brush by a groove in the handle, as in some Mühle designs.

The stand is nice for display, but it offers no advantage whatsoever in drying the brush, as shown by tests using a hydrometer[120]. Indeed, Simpson states that their brushes should simply stand on the base of the handle to dry after you've rinsed the bristles and shaken it well to remove excess water—no stand needed. (Some also dry the brush on a towel, but I don't bother.) And if you collect brushes, you would have to improvise a large rack. I use a couple of wall-mounted 4-tier spice racks to hold my collection of brushes, with the brushes standing on their bases. (In looking at the orientation of the logo on almost all brush handles, it does seem that the makers expect the brush to stand on the base of the handle.)

Brushes dry equally well with bristles up or down because capillary action is enormously stronger than gravity at that scale. (Note that sap does not pool in the roots of trees but reaches the topmost leaves through capillary action alone.)

Over time brushes may become slightly waterproof from hard-water deposits. One symptom is that the lather doesn't seem quite so nice or abundant as previously. Brushes can be easily restored by washing them with a good shampoo and conditioner. Be very careful about the shampoo: some include silicone-based additives that can make the brush less functional. The bad additives generally end in "–cone"; here's a partial list of what to avoid: cyclomethicone, cyclopentasiloxane, dimethicone, dimethinconal.

Johnson Baby Shampoo (very gentle and with a neutral pH) is a good choice—or, instead of using shampoo, soak the brush for 10-15 minutes in warm water to which you've added just a splash of white vinegar. The vinegar dissolves the hard-water (calcium) deposits, leaving the bristles no longer coated. After soaking, rinse the brush well, first in warm water, then in cold. Make sure you've rinsed away all traces of the vinegar. Bleach is a *very* bad idea: don't use it at all.

Shave Place offers various reference articles at ShaveInfo.com, including some videos on a brush cleaning method[121] that produces excellent results. You first soak the brush for about 5 minutes in warm (not hot) water with some dishwashing detergent (not the kind you put in a dishwasher, but the kind used in hand-washing dishes), swirling it from time to time. Then mix 9 parts water, 1 part white vinegar and a dash of 100% glycerin (available at a drugstore or health-food store) and soak the brush in that for about 10 minutes. Rinse the brush, and it will now be soft and water-absorbent.

As described in the later section on "Cleaning your razor," you can also use an ultrasonic cleaner to clean the brush—you immerse *only* the bristles, **not** the base of the knot. Gold Dachs makes a shaving brush cleaner[122] that's reported to work quite well. MAC brush cleaner[123] is intended for cleaning make-up brushes, but those who have cleaned their shaving brushes with it found that it did an excellent job.

Cleaning the brush may not be needed if you have soft water and are careful about rinsing the brush after use. And it certainly isn't needed so often as cleaning your razor. Remember that badger, boar, and horsehair brushes are made from actual hair, so don't do things to them that you wouldn't do to your own hair. Synthetic bristles are more forgiving and robust.

Lathering bowl [optional]

I no longer use a lathering bowl. I found that for me it works much better to load the brush and then work the lather up on my beard ("face-lathering"). But many shavers do like to use a lathering bowl.

Building the lather in a bowl does help you observe the lather as you experiment, trying different proportions of water and shaving cream or soap until you learn to get a lather you like. (A lathering bowl seems to be more frequently used with shaving cream than with shaving soap.) You can rub the lather between thumb and finger to see how protective and slick it is (and this also is done naturally in "palm-lathering," in which you brush your palm vigorously with the loaded brush, added driblets of water to your palm as needed and working that into the lather).

Thus the lathering bowl is particularly useful for making practice lathers to gain experience. For example, put a lump of shaving cream about the size of an almond in the lathering bowl, wet the brush and shake it out, then begin brushing the cream. If you use a soap, you load the brush on the puck rather than carving out a small lump of soap for the bowl.

Because the brush was shaken dry-ish, the lather will require more water, so add a tiny amount of water, work that in, and check the lather. Continue to add tiny amounts of water, each time working the added water well into the brush and lather, testing the lather, and repeating the process until the lather is obviously too wet. Along the way you will have seen lather at every stage of development, from too dry to just right to too wet. If you do that a few times, you will start to recognize the stage of lather that you most prefer. You can do the same experiment on your beard, but it's easier to observe in the bowl. Once you know the stage you want, you can develop a good lather on your beard or in the bowl.

Because a bowl is normally used as a container, the natural tendency is to think that the lathering bowl's purpose is to hold the lather, into which you dip the brush and then apply—much as a paint can holds the paint that the paintbrush applies. Not so: the lather's in the brush, not in the bowl. The bowl merely presents a surface of a convenient shape for building a lather. That the lather resides in the brush becomes obvious when you create the lather directly on your beard or on your palm (which you rinse after building the lather).

It's difficult to see how the lather's doing if the lathering bowl is white, so use a bowl that's a relatively dark color. Other than that, any roughly hemispherical bowl that's about 5″ across and 2.5″-3″ deep will work fine. Start with a cereal bowl from your kitchen or from Target, which normally has a good selection of inexpensive cereal bowls in various colors.

If you prefer a hot-water shave, fill the lathering bowl with hot water and allow it to sit (while you shower, for example). If you prefer a cold-water shave, skip this step. Empty the hot water from the bowl, rinse the brush in hot (or cold) water, and proceed. Obviously, you can use hot water from the tap to heat the bowl, even if you're going to use distilled water for the lather. Dirty Bird Pottery makes a lathering bowl that is heated as a scuttle (see next section).

With a very large brush, a lathering bowl may work better than building the lather directly on your beard. A 19mm-24mm brush is a reasonable size for face lathering, as you can work it smartly against your beard, but a really large brush may not get enough action merely against the beard. For larger brushes, a lathering bowl (or building the lather on your palm) lets you work up the lather and also adjust water amounts more easily.

Another important point: badger and synthetic brushes hold a lot of water, and if you fail to work all that water into the lather at the outset, you'll find that in the second and third pass the water drains into the lather in the brush, making it thin and worthless. So, *especially* with a brush that's both large and stiff, give the brush a good shake or two and then gently "pump" the brush (and this is where a lathering bowl is helpful), combined with the usual swirling and stirring motions. You pump the brush by working it up and down; this ensures that the water at the base of the brush gets worked into the lather. (I accomplish this now when I'm loading the brush, described below.)

Don't pump the brush so vigorously that you damage the bristles— gently but enough to work the brush's charge of water fully into the lather. Experience will be your guide. Brushes that hold much water will require a bit more shaving cream or shaving soap for a proper lather than a brush holding less water.

Some large-knot brushes, like the Omega Silvertips, are soft and flexible enough so that the pumping action usually happens automatically as you swirl and stir up the lather. With these brushes, no special pumping is required.

Suribachi bowls should be used *only* with boar brushes—and are optional even for those: they are not really necessary.

Warming scuttle [optional]

The Moss Scuttle[124] (shown at right) allows you to enjoy warm shaving lather, a real treat if you like a hot-water shave. It consists of a brush bowl sitting in, and attached to, a heating bowl (so it doesn't fall off when you empty the water).

To use: fill both bowls with water as hot as you can get it from the tap and let the bowls sit while you shower.

Then empty out all the hot water, and fill only the heating (bottom) bowl with hot water: this will keep the brush bowl hot. Rinse the brush with hot water, then load it with soap or cream and build the lather. After the first lathering, place the brush in the warmed brush bowl while you shave. Then, when you relather before the next pass, the brush and lather will still be warm.

The brush bowl should be too small to use as a lathering bowl—you want the lathered brush to fit snugly in the bowl to keep warm. The Moss scuttle comes in two sizes—small and large (see photo)—and the small size is right for all but quite large brushes.

Georgetown Pottery[125] makes a scuttle that serves the same function as the Moss Scuttle, though with a slightly different design. Dirty Bird Pottery[126] makes what in effect are heated lathering bowls (and unheated lathering bowls as well), but they also make a "brush holder" that fits the brush snugly enough to keep it (and its lather) warm.

The ideal would seem to be to combine the two ideas: a large bowl used for lathering and then filled with hot water once the lather is made, and a smaller brush bowl then placed in the hot water and used to keep the brush (and its lather) warm while you shave. The trick would be to find a way to keep the small bowl from floating and capsizing.

Dan Straus, a chemist in San Jose, discovered that the Rival Little Dipper makes a fine lathering bowl/brush warmer[127]. It has no heat setting or switch, so he just plugs it in when he awakes, and after breakfast and a shower, it's just right for warm lather.

A *thick* ceramic bowl will hold quite a bit of heat once it's hot all the way through, and can keep the lather warm for the entire shave. Others put their lathering bowl in a sink filled with hot water. Some find a pair of bowls to use in the manner of the Moss Scuttle. I usually just stand my brush on its base between passes, and the lather stays warm enough for me since my shaves take little time.

I should add that those who like the scuttle like it a *lot*—for them the warmer lather adds significant pleasure to the shave.

Water

Water is a key component of a good shave, and there's more to consider than you would at first suspect.

Temperature

When talking about "hot" water, it's important to note that water that's *too* hot is not only bad for the brush, it's also a safety hazard. Burns and scalds from hot water are among the most frequent home accidents, and so I've followed the recommendation made a generation ago by then-President Carter: set your hot-water tank's thermostat so that pure hot water coming from the tap is just right for a shower, shave, and washing dishes by hand. This finesses the safety hazard of scalding water, and it saves money: you don't pay to heat water to a temperature too high to use, and then cool it down when you use it by mixing in cold water.

At one time, dishwashers did require extremely hot water from the tap, but now dishwashers heat the water to the scalding temperatures they require.

Try turning down the hot-water heater to a temperature that allows you to use pure hot water for shaving and shower without discomfort or danger—unless you have a large family and a small hot-water heater. In that case, a lower hot-water heater temperature may cause you to run out of hot water.

If I let the water run until it reaches the maximum, hot water from my tap now runs at 116°F (47°C). I used trial and error, adjusting the hot-water tank thermostat over a period of days until the setting delivered pure hot water at a usable temperature.

Another temperature consideration is whether to shave using hot water or cold water. I consider cold-water shaving a last resort, but in fact some men like it, especially in hot weather. They say the cold water tightens the skin and makes the stubble stand erect, thus easier to shave. Some also have found that the cold water reduces skin irritation when they shave[128]. (Presumably those using cold water shave at the sink, not in the shower.)

I highly recommend you try your own experiment: do a cold-water shave for a week, a hot-water shave for a week, and another week of cold-water shaves, then decide which works best for you. You might want to schedule the experiment for summer.

Hard v. Soft

Normally you can simply use hot water from the tap to make your lather, but if you live where the water is hard—or if you think the water might be hard[129]—try using distilled or "purified" (that is, demineralized) water for your shave as described below. Demineralized water is sold cheaply in drugstores for use in steam irons, steamers, vaporizers, and the like. If the lather with that water is easier to make and more abundant, you have your answer—and one possible workaround. Obviously, using demineralized water is simpler for cold-water shaves than for hot-water shaves.

Easier than using demineralized water for the daily shave (though demineralized water is quite good for a test shave) is to soften your shaving water with citric acid, an inexpensive white crystalline powder used in canning (prevents discoloration from oxidation), sprouting (prevents mold), beer-making (to invert sugar), and as a salt substitute (like squeezing a lemon over your food). You can easily find small containers of pure citric acid on-line and often in healthfood stores and where canning or brewing supplies are sold.

Run the sink half-full of hot water and dissolve in it a pinch of two of *pure* citric acid (citric acid for canning is sometimes sold mixed with pectin). The amount to use depends on the water's hardness, so experiment, but very little is required. For 8 grains of hardness, 1 gram per liter is enough. Too much citric acid will kill the lather, but the right amount for your water works as well as using distilled water. (My own tap water is soft, so I rely on reports from those with hard water who have used citric acid to soften their shaving water.)

Use the softened water in the sink for wetting the knot to soak boar or horsehair brushes, doing your pre-shave beard wash, making lather, rinsing the razor, and splashing on your face at the end of each pass. Use tap water for the final rinse. The lather from your demineralized-water shave defines the baseline quality of lather you are going for. Men who have tried the citric acid trick are impressed by the improvement[130]. Tony the Blade commented:

> I tried it and it works really well. Improves my lather so it's back to the same standard that I had before we moved here. The other house had a soft water supply. The other thing I noticed was my DLC Weber that I used on the first couple of shaves with citric acid came away from the shave with a nice clean head. It usually was caked with soap scum, which was really noticeable on the black head. So I'll be using a pinch of citric acid for every shave now: better lather and cleaner razors. I used literally a couple of small pinches in a washbasin full of water—not too precise in the measurements but for 3 days now I've had the same improvement every time so I don't think the amount is too critical. I would guess at no more than 1/8th teaspoon.

Another man reported that he had to use a bit more citric acid, doubtless because his water was a bit harder. He used a basin of water to which he added a measured amount of citric acid, and at the end of the shave he rinsed everything in that water and drained it. If soap scum were present, he used a bit more citric acid the next time he shaved. When he reached ¼ teaspoon of citric acid for the basin of water, he found no soap scum left when the basin drained, so that's the amount he now uses.

Water hardness ranges from water so hard a cat couldn't scratch it to water of impeccable softness (such as the water of Vancouver, BC). Minimalisto of Wicked Edge made an interesting point: because some cheaper shaving soaps contain chelating agents such as EDTA, water can have a degree of hardness such that those soaps work well while extremely high-quality soaps (whose ingredients include few things with long names) produce only a so-so lather. Thus it's easy to get the idea that the cheap soaps are better, and "elite" soaps aren't what they're cracked up to be. Before making a final judgment on a soap, level the playing field by doing a shave using distilled or softened water. With soft water, the "elite" soap will usually reveal the reason for its reputation[131].

As minimalisto wrote, "If I lathered Barrister & Mann and it was just about average and did an all right job compared to Proraso or Arko, I might think the soap is just overhyped, and that I prefer Proraso! It's that spot where the water is just hard enough to affect the good soaps and bring them down to mediocrity that's dangerous." The shaver may even not suspect the water's effect since the lather he gets is acceptable to a degree—he probably thinks that his lather is as good as it gets.

One sign that the water is hard is that washing your face with soap and then rinsing leaves your face "squeaky clean" rather than slippery: the squeakiness comes from soap scum on the skin. Extremely hard water also generally leaves white deposits around faucets and valves (and on your razor).

The best long-term solution for hard water is to install a water softener. Household water softeners generally use ion-exchange, replacing calcium in the water with sodium, so that softened water is unsuitable for drinking or cooking. With this type of softener, the kitchen cold water is not softened (or you can mount a reverse-osmosis softener under the kitchen counter to remove the calcium without adding sodium, thus demineralizing water while leaving it safe to drink and use in cooking).

If you do install a water softener, look for one that recycles based on volume of water used rather than based on time (every few days). Volume-based regeneration automatically adjusts for periods of low usage (when you're away) and high usage (when you have house guests). Good volume-based softeners use two tanks: while one tank regenerates, soft water continues to be available from the other[132], thus keeping hard water from filling the hot-water tank.

Water with high mineral content is hard on the hot-water tank, the plumbing, and the valves and faucets. It's hard on skin and laundry, leaves deposits (mineral and/or soap scum) on everything (including your skin and hair), and can dull the razor blade: as the water evaporates from the blade, hard water deposits cover the cutting edge. (To prevent that, rinse the razor head in high-proof rubbing alcohol after the shave: the alcohol displaces the water and then evaporates, so there's no mineral deposit on the blade's edge.)

Some advise keeping the razor's head immersed in oil (mineral oil, for example), which also would prevent the mineral deposits from forming along the blade's edge, but the usual reason offered is to prevent the edge from oxidizing, which makes no sense: almost all blades today are made of stainless steel, and moreover the edge is coated with some non-reactive coating such as chrome, Teflon, platinum, titanium, etc. Moreover, the blade is generally discarded after a week, and if the razor's rinsed in hot water and left to dry, oxidation is unlikely (unless you're rinsing it in salt water or vinegar, which is unlikely).

If you do soak the razor's head in oil, something I definitely do **not** recommend, be sure to keep the oil in an unbreakable container: sooner or later it will slip (oil is slippery and tends to get on things, particularly as it drips from the razor as you remove it), spill, and possibly break. At least avoid the breakage.

A person using soft water for the first time will often complain that they can't rinse off the soap. What they mean is that when they rinse away the soap, their skin still feels slippery (as wet skin should). What they are missing is the stickiness they felt from soap scum adhering to their skin—that's what they've used as the sign that all the soap (which also makes the skin feel slippery) is gone. With hard water, after they rinse they feel the soap scum that remains, stuck to the skin, and so their skin doesn't feel slippery. With soft water their skin still feels slippery, so they believe that must be due to soap remaining. It's not: it's the natural condition of wet skin. (When you're trying to remove a ring that's too tight, you wet the skin to make it more slippery).

If a water softener is infeasible in your situation, you can use distilled (aka "purified") water, or add citric acid to your tap water as described above.

For a shaver accustomed to hard water a soft-water shave can be astonishingly better[133]. And some who thought their lathers were acceptable are amazed by the improvement from using demineralized or softened water.

Because hard water affects the lather from shaving cream less than that from shaving soap, I believe the idea of a "soap brush" v. "cream brush" originated with shavers whose tap water was hard. They observed that they got good lather from shaving cream but, *using the very same brush*, they could not get good lather from shaving soap. They then decided that their brush must not be a "shaving soap brush"—but the problem was the water, not the brush.

If you are the least bit unsure about the hardness of your tap water and in particular if you live in a hard-water region[134]—for example, the Midwest or Southwest of the US, the prairie provinces of Canada, or much of Australia (Adelaide's water is notoriously hard)—I urge you to try the distilled-water experiment: it's inexpensive and the results might surprise you. And it's easier than it sounds because the volume of water involved is so small.

Using distilled water

When use distilled (or "purified") water, you can do a cold-water (or, more accurately, room-temperature-water) shave; or you can heat the water on the stove or in the microwave, or use something like the Sunbeam Hot Shot[135] to heat the water in the bathroom. (The Hot Shot heats a pint of water to 180°F in a minute—too hot, so you have to let it cool a bit: turn the Hot Shot on before you shower, and by the time you're done with the shower, the water has cooled.)

You'll need relatively little water: one cup is ample. If you do a hot-water shave, a mug or bowl of water will stay comfortably warm while you shave. If you do use distilled water routinely, having a pump bottle[136] simplifies things: you can pump out a small amount of water for the pre-shave beard wash, for making lather, and for the short rinse at the end of each pass.

If you use a boar or horsehair brush, dip the brush into the distilled water before you shower. You then use that water:

- to wash your face with pre-shave soap and rinse with a splash (not a thorough rinse: residual soap contributes lubricity to the lather);
- to make the lather;
- to wet your face after each pass (two partial rinses and a final thorough rinse for a typical three-pass shave);
- to rinse lather off the razor (pour a little into a cup or bowl for this).

After very little practice, I found that a good three-pass shave requires only ½ cup water. It helps that only the final rinse must be thorough and that I don't use a moist hot towel (though for that you can use tap water rather than distilled water—and you can also use tap water, even if hard, to rinse off your hands). Depending on how hard your tap water is, you can try using a distilled/tap water mix to stretch the distilled water, but even if you use straight distilled water, a gallon (at ½ cup per shave) will last for a month, especially if you skip shaving one day a week as I do. However, using citric acid is simpler and costs less.

In reading the procedure, it might seem bothersome, but with a week's practice it becomes routine: the adaptive unconscious learns and takes over (just as it does for the much more complex tasks involved in getting dressed) so that most of the task (using distilled water or getting dressed) is done on auto-pilot, with no conscious attention or thought. In getting dressed, for example, you consciously select what to wear, and then the unconscious takes over, putting on the various pieces, tucking, smoothing, fastening, zipping, buckling, tying, and so on, while your conscious mind and attention are focused on other things entirely.

Minimal-water shaving is also handy when water is scarce, as (for example) on a camping trip. (Surely you shave when camping, right? ☺)

Shower v. Sink

I don't shave in the shower, though a shower shave provides lots of available water: easy to rinse between passes, for example. That's its only virtue, so far as I can see, and that for me is outweighed by its many disadvantages. Excess water usage is not a significant disadvantage on the assumption that anyone shaving in the shower *must* live in an area with abundant fresh water. Where I live—and in many locations—water restrictions regularly apply and shaving in the shower would be a shocking waste of water (and also a waste of the energy required to heat the water). A beginning shaver with a DE safety razor or a straight edge will often take 20 or 25 minutes or more for those first shaves. I shudder to think of the water lost, even with a low-flow showerhead.

Even apart from excess water usage, the shower shave has several significant disadvantages. For one, the noise of the running water keeps the shaver from hearing the auditory feedback from the razor's action, a significant loss. (Of course, some showerheads have a little push-valve to turn water on and off with no change in temperature, so the shave could be done with the water turned off except to rinse—but if you're doing that, why not shave at the sink?) For another, there's no place (at least in my shower) to set out my shaving stuff in an organized way. Natural-bristle brushes should not be stored in the shower, so for each shave you carry in the brush, then carry it back out. Razors get slippery with soap and are likely at some point to be dropped, and as it falls the blade may cut you—or slice off a piece—and the razor is likely to be damaged from the fall, quite apart from damage to you. The alum block is water soluble, and high-glycerin soaps turn to mush, so you can't leave either in the shower. Brushes with handles of wood also tend not to fare well in the shower.

A shower shave probably precludes the cold-water shave. You can buy shower mirrors, though many shower shavers simply shave by feel. If you use a soap mug in the shower, consider the unbreakable Marvy mug made of hard rubber; it's quite a good mug in any case. For a shaving cream to use in the shower, note Shave Place's use of plastic dispenser bottles for its shaving cream.

My recommendation: bathe in the shower, shave at the sink. But one great thing about shaving is that you get to decide for yourself. (I've not read of guys who shave in the tub, though we've seen that in movies—typically in Westerns.) But I urge you to make your decisions after some experience with each—that is, if you're a shower shaver, shave at the sink for a week, then return to shower shaving, then shave another week at the sink. That will prevent making a bad decision based merely on expectations, which often are wrong.

One reason shower shavers have given for shaving in the shower is to save time: some describe one quick pass of the razor, then out of the shower to dress, grab a bite, and run for the bus.

That process reflects prioritizing time above pleasure, and certainly the time restrictions for some (who have a tight schedule of school, work, and other demands) require efficiency. For the retired, it's easy to prioritize pleasure above time, and a shave can be a pleasure beyond the simple removal of stubble.

But consider the pleasure being sacrificed—the calming and centering ritual, the chance to focus on what you're doing and the accompanying olfactory and tactile pleasures—and compare that loss to what is gained: possibly saving as much as three minutes (but probably less) compared with shaving at the sink.

After a few years of practice and experience, my shave, from turning on the water at the sink for a pre-shave beard wash to splashing on aftershave, takes five minutes, an unhurried and relaxing five minutes. I shave without haste, taking the time I need—but experience results in efficiency, and less time is needed even though I do not rush.

I suggest that you take the time to enjoy the shave, and to shave at the sink where the shower is not a distraction. Focus on the process, and the time you take will pay off in a better and more balanced view of the day.

Running v. Still

When shaving at the sink, shavers typically take one of three approaches:

1. Fill the sink with hot water and use that for the shave: rinse your razor and your beard in the water until you finish the shave.
2. Leave the water running, rinsing your razor in the stream as needed and using that water to rinse your face between passes.
3. Turn the water on as needed to rinse razor or face, then turn it off.

Option 1 is the one to use if you're using citric acid to soften hard water. In that case, the water in the sink is used to wet the knot of a boar or horsehair brush to allow it to soften, to do the pre-shave beard wash, to make the lather, to rinse the razor and to splash on one's beard to rinse/wet it between passes

Option 2 is a bad idea, even beyond losing water you've paid to heat. The shaving problem is that running water makes a lot of noise. Keep the bathroom silent when you shave. Silence supports the contemplative mood, and silence also allows you to hear the sounds of shaving—the blade cutting through the stubble—which helps you find the optimal blade angle.

I use option 3—my lavatory has a single-lever faucet, so turning water on and off is easy, and the water is soft—but some guys prefer the first. Try both to see which works better for you, but keep the bathroom quiet: no fan, no radio, no music, and no running water—turn the tap off while the razor's on your face.

Soaking

When you shave, you find yourself soaking various things—your beard, most prominently. It gets soaked in the shower, soaked again at the sink as you wash it, perhaps soaked once beneath a hot moist towel atop the first layer of lather or a pre-shave cream, and then soaked as the lather is worked in. The more water the beard absorbs, the easier the shave and the longer the blade will last.

Some soak their shaving brush while they shower. Based on my experience, this soaking doesn't seem to noticeably help badger or synthetic brushes, but it does help horsehair, and it's important for boar brushes. Boar bristles absorb a lot more water than the others, and soaking greatly improves their performance. Horsehair brushes also become noticeably softer, but for badger I don't see from my various experiments that soaking helps—but that's me: you should try the three-week test protocol to see how you feel about it with your own brushes.

"Soaking" does not require immersing the brush: just wet the knot well before you shower and let brush sit, dripping wet, while you shower. When your shower's done, the brush will be ready. For me, this method is the most efficient.

Some put a little water atop the puck of shaving soap and allow that to soak while they shower. I tried this, and so far as I could tell, it did not help in the least. But by all means, experiment and draw your own conclusions. You can also put glycerin or Trumper's skin food on the soap and see what that does.

Latent lather: Shaving cream and shaving soap

Lather emerges from a cream or soap with the addition of water and the action of the brush. Done correctly, the result is far more efficacious—and fragrant—than dry chemical foam squirted from a pressurized can, and more pleasant than most brushless shaving creams. The traditional method—using brush and soap and cream—does, however, lack TV commercials and celebrity endorsements.

The soap or shaving cream's fragrance is to make the lather experience even more pleasant, and the fragrance is washed away with the lather. The brief life of the lather's fragrance is by design; it's a feature, not a bug. (With some soaps, you might detect a whisper of fragrance after the lather's gone.) The idea is to get the lather's fragrance offstage, as it were ("Lather fragrance: Exit left"), to give the fragrance of your aftershave or eau de toilette its time in the spotlight.

Some soapmakers, knowing that people do like their lather's fragrance, offer an aftershave and/or eau de toilette in the same fragrance as the soap: D.R. Harris offers aftershaves of the same fragrance as some of their shaving soaps and shaving creams; l'Occitane offers Cade aftershave and eau de toilette to match their Cade shaving soap and cream; Mickey Lee Soapworks has Italian Stallion shaving soap and also Italian Stallion aftershave milk.

The distinction between creams and soaps is not so strict or clear as you might imagine. Soaps come in soft formulations (for example, Vitos Red Label and Valobra are Italian soft soaps, soft enough to mash into a bowl or mug, and produce terrific lather), and some creams (that come in tubs rather than in tubes) can be quite stiff and soap-like. Figaro, an Italian shaving cream, and Dr. Selby's 3x Concentrated shaving cream are as firm as a soap, and Ginger's Garden shaving-cream soap lathers more like a shaving cream than a shaving soap.

Formulation and reformulation

Always read the ingredients in your shaving cream or shaving soap. It will take a while to pick up the lingo: for example, instead of "palm oil," you are likely to see "potassium palmate" and/or "sodium palmate," the result of using potassium hydroxide (KOH) or sodium hydroxide (NaOH) on palm oil. (Soaps with a higher proportion of KOH are softer, those with a higher proportion of NaOH are firmer.) Similarly, you will see potassium (or sodium) tallowate when tallow is used. Shea butter is often listed as Butyrospermum parkii or Vitellaria paradoxa, avocado oil as Persea gratissima oil, and so on. But you quickly become accustomed to the more common ingredients (and search engines and Wikipedia help you learn new ones), and it is useful to note the ingredients of soaps you particularly like so you can look for them in other soaps.

Generally speaking, the list of ingredients for artisanal soaps and shaving creams is shorter than the list for commercial products and also often include things (such as silk protein or organic oils) rarely found in commercial soaps. Moreover, commercial soaps includes things (various chemicals, dyes, and the like) not found in artisanal soaps. Occasionally an artisanal soapmaker will discuss his work in detail[137].

Some shaving soaps make a very fine lather: abundant, fragrant, lubricating, protective, and long-lasting. Other shaving soaps are best used as bath soaps: the lather they produce is stingy, non-lubricating, unprotective, and short-lived. The same phenomenon happens with shaving creams, though not to the same degree. Why would any company produce a soap or cream as bad as some you find?

If the bad soap is from an artisan, it is likely that the maker simply does not understand the requirements of a shaving soap. A common approach is merely to add clay to a bath soap in the expectation that this will produce a shaving soap. It does not. It produces a bath soap containing clay. Some artisans attempt to use olive oil for the soap; my own experience is that olive-oil based shaving soaps seldom work well.

If the bad soap is from a commercial enterprise, the problem is likely due to a reformulation—and reformulations are rarely announced. Modern businesses operate under constant pressure to increase profits (example: the multiblade cartridge). So sometimes, due to financial pressures, a soap, shaving cream, or other cosmetic is reformulated to cut costs and thus increase profits, thus doing a better job (from the corporate accountant's point of view: they see a cosmetic's job as the production of profit—and apparently some people also use them for something else).

Obviously some reformulations are done in order to improve the product, but depressingly often a product reformulation's main purpose is to increase profits without sacrificing too much revenue (hoping that customers who stop buying the product after reformulation will be replaced by new customers who don't know what has happened).

At a marketing seminar, I was told of a large consumer-products company that fell into this sort of trap: each of their product managers is put in charge of a product. A new product manager wants to show success to advance in the organization, and the only measure of success most businesses recognize is how much product profits increase. One easy way to accomplish an increase is to reformulate the product, substituting some cheaper ingredients for costly ones—or just omit the costly ones altogether. (Another strategy often used is to reduce the size of the container a small amount, changing the shape to disguise the diminution. Since the container is new, it is labeled "NEW!".)

Careful testing is done after reformulation to make sure that consumers do not have a significant preference for the old formulation. Once that test is passed, the product is re-released, the profits increase, and the product manager is promoted. In comes a new product manager, eager to make a mark.

The easiest way for the new product manager to increase profits is to reformulate again, using even cheaper ingredients. The process continues over several generations of product managers.

Call the original product A, and the first cheaper version B. Customers can't tell the difference. And then there is C, and customers can't distinguish C from B. Or D from C. And so on. But somewhere around F or G, the cumulative difference becomes quite noticeable, with A remembered as quite obviously better than G. At around this point product sales fall off a cliff, the product is discontinued, and the last product manager, left holding the bag, is fired or demoted. But no organizational learning occurs, so the process is repeated for other products. (It's extremely difficult to build a learning organization: Chris Argyris devoted his career to trying to understand why and wrote some very interesting books in the process.)

So this is a general warning: when someone tells you how great some particular product is, find out when they bought it. In the shaving arena, several big-name soaps and shaving creams have been reformulated over the past few years, not to the shaver's benefit (though the companies profit from the change). Floris London shaving soaps I bought some years ago are very good, but those who bought their soaps after reformulation have little good to say about it. (Floris has done a second reformulation in an effort to fix the problem.) The same is true of shaving soaps by Geo. F. Trumper: the older tubs are fine, the newer ones not so much.

It should be observed that sometimes even the original formulation is not a good shaving soap, as in some artisanal soaps—particularly, as noted, those made with olive oil. The artisanal soaps I list below are currently good; be careful in trying others; if possible, buy and test a sample.

Shaving cream

Shaving creams come in a wide variety, including unscented creams (for example, Truefitt & Hill Ultimate Comfort) for those with sensitive skin. If your skin actually *is* sensitive, as described earlier, it's a good idea to test any new product—cream, soap, aftershave, whatever—before using it on your face.

Cyril R. Salter Mint is a great summertime shaving cream and their French Vetiver is intense—as it should be. J. M. Fraser's Shaving Cream[138] has a light lemony fragrance, creates a good lather, is curiously effective at softening the beard, and gives a fine shave. Taylor of Old Bond Street Avocado has received high praise[139]:

> I couldn't agree more on the [Taylor's] avocado. The scent is nice and light but not as luxurious as some others. The real value for me is the lubricity you described [from the avocado oil (persea gratissima) in the formulation] along with zero irritation. The absence of coloring and heavier scent additives I think is what drives this. In my opinion, this benefit makes this the ideal cream for a newbie, which I am.

Shaving creams from the "Three T's" of England—Taylor of Old Bond Street, Geo. F. Trumper, and Truefit & Hill—are currently good (though their soap production has been outsourced and many say the soaps have suffered as a result). Castle Forbes is another fine shaving cream, available in lavender, lime, or cedarwood. It's pricey (better to receive as a gift than to buy). Luxury creams are also available from D.R. Harris, The Gentlemens Refinery, and others.

Some artisanal soap makers also make shaving creams so look for shaving creams on their sites. Al's Shaving specializes in shaving creams, and those he makes are highly regarded and definitely worth trying; he offers a 7-cream sampler that's quite nice. In Australia, Occam's shaving cream is well worth seeking out. Shave Place makes a lathering shaving cream that comes in a plastic dispenser bottle: you squirt some onto your brush and then build the lather—it produces a fine, thick, moisture-laden lather. The dispenser makes this an ideal shaving cream for those who shave in the shower.

You can buy shaving creams in a tube or a tub. Generally speaking, the price per ounce in a tube is twice what it is for the same cream in a tub. Some excellent shaving creams, though, are available only in a tube—Proraso shaving cream (from Italy) is one example. Other "tube only" shaving creams are Musgo Real (from Portugal), Speick (whose modest price belies its excellence) and Tabac (both from Germany), and men-ü (in the UK and US). The men-ü cream is particularly concentrated; use a tiny bead of it.

Some non-lathering shaving creams produce fine shaves. But even though the cream doesn't lather, a damp brush is a better applicator than your bare hand. For creams such as these, no water (or very little) should be added. The cream is still applied to a wet (and washed) beard. Nancy Boy shaving cream[140] is as good as any shaving cream I've used, and the Signature fragrance is wonderful. The cream itself is highly protective and lubricating. Cremo Shaving cream, Anthony Logistics, Kiss My Face, and Baxter of California are also good nonlathering creams.

Loading a brush—and indeed, getting a lather—is easier for shaving creams than for soaps, probably why novices prefer creams. The loading method depends on whether the cream comes in a tube or a bowl. (As noted above, Shave Place sells shaving cream in a pump bottle.)

Shaving cream in a tube

Use a lump of cream about the size of an almond, though a beginner might start with more—say, the size of a Brazil nut.

The shaving cream is then placed on the brush or smeared onto your cheeks to begin lathering on the face, or placed in a lathering bowl for those who use that method to work up the lather.

Shaving cream in a tub

You can dip out a lump of cream and use it as described above, but I generally just wet the brush, shake it well, and twirl the damp brush in the tub of cream to coat the tips with shaving cream, which I then use to build the lather. This requires a soft shaving cream, and the dipping/twirling should be done with care so that you do not get too much shaving cream: you want a total amount about equal in volume to an almond/brazil nut.

Some shaving creams, though, are quite firm—soap-like, almost, and those I load as I load a soap, described in the soap section below: briskly brushing the cream with a wettish brush. Coate's Limited Edition shaving cream, Figaro shaving cream, and Dr. Selby's 3x Concentrated shaving cream are examples of harder shaving creams. Use the soap instructions for those creams.

Again, the building of the lather can be done on the beard or in a bowl or using your palm. I definitely prefer to build my lather on my beard. I encourage you to experiment (as you've no doubt noticed) and try all three methods from the beginning.

Shaving cream lather using a lathering bowl

Since harder creams (e.g., Dr. Selby's 3x Concentrated shaving cream) are more like a soap, see the soap section below for how to lather those. For a soft shaving cream, put the dollop of cream in the warm bowl, take the slightly wet brush (not too wet: you can add more water, but you cannot remove water), and use a motion that's more than stirring but less than whipping to work up the lather. (If you whip too vigorously, you'll get a lot of lather, but it will be unprotective because it contains too much air. You want a stiff, dense lather that contains water more than air.) The rapid stirring motion will create a thick, creamy lather. Too much water or water added too quickly makes a lather that's bubbly and runny rather than dense.

Because shaving creams can produce quite a bit of (unprotective) lather even if you use too little shaving cream, you should experiment to make sure you're using enough—thus the note above for beginners to try a dollop the size of a Brazil nut instead of an almond. Then, as you gain experience, cut back on the amount of shaving cream until you find the right proportion. The lather should be dense enough—and contain enough water—to do a proper job.

An illustrated on-line guide[141] shows one method of lathering with a cream. In this guide, he uses water from a hot-pot (probably distilled water—I use hot water from the tap, but my water is relatively soft).

Shake water from the brush, so that the brush is damp and not wet, and then add driblets of water to the brush as you develop the lather. (If you use the sink-full-of-water method, just dip the tip of the brush into the water.) This produces an abundant and substantial lather that's just wet enough. But in practice lathers try adding small amounts of water until the lather's obviously too wet, to see what happens.

Shaving cream lather by lathering directly on your beard

This method seems much easier to me and not so finicky with the water—plus the feel of the lather is a better guide than the look of the lather.

- **For cream in a tube**, squirt out the traditional almond-sized amount and smear the cream on your (wet, washed) beard on each cheek or on the brush, then use the wet but shaken out brush to spread the cream to coat all your beard with a thin layer of shaving cream.
- **For soft cream in a tub**, shake out the wet brush and twirl it in the tub to coat the bristle tips with the shaving cream, then take that to your (wet, washed) beard and coat your entire beard with a thin layer of shaving cream.
- **For firm/hard cream in a tub**, follow the soap procedures below.

Continuing with soft shaving creams, whether from tube or tub, dip the tips of the brushes bristles in water, or run a driblet of water into the center of the brush. Briskly brush the shaving cream that coats your beard, working the water into the shaving cream and the shaving cream into the brush. Lather will quickly form. As you add water to the brush and continue to brush on your beard briskly, the lather will build. Take your time with this: you want not only to create a good lather but also to work the lather (with its load of water) into the beard to continue the softening. You may at first add too much water—making practice lathers provides the necessary experience quickly—but if you add water in small amounts, you'll easily get a fine lather. Still, in doing practice lathers, try adding too much water to see what happens. The brush itself holds plenty of lather for a multi-pass shave.

Shaving soap

Shaving soap is a nice alternative to shaving cream. Initially I found shaving cream easy to use and soap difficult, so I stopped using shaving cream altogether. As I learned how to make good lather from soap, I found that I prefer shaving soap to shaving cream and now seldom use the latter: I discovered my preference. (I do have relatively soft water, important for soap, as noted above.)

As wetshaving becomes increasingly popular—and as even cartridge shavers discover that using true lather instead of canned foam can improve their shaves remarkably—we see an increasing demand for good shaving soap even as the quality of the classic brands of shaving soaps is being undermined by reformulations (using cheaper ingredients) and outsourcing (to soap plants that make soaps for many brands). However, some traditional mainline brands still (as of now) maintain high quality—e.g., D.R. Harris.

Some soaps use animal products (inspect the ingredients list for tallow, tallowate, or lanolin), but good vegan shaving soaps are readily available.

Here are some good shaving soaps by country:

- Australia: Otoko Organics[142] (an unusual shaving soap that makes an excellent and oddly stiffish lather) and Shaver Heaven (both vegan)
- France: Martin de Candre (a top-notch soap; they say lid is just for shipping and to discard it once you start using it so soap can dry) and Institut Karitè (which also has a good aftershave balm)
- Germany: Tabac, Klar Seifen, Speick, and the soap known variously as Dr. Ditman, Gold Dachs, and Rivivage
- Italy: Tcheon Fung Sing, an extremely nice artisanal soap; Virgilio Valobra (offers a soft soap and a shave stick), Cella, and Vitos (Red Label), available in 1 kg blocks: tear off a piece, mash it into a tub.
- Spain: La Toja
- UK: D.R. Harris, Castle Forbes, and Mitchell's Wool Fat

Essence of Scotland Sweet Gale[143] has ingredients that include bog myrtle, honey, mixed spices, cedarwood, and Aberfeldy single-malt Scotch whisky. The fragrances of honey and scotch remind me of a Rusty Nail cocktail—a pleasant association for me.

Creed's Green Irish Tweed is spectacularly expensive, but a superb soap. Dr. Selby's 3x Concentrated Shaving Cream, already mentioned, is firm as a hard soap and makes an excellent lather.

But the situation is fluid. Even as some established brands fall in quality, new artisanal soapmakers appear, and the best of those artisanal soaps now equal or exceed the quality of traditional brands. The demand for good shaving soaps is growing rapidly, and any artisan's production is necessarily somewhat limited (sometimes very limited). However, barriers to entry are relatively low—nothing like the intricacies of manufacturing a razor—and one can start on a small scale and, with success, gradually increase production.

Thus we see a large number of new (and often excellent) artisan soapmakers arising to meet the increasing demand: new soapmakers appear every month or two. Search Etsy for "shaving soap," for example.

It should be noted that some artisanal shaving soaps don't work well: the artisan may not be a wetshaver, and some of the new soaps will be best used as bath soaps. Some (often those with olive oil) will not form a lather.

In view of the variable quality of shaving soaps and the continually changing situation with commercial brands, it's wise to seek samples (see sources in the Appendix) and to read reviews in the various shaving forums. It's also a good idea to read soap ingredients carefully—you can search for definitions of unfamiliar ingredients, but when you read the ingredients of a soap you really like, then you get an idea of what to look for in future soaps.

Look at the ingredients for good artisanal shaving soaps such as these:
- Al's Shaving – alsshaving.com
- Barrister & Mann* - barristerandmann.com
- Bathhouse Soapery – bathhousesoap.com
- Catie's Bubbles – catiesbubbles.com
- Chiseled Face Groomatorium – chiseledface.com
- Cold River Soap Works – coldriversoapworks.com
- Dapper Dragon – dapperdragon.com
- Ginger's Garden – gingersgarden.com
- Green Mountain Soap* - gmsoap.com
- The Holy Black Trading Co. – theholyblack.com
- Honeybee Soaps – honeybeesoaps.net
- Huntlee - US Wickham: bullgooseshaving.com/brands/Huntlee.html
- Kell's Original – kellsoriginal.com
- LA Shaving Soap Company - lashavingsoap.com
- Latha – barristerandmann.com/collections/latha
- Maggard's Artisanal – maggardrazors.com

- Mama Bear – mamabearsoaps.com
- Mickey Lee Soapworks – mickeyleesoapworks.com
- Mike's Natural Soaps* - mikesnaturalsoaps.com
- Mystic Water – mystic4men.com
- Nanny's Silly Soap Company - nannyssillysoap.com (in UK)
- Otoko Organics - otoko.com.au (in Australia)
- Phoenix Artisan (5" puck) – phoenixartisanaccoutrements.com
- Queen Charlotte Soaps – queencharlottesoaps.com
- Reef Point – reefpointsoaps.com
- Saint Charles Shave – saintcharlesshave.com
- Shannon's Soaps – shannonssoaps.com
- The Shave Den Shop – theshavedenshop.com
- Shaver Heaven – shaverheaven.com.au (in Australia)
- Soap Commander – soapcommander.com
- Soapy Bathman – soapybathman.ca (in Canada)
- Soap Smooth (formerly Seifenglatt) – soapsmooth.com
- Stirling Soap Company* - stirlingsoap.com
- Strop Shoppe – stropshoppe.com
- Through the Fire Fine Craft – ttffcraft.com
- Tiki Bar Soap – tikibarsoap.com
- WhollyKaw – whollykaw.com
- Wickham (in the UK; 5" puck) – w-soap.co.uk

For those that are starred, I modify my usual loading technique somewhat. The starred soaps are very thirsty, and I have found that I get the best lather if I add small amounts of water *while I load the brush.*

It's worth noting that many of the vendors above offer aftershave splashes, balms, and milks, eau de toilettes, and other grooming products. I particularly like aftershaves from Ginger's Garden, Mickey Lee Soapworks, Saint Charles Shave, The Shave Den Shop, Stirling Soap Company and others. The products are available directly from their makers but also through an increasing number of vendors, including BullGoose Shaving, Maggard Razors, Phoenix Artisan Accoutrements, and Shave Revolution in the US, Italian Barber in Canada, and Shaving Station and The Shaving Time Company in the UK. As demand increases more on-line vendors will carry a good selection of artisanal products.

If you have skin sensitivities, get samples to test as previously described. Some with sensitive skin have reported that some soaps have enough essential or fragrance oils to trigger a skin reaction (skin turns red and hot for some minutes). Most vendors provide unscented versions as an option.

If an artisanal vendor offers a full range of products—beyond shaving soaps—those products are worth exploring. Some of the listed soaps are really exceptional. Some I particularly like are by Catie's Bubbles, Mickey Lee Soapworks, Otoko Organics, Phoenix Artisan Accoutrements, Shaver Heaven, Strop Shoppe, WhollyKaw, and Wickham, but all in the list above are good.

The ingredients of the better artisanal soaps are extremely good. Strop Shoppe, for example, whose soaps make a particularly rich lather, has as the ingredients of one of its Special Edition soaps:

Stearic Acid, Tallow, Glycerin, Ricinus communis (Castor) Seed Oil, Cocos nucifera (Coconut) Oil, Theobroma cacao (Cocoa) Seed Butter, Butyrospermum parkii (Shea) Butter, Blend of Fragrances.

The ingredients for Mickey Lee Soapworks The Drunken Goat are:

Stearic Acid, Tallow, Coconut Oil, Guinness, Goat Milk, Potassium Hydroxide, Sodium Hydroxide, Vegetable Glycerin, Castor Oil, Shea Butter, Lanolin, Fragrance.

The ingredients in WhollyKaw's soap show that it is vegan—that is, it contains no animal products such as tallow, tallowate, or lanolin:

Vegetable Stearic Acid, Organic Coconut Oil, Distilled Water, Sodium Hydroxide, Potassium Hydroxide, Glycerin, Essential Oils, Fragrance Oils

In contrast, look at the lengthy list of ingredients of Arko's shave stick:

Potassium Tallowate, Stearic Acid, Potassium Cocoate, Aqua, Sodium Palm Kernelate, Glycerin, Parfum, Parafinium, Liquidum, Tetrasodium EDTA, Etidronic Acid, Disodium Distrylbiphenly, Disuffonate Amyl Cinnamel, Citronellol, Geraniol, Hexyl Cinnamal, Linalool

And, of course, you can make your own shaving soap. You can find various recipes on the Web, but one easy way is to use Bramble Berry's melt-and-pour shaving soap base[144]. Other recipe links are in the endnote.

Soap in mug or bowl

The first—and critical—step is to load the brush with enough soap to create a good lather. Some use a damp brush, some prefer a wet brush. I was a wet-brush man until I ran into a soap getting rave reviews from which I could create only mediocre lathers. I finally tried using the damp-brush method with it and was bowled over by the lather quality. So I used that method with several other soaps that many had praised and that for me had not lived up to their promise— Stirling soap first, but then also Barrister & Mann, Dapper Dan, and Mike's Natural—working up the lather using the damp-brush method, and again was stunned by how much better the lather was than my wet-brush lathers from those same soaps. And I started to wonder whether *all* my soaps would seem better with the change in method from wet-brush to damp-brush. They do.

The problem with the wet-brush method is that while you start with a lot of water—using a dripping wet brush—much of the water spills away when you start loading the brush (thus you hold the tub on the side over the sink). That means for some soaps you don't load enough soap and/or you don't work enough water into soap as you load the brush. With the damp-brush method— wet brush well, then give it a medium shake or two (experiment)—you start by making a sort of paste of soap on the brush and add water until you get the lather you want—thus potentially adding more water than you would normally get using the wet-brush method. I now use only the damp-brush method.

Damp-brush method: Squeeze some water from the brush or shake the brush once or twice so that the brush is wettish/damp rather than dripping wet. Brush the soap briskly to load the brush, coating it with a paste of soap. You can add a driblet or two of water as you load the brush. You can then move the loaded brush to the beard, to a lathering bowl, or to the palm of your other hand.

Palm lathering: Brush your palm vigorously with the loaded brush. From time to time extend your palm under water dribbling from the tap and brush vigorously to work the water into the lather, then extend your palm for another driblet of water, brush vigorously to work it into the lather, and so on, until you have the lather you want. If you have water in the sink that you have softened with citric acid, dip up a small amount of that with your closed fingers.

The brush grows noticeably larger as more water is worked into the lather, and with your hand you can feel the slickness and thickness of the developing lather. At one time this method seemed finicky to me, but with experience I quickly learned how much water to add and how rapidly to add it.

Face lathering: Much the same as palm lathering, except you are working the lather up on your beard, adding small amounts of water as needed, then working that into the lather on your beard. You can run a driblet of water into the center of the brush, or dip the tips of the brush into softened water in the sink. This is the method I use, since while I work up the lather I also soften the beard.

Bowl lathering: Much the same as the above methods, but done using a bowl. Note that it's the shape of the bowl that helps you fold lather back into the brush; you're not attempting to fill the bowl with lather, as a lather reservoir. The lather's in the brush, not in the bowl.

Wet-brush method: Wet the brush fully, hold the tub or mug or puck of soap on its side over the sink, and for 30 seconds brush the soap briskly and also firmly—if the brush has a 2" loft, get the top of the handle to 1" from the surface of the soap. At first, water and loose, sloppy lather will spill into the sink, but keep brushing. Soon you'll see real lather forming, but continue the brushing until you see no large bubbles: you want the brush fully loaded with soap. This will take anywhere from 10-20 seconds for most soaps. With hard water, use citric acid to soften the water in the sink.

Not all brushes will spill water: I used two Simpson brushes recently, a Chubby 1 Best and a Duke 3 Best, following the wet-brush method described, and the water from the brush mixed right in with the lather. This is probably because the dense, stubby knots of these brushes hold less water (and less lather) than the sort of puffy, long-lofted knot that I personally prefer.

You can use a bowl or your palm for this method as well, but I move the loaded brush to my (wet, washed) beard and continue to work the lather up and into the stubble. I have never once found that I had too wet a lather, but sometimes I did need to add a little water because the extended loading picks up a good amount of soap. Adding water is easy: run a driblet of water into the center of the brush, or dip the tips of the brush into the water in the sink, and then work that into the lather.

I recommend you try both methods, spending at least a week on each. As I note, with some soaps the damp-brush method works noticeably better than the wet-brush method, so experiment with both methods. For me, the damp-brush method has worked better overall.

For both methods, making good lather is a matter of experience, so get as much experience as quickly as you can by making practice lathers. Try loading for the full 30 seconds, then make a lather with a 25-second loading period, then a 20-second loading period. (I normally require only 10 seconds to fully load the brush, even if the soap is a totally dry hard soap and the brush is soft and fluffy— but my tap water is fairly soft.)

Try starting with a lather that's clearly too dry (for example, a damp brush fully loaded with soap) and adding just a little water as you work the brush with the soap. As you work in the water, feel the lather between thumb and forefinger. (Palm lathering makes this easy, but you can do it with any method.) At first, it will be almost sticky. Then, as you hit the sweet spot, the appearance of the lather will change, and it will feel slick. As you continue adding water, you'll find that soon the lather becomes sticky once more.

After several practice lathers, using the same soap each time, you'll know the look and the feel of a good lather. You can then transfer this knowledge to other soaps, which may require a different amount of water for the sweet spot. After you know it, the sweet spot is clear—some say the lather "explodes" at that point, meaning that the lather seems to change state.

You'll note the continuing theme in shaving: the need to experiment to find what works well for you and to gain experience. Guidance (as from this book or from videos) can be helpful, but the best teaching and the truest test are found in your own experience, and practice builds experience efficiently. The more you practice, the better you'll become. Fairly soon, you won't need to time the loading: you'll know from experience when your brush is sufficiently loaded and when to add water as you work the lather.

Shave Place has more information[145] on lathering from both soaps and creams. Razor-skipping when you shave (razor head not gliding smoothly across your skin, but seeming to "stick" and then skip) might be due to hard water, but it also might be a problem with the lather. If you switch creams and soaps a lot (trying different samples, for example), you may not hit the sweet spot for a particular cream or soap, using too much (or too little) water.

Use the brush to work the lather thoroughly into your beard. You need only enough lather to fully cover the whiskers—that is, the lather need not be deep on your face. To give the lather a chance to do its work, spend a little more time working the lather into the stubble on your first pass than on the later passes. Keep the lathered brush (whether using cream or soap) handy. After each pass, rinse your beard (it is more wetting than rinsing the beard—a splash of water will do) and re-lather your beard prior to the next pass. Lather is always applied to a wet beard. Each pass requires a lathered (and thus lubricated and protected) beard.

Take a look at this excellent on-line tutorial[146] (with photos). I don't bother with putting water on the soap—I experimented with the three-week protocol (week with, week without, another week with); it made zero difference in performance but did add a step and required that I remembered to do it before the shave actually started—and I have enough trouble remembering to wet a boar or horsehair brush before I shower. I want to minimize what I must remember, and just let each step lead to the next. Having to do one special step totally out of the flow and that moreover doesn't improve things—well, that's really not what I'm looking for.

But definitely do your own experiments: that's how you learn what works for you and what doesn't. And what you expect to happen may well turn out to be not at all what does happen.

A video referenced earlier[147] shows the quick creation of lather. The loading is 10 seconds, and working up the lather took 30 seconds. However, in the demo I was working with a dry beard, and that is harder than when I do my usual pre-shave beard wash. The same process works with a glycerin soap like Col. Conk[148].

You'll note that Col. Conk fills the (plastic) tub to the very brim, and this is not a problem for loading the brush. Indeed, the classic English shaving soaps sold in wooden tubs are filled to within 1/4" of the brim, as is (for example) Martin de Candre and Catie's Bubbles. Despite the fact that full tubs do not present a loading problem, some vendors provide a *lot* of space above the soap, resulting in containers whose height exaggerates the amount of soap contained.

For example, take a look at this photo of two (excellent) artisanal soaps. The container on the left holds six ounces of soap with *lots* of space for loading the brush. The container on the right holds eight ounces of soap and is filled to the brim—but it is absolutely no problem to load the brush even so. As you can tell, I prefer containers without the superfluous space. I stack my soaps[149] and very tall containers take up too much room.

If the lather is inadequate (thin and sparse), the cause is almost always that either the brush is insufficiently loaded or the water is hard. Insufficient loading can be from brushing the soap too lightly or for too short a time or both.

I have found that horsehair brushes work best (for me) for making a good, creamy lather. Boar brushes also work well (and particularly require extended loading), and better as they become broken in. Badger and artificial badger make and hold a good amount of lather, but with these the novice has a tendency to stop loading the brush too soon: try for 30 seconds initially, then gradually reduce the time as you gain experience.

Soap as a shave stick

A shave stick is shaving soap in stick form. Shave sticks are pleasant to use if you have a normal beard: the stubble scrapes the soap from the shave stick when you rub it against the grain of your beard. Two types of beards present a challenge. A beard that's sparse and soft, as on a man just beginning to shave, will not rub off enough soap to make a good lather. However, as shown in the (terrific) movie *The Dam Busters* (1955), a shave stick can also be used as an extraordinarily thick puck of small diameter, with the shaver loading the brush by brushing the end of the stick, as if loading from a puck.

In contrast, a heavy, thick, cheesegrater beard will scrape off *too much* soap, so that the lather will be soap-heavy and require a *lot* of water to keep it from being sticky. Men with this sort of thick, tough beard rub the sick only on the chin and around the mouth (the Van Dyke area), work the lather up there and then work it into the rest of the beard. Another possibility, is for men with very tough beards rub the stick *with* the grain instead of against the grain.

Chuck Falzone pointed out hard water requires loading more soap into the brush—thus men who shave with hard water prefer stiff, scrubby brushes that scrape up more soap (the notorious "shaving soap brush"). So rubbing a shave stick over the beard may not scrape off enough soap if the water's quite hard. The best solution is to use citric acid to soften the water (described above).

Shave sticks work great for travel: they require no lathering bowl and their physical format is compact. D.R. Harris, Lea, Palmolive, Speick, and Valobra make excellent shave sticks, as do many artisanal soapmakers.

Some good soaps are available only as shave sticks (Arko, for example), and men who do not like to use shave sticks on their beard can use the stick as a puck, as described above, or grate the stick and press the gratings into a mug or bowl to be used as a regular puck. I haven't tried this because I enjoy using a shave stick in the traditional way of rubbing it on my beard. (Try it.)

Some shave sticks don't have a container and are simply cylinders of soap, perhaps wrapped in foil or paper. These can be packed for travel in a tall plastic prescription pill bottle. You can also make your own shave sticks from any easily melted shaving soap (not triple-milled soaps). Melt the shaving soap and pour it into a shave stick container. It's a simple process[150], but be careful not to get the soap too hot, lest you lose or alter the fragrance. You can also make your own shave sticks from the Bramble Berry melt-and-pour shaving soap base.

As noted above, in using a shave stick you load your beard with soap, rather than your brush. After washing and rinsing your beard, rub the stick against the grain of your wet beard—over the entire beard for a normal beard, over only the Van Dyke area (or only with the grain) for a tough thick beard. I have never found it necessary to wet the shave stick, but you may wish to experiment with using the shave stick dry and then on another shave using it wet to see which works best for you. Wetting the stick seems to help when the humidity is extremely low (as in centrally heated houses in very cold weather).

Once your beard is well soaped, begin brushing briskly all over your beard with your wet shaving brush. Lather will appear, as if by magic. Continue brushing until the brush is fully loaded with lather, which also works the lather into your beard. Normally, a lathering bowl is not used with a shave stick, but it certainly would be possible. Try it and see if you like it.

Superlather

A "superlather" uses both shaving soap and shaving cream—best seen in an on-line video[151]. Use a lathering bowl and begin to build the lather from a shaving soap—but also add a dab of shaving cream and work that into the lather as well. Superlathers are generally extra thick and luxurious. StraightRazorPlace has a good and detailed tutorial on making a superlather, with photographs[152].

Another way to generate superlather: use a shave stick to apply soap to your prepped and wet beard, then twirl the brush in shaving cream and lather on your beard. Superlather a thick, luxurious lather. A man in Quebec who doesn't particularly like either l'Occitane Cade shaving soap or l'Occitane Cade shaving cream by itself found that the two work spectacularly together in a superlather.

EIGHT

The blade

THE blade and razor are the key components of the shave itself (as distinct from the prep). Novices tend to focus more on the razor because it's more obviously interesting than the blade—and also much more expensive. Yet the comfort and smoothness of your shave, once your prep and technique are good, will be about 80% from the blade and 20% from the razor.

High-quality double-edged blades generally run 25¢-55¢ each in a pack of 5 or 10 and as low as 7¢-14¢ each if you look around for bulk lots—for example, on eBay or from blade vendors on-line. As noted earlier, Derby blades are now available on Amazon for $12.93/200 (with average blade life, that amounts to about $3.37 for a year's supply of blades), but Derby blades don't work for everyone. In fact, they don't work for me: they seem tuggy. (I like Astra Superior Platinum blades, which I got for 9¢ per blade.) Blades come from Germany, Turkey, Pakistan, India, Japan, Sweden, Egypt, Israel, the UK, the US, Russia, Poland, and other countries.

With the right cutting technique on a well-prepped beard, the typical blade lasts from one shave to seven or more, depending on the brand of blade, the razor used, and the individual (the thoroughness of his prep, the nature of his beard (soft and sparse, thick and wiry, or in between), his skin (oily or dry or in between, highly sensitive or tough as leather or in between), and his technique. A range of 3-6 days is typical. There's no sense in trying to stretch a blade beyond its life—some blades will die gracefully, simply starting to pull and tug as they become dull, but others go out with a bang and start nicking. Change the blade as soon as your shave is unsatisfactory: that's how you determine the blade's life.

Double-edged blades cost substantially less than today's disposable multiblade plastic cartridges, which run as high as $3.50 each in the US and $8 each in some other countries, and the usual rationalization for buying lots of wonderful shaving equipment is that you'll be money ahead (eventually— sometime in the next 20 to 30 years) because you save so much on blades.

Remember: the common story is that blades are where Gillette makes its money—give away the razor, sell the blades, and over time, the total spent on blades is much more than the price of the razor. (The true story is more complicated[153].) Certainly with multiblade cartridges costing what they do, double-edged blades save you money immediately and over time will save a lot.

Finding the right blade

DE blades offer three surprises. The first, already noted, is how *smoothly* and *easily* the DE blade cuts through the stubble compared to a cartridge razor. Using a multiblade cartridge means pulling 3-7 blades simultaneously through the stubble, so naturally the effort required is 3-7 times what is needed to pull a single blade through stubble. Keeping a cartridge razor on the face while cutting against such resistance seems to require much more pressure than a DE razor needs: thus cartridge shavers develop the (bad) habit of pressing hard—a habit that causes serious problems with a DE razor.

A second surprise for DE novices is how greatly brands of DE blades differ in sharpness and smoothness. One shaver wrote:

> Just started wetshaving 2 weeks ago... have only used Merkur blades since they came with the razor.
>
> Leisureguy suggested I order a 5-blade sampler with plan to try the blades in this order: Merkur -> Israeli -> Derby -> Gillette -> Feather
>
> I rec'd my sampler yesterday and tried the Israeli this morning... WOW!!
>
> I could not believe the difference. My best shave so far by leaps and bounds. The razor was gliding across my face and by the 3rd pass it was the closest most comfortable shave I have had yet.

The third—and greatest—surprise is that different men can experience very different performance from any given brand of blade. This perhaps should not be a surprise: different men often use different prep, have beards that range from sparse and soft to thick and wiry, have different sensitivities of skin, use different techniques, and have different razors. Often the *only* thing in common *is* the brand of blade, so no great surprise that the experience is different.

But one's own experience is so vivid and immediate that many find it extremely difficult to grasp that someone else using the same brand of blade can have a different experience. Thus you find occasional suggestions like "Don't even bother to try brand X—just throw them out." They don't get it.

The source of the difficulty is attributing to the blade characteristics that exist only in relation to a user. It's like asking, "Does fried liver have a good taste?" That sounds as though the taste is in the fried liver (with onions: yum!), but since some relish fried liver and others blanch at the thought (the fried liver itself being the same in each case) it's obvious that there's more in play than just the fried liver. The same with blades: "Does this blade cut easily and smoothly, or is it harsh and tuggy?" has no answer except in relation to the entire situation: the person, the razor, and the blade.

Changing any of those three—the person, the razor, and/or the blade—changes the system, and as a result the shave can go from good to bad, or from bad to good, or from good to great. Changes can be any combination of:

- **The person**: The change can be a different person altogether, or the same person changing technique and/or prep (procedure, products, or water); or
- **The razor**: The change can be a different razor altogether, or the same razor using different pressure or a different angle or (in adjustable razors) a different setting or (in a three-piece razor) a different handle; or
- **The blade**: The change can be a different brand of blade or the same blade changed through use (becoming dull).

The performance of a given brand of blade can vary not only from one person to another, but also from one *razor* to another. You may find that a brand that's uncomfortably harsh in one razor will feel smooth and comfortable in another, presumably due to small differences between the two razors in blade angle, guard placement, blade exposure, head design, and the like. For example, Feather blades do not work well for me in most razors, but are terrific in the Feather AS-D1/2, the Gillette Tech, and some others. Kai blades are terrific for me in most razors, but I found that a Kai blade in a Weber was harsh (though the Weber is excellent with other brands). And if the person is changed—to someone other than me—a Kai blade in a Weber may be fine, and indeed I heard from someone that he loves that combination: for him, it works.

Since a blade that someone else likes may not work for you (or your razor)—and a blade that they hate might work fine for you (in your razor)—trying blades yourself is the *only* way to find your own "best blade(s)." Dismiss comments such as "this blade is excellent" or "this blade is terrible." Those reflect *the speaker*'s experience. You *must* use the blades yourself to actually know how the blade will work *for you*.

When someone says a brand "doesn't work" for him, he means the blade tugs at the whiskers rather than cutting easily, or he can't seem to avoid nicks and/or skin irritation even when he's being careful with prep, blade angle, and razor pressure.

The unpredictability of a shaver's response to any given brand of blade is mysterious but readily observed: Each brand has some who love it, some who hate it, and some who are indifferent[154]. Some brands have a preponderance one way or the other, but even if only a few hate (or love) a brand, you may be one of those few. You can't use the brand statistically: "I love this brand of blade 60%, and hate it 35%, and am indifferent 5%."

With an individual shaver and a particular blade and razor, the judgment is 100%, whether love, hate, or indifferent. Each individual shaver *must* try multiple brands to find the brand(s) that work best for him, rather than simply pick those that are (statistically) popular. For each new razor, he *must* do some renewed blade exploration. If he never ventures beyond the popular brands, he may never find his own ideal blade. Fear of the new defeats many.

If it were not like this—if all shavers responded in the same way to a blade, independent of the razor (and many novices believe this is the case and simply ask "Which blade is sharpest?" as if that would be the best blade for them and their razor)—then there would be only one brand of blade: THE blade. Perhaps it would be sold in different colors of packages, or with different decorations printed on the blade, but everyone would use it because it is the universal "best" blade.

But life is not like that, and so blade sampler packs were developed to allow a shaver to try a wide variety of brands through one purchase.

I suggest that you get a large sampler pack, along with as many brands as you can buy locally. Samplers that have only one blade per brand are useless: don't get those. Initially, you won't be trying all the blades—that's for later. At first, try just a few brands: three or four. Guys who like Derby blades will suggest you start with Derby; guys who like Personnas will suggest that; and so on. Since you cannot know which brand(s) will work for you, just pick any brand to start with. One easy way: test them alphabetically.

Try three or four brands, pick the best of the lot, and **stick with that brand for two months.** (You'll have to buy a few packs of that brand, since the sampler will have only one pack.) By keeping the brand of blade constant and using the same razor, any problems that arise will be due to your prep and/or your technique, so you can focus on fixing those. And at the end of two months, you'll *really* know the feel of that brand, so when you try a different brand the differences are much more obvious.

After a couple of months, your prep will be solid: you can easily create an excellent lather, and when you bring blade to beard, your beard is ready for the razor. Moreover, when you shave, you're not hesitant: your strokes are smooth and efficient, you never have razor burn, and nicks are infrequent. You enjoy your shave, and the result is a smooth face and a jolly outlook.

Why explore?

Of course, once you're getting good shaves, you might think, "Why try another brand? This one's doing okay. Better just to stick with it." Indeed some shavers do stick with the first brand they encounter that gives them a passable shave. I've read comments along the lines of "This brand tugs a lot, but when I'm finished, my face is smooth, so it's a good blade." Or, in the case of guys who ask, "Which blade is sharpest?" and then use only Feathers even if they find they suffer chronic razor burn and constant nicks—they assume that's just what DE shaving is like because they're using the best blade available.

Shaving shouldn't be like that. If you find that a blade tugs a lot or feels harsh or seems to scrape, and you're pretty sure you use good technique (covered later), it's not a good brand for you. Shaving is about the process as well as the end result: both should be pleasurable, and the blade is a critical factor.

By continuing to explore even after you're getting good shaves with a particular brand, you might find a blade that takes your shave to a whole new level of excellence. And note that the best brand of blade for you may not one of the popular brands. Don't dismiss popular brands, but don't try only those.

It may happen, of course, that your best brand is the brand you're already using—though, if you haven't tried many different brands, that's unlikely: the range of blades is quite large, you'll discover. And it may be that none of the new brands you try will really astonish you with the excellence of the shave. But it's more likely that you'll find a blade better than you imagined possible. You have much to gain and little to lose from trying a new brand occasionally.

To maximize your chances of finding a great brand (for you), try as many brands as you can. If you're lucky, you'll find a blade whose excellence is beyond what you imagined possible. At the very least, you can enjoy some inexpensive exploration and learning. Blade acquisition disorder is the least costly of all the shaving-related acquisition disorders, much cheaper than acquisition disorders for razors, shaving creams, brushes, shaving soaps, and aftershaves.

Because brands occasionally go out of production with no warning, you might want to buy a few hundred blades when you do find a superb brand. (I bitterly regret to this day not laying in a stash of Astra Keramik Platinum blades before they unexpectedly vanished from the scene.) You may well find a later brand that's even better than your stash brand, but you can readily sell blades on the forums or through Reddit's /r/Shave_Bazaar. And since that one works well (for you), you may want to keep it, since it may be the best brand in a new razor.

How to explore

After two months of sticking with that first good brand, you're ready to find whether your shave can be improved. If you followed the suggestion above, you already have the sampler pack with the greatest number of brands. If not, get it now, or buy sample blades from Tryablade.com. And whenever you order shaving supplies—a new shaving soap or shaving cream, for example—include in the order a few packs of different brands you've not yet tried.

When you start trying new brands, you're looking for a blade that produces a significantly smoother, easier, and more comfortable shave than your current brand, with no nicks or burn—a "transcendent" blade that takes your shave to a new level.

Every 4-8 weeks, try one blade of a new brand. (I recommend every 4 weeks for your first two years to increase the odds of finding a transcendent blade in that time; once you've found such a great brand, drop the frequency of testing to every 6-8 weeks, but do continue to explore.)

If the new blade you tried is better than your regular brand, then that becomes your new regular brand—the one you use daily. If it's not, return to your regular brand for another 4-8 weeks.

Most at some point find a brand that makes them realize until then they had not really understood what "a good shave" means.

Save the remaining blades of brands that don't work so well—in your next razor they might be fine. And continue to try new brands for some years, at the rate of a new brand every 4-8 weeks.

If you have more than one razor, try each new brand in another razor before you give up on it. A blade that's terrible in the Merkur 34C might be wonderful in a Gillette Super Speed and vice versa. Also, note that some blades seem dull for the first shave or two, until the coating that covers the edge is worn away. Sputnik, Dorco 301, Tiger, and Crystal, among others, are like this.

By using the approach described above, you're always comparing just two brands: your best so far (your current regular brand) and a new brand. That makes the comparison easy, and by always shaving a few weeks using your best brand to date before each test, you not only get a break from testing, you test when you're freshly reminded of what a blade that's good for you feels like before you try the next new brand—and testing won't feel overwhelming.

Sometimes two different brands seem equal in quality. In that case, the obvious choice is to use the cheaper as your regular brand. Remember that some brands will not shave smoothly for the first shave or two—your own response to a blade should be your guide, but try for three shaves at least before you decide a blade is dull. And also remember that a brand that's bad in one razor may be excellent in another.

As you explore, you'll find that blades fall into one of three classes:

1. **Some won't work for you**. For such a brand, write on an envelope the name of the brand, the date, why the blade's not good for you (too

dull, nicks too frequently, irritates your skin—whatever), put the remaining blades of that brand into the envelope, and put it aside. A year or so later, try the brand again to see whether things (your prep, technique, razor, etc.) have changed and the brand is now good for you. If it's still not your cup of tea, pass the blades along to someone else—for him, they could be a "best blade".

2. **Some will work fine**—just as good as the blade you've been using, or perhaps even a little better. Add these to your rotation for variety.

3. If you're lucky, **one or two will make you say, "Wow!"** These blades are, for you, truly exceptional: they shave so smoothly, so easily, so readily that it's as though you've not really had a great shave before.

My own current best brands include Personna Lab Blue, Astra Superior Platinum, Voskhod, Gillette 7 O'Clock SharpEdge, and some others.

Once I liked Feather and Tiger blades, but then I decided that they were too ready to nick for no reason. They seemed like a high-powered but unstable motorcycle: great performance but unpredictable. And yet I find that Feather blades work extremely well for me in the Feather AS-D1 and AS-D2 razors, the 1940's Super Speed, the Schick Krona, and the Gillette Tech.

It's the same story with Gillette 7 O'Clock SharpEdge blades (not to be confused with the 7AM brand). When I first tried them, they seemed too sharp for comfortable use—not erratic, just very sharp. I set them aside and continued with other brands. By the time I got around to trying them again, they were perfect. It's just as your music teacher told you: daily practice improves your skill (as is also shown by how the time required for a shave gradually diminishes).

With a microscope you can see the actual differences in the edges of different brands. Microphotographs of the edges of several common brands show clear differences. The Treet Blue Special clearly has a well-sharpened edge—still, it doesn't work for some shavers, though it works extremely well for others (including me). A series of reviews[155] on ShaveMyFace of different brands of blades has a microphotograph of each blade being reviewed. The reviews are helpful, though the reviewer's experience of the blade may not match yours. Again: different men often respond quite differently to the same brand of blade—an idea that's extremely difficult to internalize.

It's worth noting that cartridge shavers get few choices of brands and types of blades—many fewer than DE shavers have, who can also choose among various kinds of steel (carbon, stainless, tungsten stainless, etc.) and various kinds of coatings (platinum, chromium, Teflon, etc.). Cartridge razors have to make do with the very few varieties available—and those that are available may fall far short of the shave that a "best blade" for you can deliver.

Carbon-steel blades

Some blades (Treet Blue Special, Treet DuraSharp HiTech Steel, Treet Classic) are made of carbon steel rather than stainless steel. I know from using knives (and reading about straight razors) that carbon steel can take a sharper edge than stainless steel, but carbon steel does tend to rust. So if you find you like a carbon-steel blade, you have three choices:

1. Use a new blade for each shave (they're cheap).
2. Dry the blade after each use (*not* by rubbing it with a cloth but, for example, by rinsing it under hot water and then shaking it well or using a hair dryer).
3. Easiest: After shaving, rinse the razor in hot water, give it a good shake, swish the head in 91% or 99% rubbing alcohol, and then put it in a rack to dry. The alcohol displaces the water and then evaporates, leaving the blade dry so that it doesn't rust. (You will recall the same technique is used in hard-water areas to avoid mineral deposits forming along the edge as water evaporates.)

I go with option 3, using an inexpensive 99% rubbing alcohol I buy at the local Safeway supermarket. I use a squat, wide-mouth jar that originally contained a food product: the mouth is large enough to accept the razor head, and a commercial jar's lid opens/shuts with one quarter-turn.

If you do use alcohol for your straight or DE razor, simply dip the razor in the alcohol and remove it: never let it rest there for long: it will discolor steel and ruin resin handles. Avoid bleach like the plague: it destroys metal quickly.

In the Great Depression (long before stainless blades arrived), small hones were made to resharpen double-edged blades, which at that time were all made of carbon steel. You can occasionally find such hones on eBay. They don't work on coated stainless blades, and I don't think they're worth the effort on carbon-steel blades. My blades at 9¢ each last a week: $4.68/year. If I *doubled* their life, it would save $2.34/year: less than 5¢/week.

More about blades

For most brands, the manufacturer's name and other information are printed on the blades, so the two sides—top and bottom—look different. You can put the blade in the razor with either side on top: it makes no difference. Since you use both edges of the razor as you shave—when one side of the razor has collected enough lather, you switch to the other side for a while before you rinse the razor—the blade's two edges thus get about the same wear per shave.

Merkur manufactures both blades and razors, so they naturally include their own blades with the razors they sell. Unfortunately, for the majority of men (and thus probably for you) Merkur blades are terrible (though, of course, some men find them absolutely wonderful—but relatively few). If you get a Merkur razor, trying some other brands is particularly important.

Some blades are made of a kind of stainless that rusts to a degree and will leave brown stains inside the razor, between cap and baseplate. This discoloration, generally called "tea stain" because of its color, is easily removed with a soft toothbrush and regular toothpaste. When the razor is made of stainless steel, owners sometimes worry that the razor's rusting. It's not; it's the blade. For example, Gillette Rubie blades tend to produce tea stains.

Some novices wonder whether turning the blade over after a few shaves will make it last longer. It might, but given the price of blades, it doesn't seem to be worth the effort: as noted above, even *doubling* a blade's life saves little over a year. Moreover, it's a good idea to avoid handling the blade, whose cutting edge is delicate and easily damaged. But try it if you like: experiment.

Some, as previously noted, find that a given brand of blade works well for them in one razor, but not in another. For example, a very sharp blade might work well for them in a Gillette Tech but not in a Merkur 34C. The practice of shaving is an on-going series of experiments that you perform.

If you find a brand harsh, you can pull each edge of a new blade through a wine cork before using the blade ("corking" the blade). This tames the blade's edge while leaving it still sharp enough to shave. But it's better to find a brand that works for you without corking. Also, a blade's edge is easily damaged, so the result of corking can be a blade that's much the worse for it—and for you. So my own inclination is to explore more brands of blades before I try corking a brand I have. Others like to do the corking. You decide for yourself which you want to do.

I do want to provide one blade warning. I had a chrome Merkur 37C slant that provided me with lovely, perfect shaves even when I used it with a Feather blade—and never a nick. So I decided I had to have a 37G: the slant in gold. I sold the 37C, got the 37G, loaded it with a new Feather blade, and... Nick City! I was aghast. I tried again the next day: still many nicks. I was despondent, but then I tried a new Feather blade, replacing the one in the razor.

I got a perfect, lovely shave, with nary a nick. So it was a bad blade. I knew that *could* happen, but that was my first experience of it. I think I would have immediately tried another blade if: (a) it had not been my first shave with the new razor (thus blaming the razor instead of the blade, still thinking that all blades of a given brand were identical); and (b) it wasn't the first time I had encountered an instance of a dud blade (it's rare); and (c) I hadn't panicked, thinking I had just sold the one slant that would work for me.

Lesson learned: if you have a bad shave with a new razor, try changing the blade. And if you then have a bad shave with the new blade, try a different brand of blade. Don't jump to the conclusion, as I did, that the razor is the problem. Experiment.

Blade disposal

Razor blades remain quite sharp even when too dull for shaving, so disposal requires some care. Plastic blade dispensers (increasingly rare as manufacturers cut costs: cardboard boxes are cheaper) usually have a "used-blade" compartment for safe disposal.

If your brand lacks a plastic dispenser, use a special receptacle for used blades. Do **not** simply toss the blades into the trash—razor blades can all too readily cut through plastic trash bags and into the hands lifting the bag. Proper disposal of sharps is *always* worth doing with care. States and cities often have laws and ordinances regulating the disposal of biohazard sharps, and blades belong to this category. (Call your local waste management company or municipal department for more information on appropriate sharps containers and where to dispose of them.)

You can easily find commercially made disposal safes for razors—some pharmacies even provide free sharps containers. The Feather Blade Safe[156] works well, and Pacific Handy Cutters makes a wall-mounted blade bank[157].

But it's also very easy to make quite a good blade safe. Take a small can—for example, a small can of evaporated milk or tomato juice—and drain the contents by punching two small holes in the bottom. Rinse out the can, using the two holes. Then use a hacksaw or a thin Dremel blade to cut a slit in the side, just under the top. Make the slit just wide enough to admit a double-edged blade.

The can then sits on a high shelf (out of reach of toddlers) and you discard the blades through the slit. When the can is full, a tap of a hammer permanently seals it shut. The result is an opaque, unbreakable blade safe that has no lid to open and looks boring. I used one; it took a little over six years of six-days-a-week shaving to fill it. Note, however, that this homemade container, though safe, may or may not meet local requirements for a sharps container.

Others suggest using coin banks. I recommend against this because a coin bank looks interesting to a young child, especially with the rattle—*wealth!*—and most coin banks can be opened so the coins can be removed. A toddler will be surprised by how sharp the "coins" turn out to be—and you will feel awful.

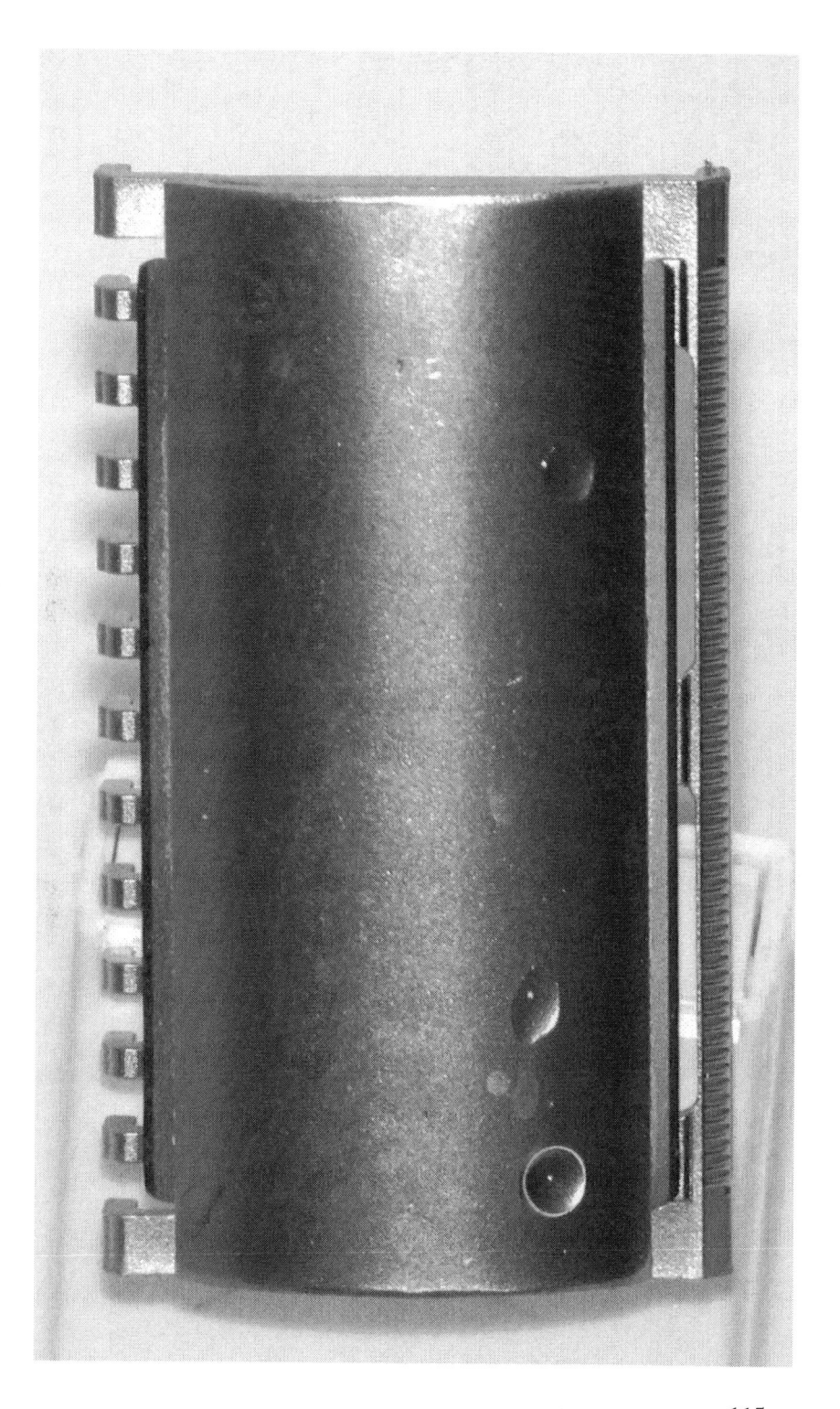

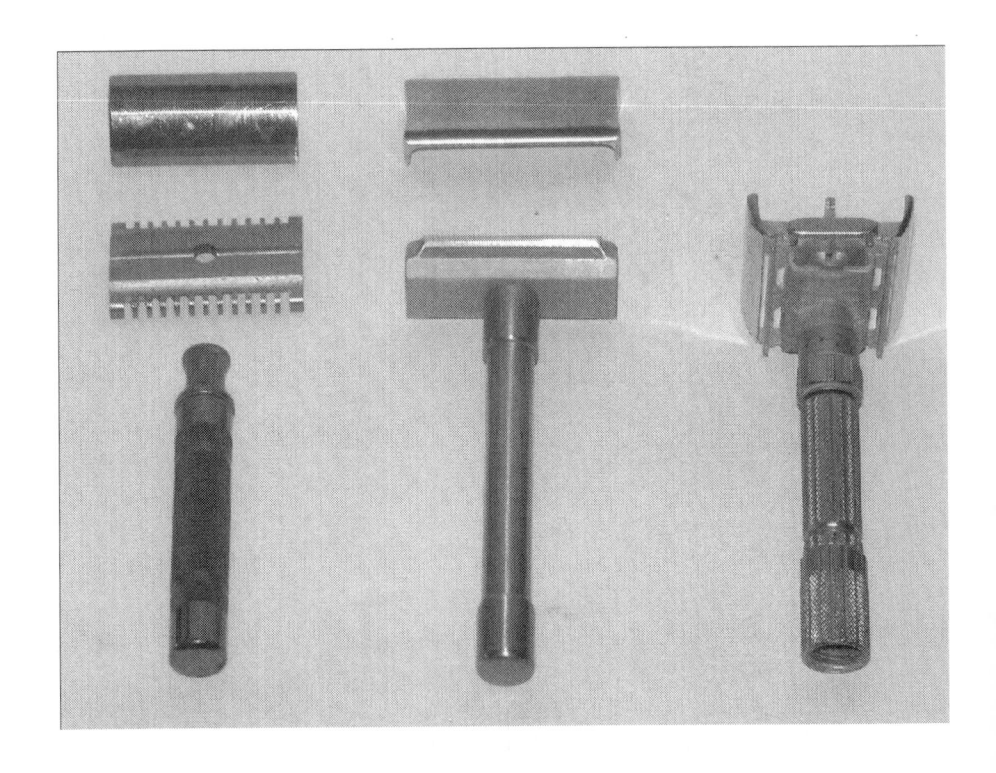

NINE

The razor

THE focus of this book is the DE safety razor (see photo opposite). Before the safety razor, there was the straight razor, but once the safety razor arrived, it quickly displaced the straight razor[158].

The disposable double-edged blade is the very core of the safety razor system, and it was the blade that gave King Camp Gillette his opportunity and the challenge: to manufacture a sharp, disposable blade from thin, stamped steel. The safety razor holds the blade and presents the edge with a specific exposure and angle. The safety razor can be:

Three-piece (like the early Gillette razors and the Edwin Jagger DE8x series: top, baseplate, and handle) – *left opposite*: a Gillette NEW (introduced in 1930); this type is the easiest to pack since it's lies flat once disassembled; it's also the sturdiest;

Two-piece (like several Merkur razors: the Futur, the 34C Hefty Classic ("HD"), the Progress, and the 37C/39C slants: top and baseplate-handle) – *center opposite*: a Pils razor; or

One-piece (like the Merkur Vision, Gillette Super Speed, and other twist-to-open (TTO) razors: twisting the knob at the bottom one way opens butterfly doors for changing blades, the other closes them to grip the blade for shaving) – *right opposite*: a Gillette Fat Boy. One-piece razors are the most fragile and prone to damage if dropped: lots of moving parts and insecure joints.

Novices sometimes call DE safety razors "handles" and call DE blades "razors," apparently a back-formation from cartridge razors, since in a sense the cartridge is a razor (in that it holds the blades) and the other part of system does nothing other than provide a handle and hold the cartridge, allowing it to pivot. In contrast, the DE safety razor actually has a job to do beyond holding the blade and providing a handle: the razor presents the blade at a particular angle and exposure and the placement of the guard and the design of guard and cap have a significant effect on the feel and quality of the shave.

DE blades are just that: blades. They are not "razors," but they are loaded *into* (DE safety) razors. Those razors *have* handles, but they are not themselves "handles." Handles for three-piece DE safety razors are available from a variety of vendors, and those handles are exactly that: handles, not razors.

A beginning shaver will sometimes assemble a three-piece razor with the baseplate upside down, which generally results in the razor not cutting at all. If the guard is scalloped on one side, those scallops are on the top side of the baseplate: toward the cap, away from the handle. Inspect the razor closely before removing the baseplate, and when putting in the blade, make sure the baseplate is right-side up before tightening the cap.

In the photo at the right are two baseplates from Edwin Jagger razors. The baseplate at the top is right-side-up, and the side shown faces the cap. The baseplate at the bottom is upside-down, and the top of the handle fits into the circular depression in the bottom of the baseplate.

To load a three-piece razor: locate the alignment studs. These usually are on the cap (two studs, one on each side of the threaded stud in the center), but on some razors the alignment studs are on the baseplate (as on the Pils and the iKon S3S), and some razors use four corner brackets.

If the alignment studs are on the cap, place the cap upside-down in the palm of your hand, drop/push a fresh blade over the studs for proper alignment, then place the baseplate (scalloped edges facing the cap) on the blade and screw the handle onto the threaded stud projecting through the baseplate.

If the alignment studs are on the baseplate, place the blade onto baseplate, over the alignment students, and then place the cap over that and tighten the handle.

Two-piece razors, with the baseplate and the handle joined into a single unit, must solve the problem of how to attach the cap to the baseplate+handle. The usual attachment is threaded; the challenge then is how to turn the threads while the cap stays in a fixed orientation with respect to the baseplate+handle. The usual approach (used in the Merkur 34C among others) is to have a threaded shaft that can rotate independently inside the hollow handle, the shaft turned by a knob at the bottom and engaging the threads on the cap's threaded stud. Generally a friction ring allows easy rotation and prevents the shaft from falling out while enabling you to remove the shaft for cleaning.

Another approach, used by the Pils shown and by some iKon two-piece razors, is to attached the handle to the baseplate with a bearing so that the handle rotates independently of the baseplate. In this case, the action is much like a three-piece razor.

A third approach, seen in the Merkur Futur, is to do away altogether with a threaded attachment (and the corresponding requirement for easy rotation) and instead attach the cap to the baseplate with a snap-on connection. A snap-on cap has recently been proposed for a new razor on Kickstarter as well.

Shave Place also has a good explanation (with photos) that explains these three types of razors[159].

In razors that use double-edged blades, the blade is held between the cap and the baseplate, with only the edge exposed. As the razor is tightened to grip the blade, the cap bends the blade over the slight hump of the baseplate, which makes the edge rigid.

The blade's rigidity is a consequence of the fact that the Gaussian curvature of a flat surface is always zero: if the flat surface has non-zero curvature in one direction (that is, it's curved that direction), then it must have zero curvature (that is, be straight) in the other direction, since the product of the two—the Gaussian curvature—must be zero. The Gaussian curvature of a cylindrical surface is zero because if you cut the cylinder along its side, the surface will then lie flat, and flat surfaces always have a Gaussian curvature of zero. And since the cylinder's side curves in one direction (around the cylinder: non-zero curvature), it cannot curve in the other (since the product must be zero). Thus flat paper that lacks rigidity will become somewhat rigid after you roll it into a cylinder: though the resulting rod may be weak, it resists bending. For the same reason you make a slight fold along the length of a slice of (flat) pizza: so that it won't bend when you pick it up (i.e., to prevent it from curving in the other direction). And that's why metal tape measures are curved across their width: so they're rigid lengthwise and resist bending when the tape's extended.

The razor head, once assembled and tightened, presents the cutting edge at a specific angle—an angle that differs slightly for different razors—and with the edge carefully placed with respect to guard and cap. (Single-edged blades, like those used in GEM razors and Schick Injectors and the Mongoose, are rigid to start with because they are made of thicker steel, and thus do not have to be bent in the razor's grip as do thin double-edged blades.)

Novices sometimes fail to tighten the razor sufficiently after inserting the (double-edged) blade. The cap must be seated firmly onto the blade, to bend it over the baseplate (for rigidity) and also hold it securely so that the edge doesn't flap up and down—flutter—in use. (The Futur's design cleverly finesses this error: the top *snaps* on, so if it's properly in place, it's holding firmly.) In razors made of plated Zamak (a zinc alloy), over-tightening the cap will stress and eventually break the cap's threaded stud: be careful. (Photos of broken razors seem always to show the broken Zamak stud stuck in the handle.)

The question is often asked: *how* tight should the cap be? So, a little scenario. You're going on a picnic. Just before you pack the jar of pickles, you open it to eat one. Then you put the lid back on and put the jar on its side in the basket. *That* tight: tight enough so the jar won't leak and the lid will stay on, but not so tight that even a child would have any trouble removing the lid at the picnic.

The reason to tighten the cap carefully is that an insufficiently tightened razor becomes a bloodletting threshing machine. Although the blade is rigid along its edge (because of the bend over the hump) it can still flutter up and down, flexible parallel to the edge. This is particularly an issue with one-piece (TTO) razors. In the Gillette Fat Boy, for example, resistance is encountered just at the point where a final quarter-turn is needed: that last bit of resistance is similar to that of a lock nut—easy tightening until the end, then more torque required for the final quarter turn to lock the razor. Do the extra quarter-turn.

A **razor stand** is optional: I store my razors lying on their side across a shallow shelf. You can buy a stand for a single razor from various places, or you can use a test-tube rack for multiple razors: the razors in current use. A razor stand or rack is used because you want the razor out where it can dry after you shave. Do not put it into a drawer—it won't dry well and the blade's edge is more likely to be damaged in a drawer (much as you do not put your quality kitchen knives in a drawer but keep them in a knife rack). A blade whose edge you nick will nick you in return.

An important note on razor safety: If you have a toddler who admires and imitates you, then leaving a razor in the open within the toddler's reach is an extremely bad idea that, in a worst-case scenario, can lead to an interview with Child Protective Services. When such a thing happens—and it unfortunately does happen, though thankfully not often—then the parent will face some harsh accusations from the child once he or she reaches adolescence, and some hard-to-answer questions. Better to be safe than sorry: keep the razor out of sight and above a child's reach.

The grip

The razor is held, generally by the thumb and forefinger with an assist from the middle finger, lightly but firmly, much as you would hold (say) a small lizard: firmly enough so that it does not escape, but not so firmly as to injure it. This photo shows my (right-hand) grip using the Silvertone/Sodial/RiMei razor.

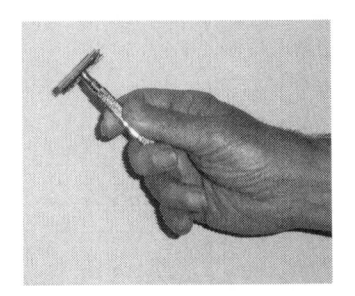

Handles

Three-piece razors use standard threads[160], so that one razor's handle can usually (but not always) be attached to another's head: a "Frankenrazor". Some manufacturers of new stainless three-piece razors offer a choice of handles and even sell handles and heads separately. Handles are available from Above the Tie, Elite Razor, iKon, Maggard Razors, Pens of the Forest[161], UFO Razor Handles, Weber, and Wolfman Razors. Because handles are relatively easy to make, it's likely that we shall soon see more handles from artisan makers appear on the market—part of the current overall burgeoning of DE shaving.

A solid metal handle (stainless, brass, or bronze) can greatly change the heft and feel of a razor whose original handle is much lighter because it is hollow or made of resin or aluminum. The difference in handle weight, diameter, knurling, and look produces a noticeably different shaving experience—and the same handle can be used on different three-piece razors, illustrating another advantage of the three-piece format: interchangeable parts. A Gillette Tech head on a Wolfman handle or a Gillette NEW on a Stealth handle is very nice indeed.

The Merkur Classic head and the newer Edwin Jagger head are available from Elite Razor in various handle materials: stone, resin, wood, and snakeskin (with clear plastic coating). I have two razors from Elite: a Merkur model (white quartz with gold lacings) and an Edwin Jagger model (red jasper). Both are *very* nice to use: the heavier weight makes shaving a dream. Elite Razor also uses semi-precious stone for the handle and knob on the Merkur Progress.

Pens of the Forest, BadgerBrush.net, and Penchetta make razors with custom handles. Penchetta also sells kits for you to make your own razor: they provide the head, you make the handle.

Since handles are available for separate purchase, you can also buy a razor head by itself and combine it with your own handle—one you've made or a handle you've purchased separately—to make a complete razor. Edwin Jagger sells their razor head separately[162], and high-end razors are now often sold unbundled: you can buy the head separately and even the cap and the baseplate separately, with or without a handle. Above the Tie, iKon, and Wolfman Razors currently offer their stainless steel premium razors unbundled.

The rule for razor handles, I've discovered, is that a heavier handle generally improves the feel of the razor, but a lighter handle can make the razor feel top-heavy and awkward. For example, I tried an Edwin Jagger DE86bl (faux-ebony handle) handle with the Shavecraft #102 slant head, and it didn't feel right at all. In contrast, with the #102 head a Maggard handle or an iKon Bulldog or OSS handle works fine because the heavier handle balances the head nicely.

A heavy handle puts the center of mass down in the handle, and the razor feels agile; a light handle puts the center of mass toward (or even in) the head, making the razor feel unbalanced and head-heavy.

A UFO aluminum bronze handle, fairly hefty at 95g, was quite comfortable with the Standard head—the razor felt even better than with its original (Standard) handle, made of aluminum and weighing 31g.

Smooth handles vs. knurled handles

Razors are commonly available with smooth handles—resin (faux ivory and faux ebony, typically), stone, wood, bone, and chromed metal. Since in shaving one's hands are often wet, you may think such handles would be slippery. Obviously, if the handle is wet *and* soapy, it will indeed be slippery, but soap is readily rinsed away. A smooth handle is indeed slippery when soapy, but even a knurled handle is slippery when soapy unless the knurling is extremely aggressive—more aggressive than on most razors. I tested a Merkur 37C and a Gillette Fat Boy, which have knurled handles, and I found the grip was slippery when my hands were wet and soapy; when the soap was rinsed away, I had a secure grip with wet hands, as I do with wet (but not soapy) hands on a smooth handle.

Based on a poll I ran on the Shave Nook forum, a wet smooth handle presents no problem at all for 80% of shavers, though 20% do find that a wet smooth handle is slippery—particularly a chrome smooth handle—but for most the slipperiness declines over a week or two. The decline in slipperiness may be due to a polish wearing off through use and/or the shaver unconsciously adjusting his grip to make it more secure.

If you have a smooth-handled razor and you're one of the unlucky 20%, the simplest solution is to brush your wet fingers over an alum block; your grip on the razor will then be secure. A more complicated and less elegant solution is to wrap the handle with some non-slip tape or use a different handle, but the alum block is right at hand, as it were, and it works. And as noted above, the problem in many cases diminishes over time as you use the razor.

Open-comb vs. safety bar

Some razors have an "open-comb" guard—separated teeth instead of a solid bar. Open-comb razors have the blade either resting on the teeth (the Merkur and old Gillettes) or just above the teeth (the improvement introduced with the Gillette NEW IMPROVED (1921) and used in later models like the NEW (1931)).

The other common type of guard is a solid bar placed just below and in front of the blade, parallel to the cutting edge. A razor with a safety bar is often called a "straight-bar" or "bar-guard" razor. Bar guards are much more common than open-comb guards.

The open comb was the original design, with the bar guard introduced later. The bar guard is easier to manufacture and it's less fragile. If you drop an open-comb razor, you're likely to bend a corner tooth. The straight bar does, however, squeegee away the lather, whereas the open comb leaves some lather in place as the blade hits the stubble. In practice, however, bar-guard razors shave perfectly well despite the fact that the lather's just left the stubble.

If you are cutting very long stubble—as for men who shave once a week instead of every day or two—an open-comb guard allows the blade to strike stubble still standing upright, but a bar guard will push the stubble over and might make it a bit harder to cut.

Another advantage of an open comb razor when shaving very long stubble is that it does not easily clog. In a bar-guard razor, the cut stubble must pass between guard and blade, and long stubble can clog the opening. An open-comb razor presents no barrier to cut stubble and so does not clog. Still, a Merkur Progress (a bar-guard razor) cuts long stubble perfectly well without clogging, and for a man who shaves every day or two, bar-guard razors are fine.

An open-comb razor feels different from a bar-guard razor, but you can get a good shave with either. Most men use bar-guard razors simply because that design is more common. The quality of the shave is due to the prep, the blade, the overall razor design, and your technique, not the shape of the guard.

One common (but odd) assumption is that open-comb razors are more aggressive than bar-guard razors. However, aggressiveness is not determined by the shape of the guard. The degree to which a razor is aggressive (or not) depends rather on the placement of the guard with respect to the cutting edge—how far in front, how far below—the angle at which the blade is presented, blade exposure and blade gap, convexity of the razor's cap, and so on. In other words, the entire head design, including blade setback and angle, determines whether a razor is aggressive or not. "Open-comb razors are aggressive" is no more true than "Bar-guard razors are mild." For example, the Parker 24C and 26C (same head, different handles), the iKon Shavecraft #101, and the various iKon stainless open-comb razors are all extremely comfortable while still being extremely efficient.

Slant razors

The slant is an intriguing razor with an intriguing history[163]. Patented by Thomas Wild in England on 6 February 1905[164], the slant razor holds the blade's edge at an angle. And because the blade is mounted at an angle, the slant razor provides

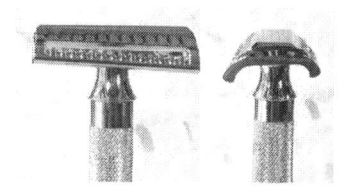

effortless, smooth shaves when used with a blade that works well for you. On the other hand, in polls for the best razor for a beginning shaver, *no one* suggests that a novice start with a slant. (The Stealth slant is mild enough on the face (though still aggressive on the stubble) that it may be suitable as a first razor.) When one has learned good technique, the slant seems tailor-made for the combination of thick, wiry beard and sensitive skin—a combination often found in, for example, redheaded men. In my opinion, **a slant should be your second razor**. Indeed, for many a slant is a "destination razor": a razor so good that those who buy it lose all temptation to move to another razor.

A slanted blade—whether razor, guillotine, or mandoline—encounters less cutting resistance than a blade that simply pushes through with a straight-on chop. Cutting with a shearing force works much better and more easily than cutting with a compressive force. If you are cutting tomatoes, for example, sliding the knife over the tomato or using a slanted-blade mandoline (shearing force) cuts readily, but pressing the knife in a direct downward cut (compressive force) squashes the tomato.

Thus the slant's advantage is directly proportional to the degree to which a man's beard resists cutting: those with thick, tough, coarse, wiry beards will love a slant; those with a beard that's finer and easily cut may not even notice the difference and get the idea that people praising the slant are simply fooling themselves—but the difference is an example of YMMV, in this instance due to a difference in beards. Your own experience may differ from another's.

The slant works best with a sharp blade, but as with any new razor, you will have to do some blade exploration to find your best brand for the new razor. Once you're getting consistently good shaves with your current safety razor—that is, your technique (maintaining the correct pressure and angle) is solid—then I recommend you try a slant.

The main reason for first developing good technique is that slants require very light pressure. As noted above, use the same pressure you'd use if you had really terrible sunburn and the razor were an uncomfortably hot metal rod: still touch the skin, but barely.

Slants feel extremely mild and gentle on the skin, despite their fierce efficiency in removing stubble. I believe that the mild, gentle feeling results from two causes. First, the razor doesn't really press at all on the face, and thus there is little pressure against the skin. Second, the slanted blade encounters less cutting resistance than a regular razor, and thus the slant does not press so hard against the stubble, and so the stubble does not press so hard against the skin. The net result of noticeably reduced pressure in both directions—toward the skin and toward the stubble—makes the razor feel mild even while it efficiently strips off the stubble.

Once your technique is polished, a slant can take you to a new level of shaving ease, comfort, and closeness. A poll I ran on ShaveNook.com showed that about 70% of those who try a Slant Bar love it—though it doesn't work for about 7%. (Nothing in shaving works for everyone, mind.) And about 23% don't notice any improvement over their regular razor. Still, when the beard is tough, the slant works very well indeed[165]. If you try a slant and it doesn't work initially, put it aside a few months and then try it again: often the problems do not reappear.

The slant is handled *exactly* as a regular safety razor. The difference in performance is due not to any manipulation on your part (as in the "Gillette slide,"[166] another way to use a shearing force rather than compressive force to cut the stubble) but rather to the slant of the blade in the razor. Instead of chopping directly through each whisker (compressive cutting), the slanted blade *shears* through the whiskers when you pull the razor normally. In effect, the slant packages the Gillette slide into a razor that you use in the usual way.

The guillotine superseded an earlier device for decapitation, the Scottish Maiden, because the Scottish Maiden's blade is straight across and cuts with compressive force, whereas the guillotine's angled blade uses a shearing force and slices rather than chops. The guillotine proved far superior, since the Scottish Maiden's blade, even when sharp, tended to crush rather than cut the victim's neck. Similarly, mandolines most often use a slanted blade[167].

I believe that very fine stubble, when fully wetted and flexible, similarly tends to be "crushed" by a standard non-slant razor. Rather than cutting the fine, flexible stubble, the blade's compressive-force cutting action simply pushes the stubble over, flattening it against the skin. After the shave, once the stubble has dried and regained its copper-wire strength, you feel a rough patch.

The slanted blade, in contrast, does not push directly against stubble, but shears through it, and with less force the stubble is not pushed over. A slanted blade encounters less cutting resistance from the stubble—that is, the slanted blade exerts less force against the stubble than would a regular razor.

Shaving stubble on the neck is often a challenge because of grain weirdness and how a straight-bar razor pushes directly against the stubble (the stubble in turn pushing against the neck's soft skin). The slant, shearing the stubble, encounters little resistance, and since it does not push so hard against the stubble, the stubble in turn does not push so hard against the skin: comfort!

The slant razor's blade automatically does the shearing by virtue of its slant. Again: You do not wield a slant any differently than you would, say, a normal razor. Shave with light touch and proper angle and don't even think about the fact that it's a slant (or a normal razor). The way the razor is constructed will take care of the cutting. Again: *light* pressure with a slant razor.

When the slanted position of the blade in a slant razor is described, many shavers immediately start to think how they might get the same effect using a regular straight-bar razor. For example, you might slant the razor's head with respect to the cutting path, thus presenting the blade at a slant.

However, slanting razor's head or using the Gillette slide both require, in addition to careful focus and good coordination, some maneuvering room—to use either technique on your upper lip—WTG, XTG, or ATG—is difficult. In contrast, one wields the slant just as though it were a regular razor, using the same technique (and a light touch). The slant does the work, and you don't have to master any new moves. Judge the slant after experiencing it.

Vintage slants are often available—the Hoffritz, for example, is a rebranded Merkur. Slants in current production include two by Merkur, the 37C and the 39C. Both of those have the same head design, with the 39C having a handle substantially heavier and longer than the 37C. (I vastly prefer the 37C of the two: the 39C's spirally engraved handle tends to twist in my hand.)

iKon offers three stainless steel slants with the same head design: one plain head, one DLC coated, and one with a B1 coating, similar to an anodized finish and quite tough. iKon also offers the Shavecraft #102, sold both as a complete razor and as the head by itself.

The #102 is unique among current slants because it simply slants the blade without twisting it. As a result, the #102's head is asymmetric (unlike slants that twist the blade): the slant on one side is from upper left to lower right and on the other from upper right to lower left. This asymmetry has no effect on performance and in use you cannot feel the difference. Like the Shavecraft #101 open-comb razor, the #102 has a head of cast aluminum. The #102 performs extremely well and seems to me the best bang for the buck among the modern-day slants—and in fact it is the slant that I most often use.

Italian Barber's RazoRock line has two excellent slants that share a common design. The Stealth, CNC machined from aluminum or from stainless steel, is probably the most forgiving of current slants. Because of this, I believe the Stealth will work well even as a first razor for a novice shaver, but have not seen that put that to the test, partly because of the Stealth's limited availability.

Above the Tie has two slant heads made from machined stainless steel with great precision, the S1 (bar guard) and the S2 (open comb). I found the S1 extremely comfortable, the S2 much less so—but ATT baseplates are tuned to a narrow range, and some like the S2. ATT offers a 30-day money-back guarantee, so you can test them. ATT's slants cost almost 2.5 times as much as the #102.

Additional slants are expected from other vendors and manufacturers within the next few months. Indeed, DE razors in general are coming to market at an accelerating pace.

Why the sudden burst of activity? At the time of the previous edition exactly one slant head was in current production: the Merkur slant, available with two handles (the 37C and the 39C). Now you have a choice of those two plus three iKon stainless slants, the iKon Shavecraft #102, two Stealth models, and two models from Above the Tie: from two models to ten in just a couple of years. I wrote an article[168] to explore the reasons. In my view, the same engine that drives the rapid growth of the DE safety razor (namely, that men who try it overwhelmingly find it does a better job at lower cost and makes shaving enjoyable, so they (a) stick with it and (b) tell their friends, who then try it, which results in an accelerating growth) also applies to the slant (men who try it overwhelmingly find it does a better job, so they stick with it and tell their friends). Just as DE shaving is cannibalizing the cartridge razor market, so the slant is cannibalizing the DE market, though starting later and thus still growing. So new slants are coming onto the market because of increasing demand for slants, just as the many new DE razors are the result of increasing demand.

Describing razor performance: Comfort and efficiency

Razor performance is best described using two independent dimensions, comfort and efficiency. Comfort can be "uncomfortable," "comfortable," or "very comfortable; efficiency can be "inefficient," "efficient," or "very efficient."

By "comfort," I mean "shaves smoothly and is not inclined to nick and *feels* not inclined to nick"—the sort of razor where you can relax and enjoy the shave without having to be constantly on your guard against nicks.

By "efficient," I mean "removes stubble easily and effectively with no pressure required"—a very efficient razor will result in swaths of BBS skin after two passes and often produces a BBS result overall in three passes.

Two terms more commonly used to describe razor performance are "mild" and "aggressive." Indeed, many believe razor performance is a linear scale that ranges from "mild" at one extreme to "aggressive" at the other. You sometimes see razors linearly ranked on performance in a simple list (from "mildest" to "most aggressive" is the idea). One such list uses blade gap, based on the (mistaken) idea that blade gap determines a razor's feel and performance. A linear ranking, though simple, turns out to work poorly. (Einstein famously observed that one should make things as simple as possible, but not simpler. Using a linear ranking for razors makes things simpler than possible, though linear rankings do indeed work in other contexts—age, for example, or height.)

The shaving performance of a razor is primarily due to its head design (and to blade choice, of course): the blade gap, setback from the guard, guard position in relation to the blade's edge and the cap, blade angle and exposure, the height and configuration of cap, and so on. Very small differences as measured can make noticeable differences in feel and performance, and the entire package affects the shave: that is, you can't simply look at the blade gap (or at the type of guard) and know from that how well the razor will shave. (Note that razor feel and performance—the experience the shaver has in using the razor—also depends heavily on blade choice and the individual shaver's beard, skin, prep, and technique.)

In terms of the two dimensions described above, razors that people call "mild" typically lie in the comfortable-inefficient quadrant—but "mild," like "aggressive," has two meanings.

When someone says a razor is "too mild," they are clearly referring to its being too inefficient. (No one would complain about a razor's being "too comfortable.") On the other hand, when someone wants a "milder" razor, he's clearly referring to comfort (since no one would want a razor that's less efficient in cutting than his current razor).

Razors that people call "aggressive" typically lie in the uncomfortable-efficient quadrant. When someone says a razor is "too aggressive," they clearly are referring to its (lack of) comfort: they mean that the razor is uncomfortable. "Too aggressive" means "harsh." (No one would complain about a razor's being "too efficient.") On the other hand, when someone wants a "more aggressive" razor, he's clearly referring to efficiency (since no one would wants a razor that's more uncomfortable).

Razors that lie in the uncomfortable-inefficient quadrant can, I think, simply be called "bad": no one would want such a razor, so razors that are both uncomfortable and inefficient fail quickly in the market.

That leaves only one quadrant to be named: the comfortable-efficient razors. For most, examples of these are the slants, the Standard, the iKon Shavecraft #101, the Feather AS-D1/2 with a Feather blade, the Above The Tie with the baseplate that works best for you, the Wolfman razors, the Parker 24C and 26C (same head), a Gillette Tech with a Feather blade, a Gillette NEW with a brand of blade that's good for you, and some others. Razors in this category are often "destination razors": the razor at which the search for improvement stops.

"Comfortable-efficient" would work as a name, but the one-axis idea (a single scale running from "mild" to "aggressive") is so prevalent that if a razor is called "comfortable-efficient," some will immediately ask, "So, is it mild? or aggressive?"

To forestall that question I suggest the term "mild-aggressive" for this category. If the question is asked, the answer is easy: "Both. It's mild and gentle on the face, but aggressive and efficient in removing stubble." So I describe razors by the quadrant into which they fall:

	Inefficient	Efficient
Comfortable	"Mild"	"Mild-Aggressive"
Uncomfortable	"Bad"	"Aggressive"

The Weishi razor ("Mild") falls into the comfortable-inefficient quadrant, the Mühle R41 ("Aggressive") into the uncomfortable-efficient quadrant. Obviously, as in all of shaving, YMMV plays a role and some like the R41—but for most, I think, it borders on harsh, and for some it definitely crosses the border.

Now consider how to explain the action of a slant razor to someone who has not used one. First, you say that it is a very comfortable razor, gentle on the face (and he thinks, "So it's a mild razor"), and yet at the same time it is noticeably more efficient than a bar-guard razor, removing more stubble faster (and he thinks, "Ah! So it's an *aggressive* razor.").

The problem is that "mild" and "aggressive" don't co-exist easily in one's mind, so one of those two descriptors tends to be dropped. For example, with slants it's usually "mild" that's not mentioned, and for the Feather AS-D1/2 it's usually "aggressive" that's omitted. Thus many first-time slant users expect the slant to be what they think of as an "aggressive" razor—namely, a razor that, while efficient, is also uncomfortable—so they're surprised by how gentle it is. But in describing a slant, "aggressive" refers only to efficiency, not level of comfort. Similarly, those using a Feather AS-D1/2 with a Feather blade expect the comfort, since the razor was described to them as "mild," but are surprised by its efficiency, since it removes stubble aggressively. Describing both those razors as "mild-aggressive" (or "comfortable-efficient") might communicate better their feel and performance.

What is "pot metal" and why do I care?

You sometimes see "pot-metal" razors strongly condemned, a mistaken attitude in my opinion. Wikipedia notes, "The term 'pot metal' came about due to the practice at automobile factories in the early 20th century of gathering up non-ferrous metal scraps from the manufacturing processes and melting them in one pot to form into cast products."[169] Modern manufacturing methods require standardized materials, so a standardized zinc alloy, Zamak, is commonly used, not a collection of random scraps. Zamak has the advantages of being amenable to casting, reasonably strong, and relatively inexpensive. The last characteristic is important: razors made of Zamak can be priced lower than razors using more expensive materials, and most consumers turn out to prefer lower prices.

Back in the day, DE razors like vintage Gillettes (not vintage at the time, of course: they were then "pre-vintage," as are razors made today) were made of brass and plated with nickel (most common) or gold, rhodium, or silver. Today some razors are made of stainless steel (with heads machined or sintered[170]), and some are made from aluminum (Standard, Stealth, and Baby Smooth).

Zamak is brittle and does not have much tensile strength—unlike brass, stainless steel, and aluminum—so a Zamak razor may break if dropped. This seems to be a deal-breaker for many, but consider that most don't think twice about buying a smartphone, even though it costs substantially more than a Zamak razor and is more likely than the razor to break if dropped.

Also, if you tighten the handle of a Zamak razor too tightly, the cap's threaded post eventually weakens and will finally break off in the handle. Ideally, the cap should be made of (plated) brass rather than Zamak. (Zamak baseplates are not a problem, since baseplates are not subject to the stress that the cap's threaded post gets.) So far, I know of no manufacturer that has done this.

Some do believe that it's best to pay more to get a razor less apt to break if dropped or repeatedly over-tightened. The same men will probably avoid straight razors altogether, since a straight is much more likely than a DE razor to be damaged if dropped and also may inflict a nasty wound. Moreover, a typical straight razor costs significantly more than a Zamak razor. So those who avoid Zamak razors will also avoid straight razors for much the same reasons, only more so.

I consider the concern about fragility to be overblown, perhaps because I own many breakable things that I enjoy (china, glassware, vases, Zamak razors, and so on). Sometimes one breaks. That's life (with a capital "F," as my friend Spaeth used to say): breakable things do occasionally break—but they are nice while they last, so enjoy them.

Handle your razor with reasonable care and don't over-tighten the handle, and the razor will last indefinitely. I have yet to break a razor, mainly because I am careful not to drop them (and when I have, they fell on the bathmat and did not break). If you truly are concerned, buy a vintage Gillette (plated brass) or a modern razor made of stainless steel or aluminum—and don't buy a straight razor or a smartphone.

Still: if you do want a sturdy razor, you can find stainless and aluminum razors, the Fatip is brass, and vintage Gillettes abound.

A gamut of razors

The current renascence of DE shaving has produced a rapidly growing demand. In response to this demand, new razor manufacturers are emerging and established manufacturers are coming out with new models.

This section is but a sampling of what's available now and obviously does not include razors yet to be produced. Quite a few of the razors described will continue to be available, but this list is not comprehensive: it is merely to indicate the range of what's available. Keep your eyes open and check the forums to learn about new razors as DE shaving continues to grow and to cross over from a niche market into the mainstream.

Calling these new DE razors "modern" strikes some as odd, since the cartridge razor + canned foam system is sold as the modern rebuttal to the traditional shave. But the emergence of these new razors—traditional in the sense of being DE razors, but modern in the sense of using new designs, new materials, and new manufacturing techniques—presents a problem in nomenclature. They are not really traditional, and yet they are not what most consider to be the modern way of shaving (cartridges and canned foam). I suggest this new breed of DE razors be called "post-modern" razors. ☺

Razors vary in feel and in performance, and some find that a razor that's good for the first pass is a bit much for the later passes. Bruce Everiss describes in detail how to efficiently use a different razor per pass[171]. It's quite easy, in practice: since you rinse the razor at the end of each pass, you simply put down the razor after rinsing it and pick up the next razor in the sequence.

Whenever you get a new razor, you must do some experimentation to learn how best to handle it—and that includes doing some renewed blade exploration as well: a blade that's best in one razor may not be best (or even good) in another.

Above the Tie

Above the Tie makes premium razors from precision-machined stainless steel. The razors are sold in three ways: individually, in sets with multiple baseplates of different blade exposures, and unbundled (handle, cap, and baseplate sold separately). They offer a 30-day no-questions-asked guarantee, which is useful since the baseplates are carefully tuned to different shaving characteristics: they offer M (mild), R (regular), and H (heavy), with 1 denoting bar guard and 2 open comb. Thus M1 is a mild bar-guard baseplate, and R2 is a regular open-comb baseplate. For me, the R1 is a top-notch razor, extremely comfortable and extremely efficient, and the S1 likewise. However, the other baseplate options were not so comfortable and the H1 was downright uncomfortable. So test any you choose and remember the 30-day guarantee: it should be easy to determine whether the M is too inefficient or the H too uncomfortable.

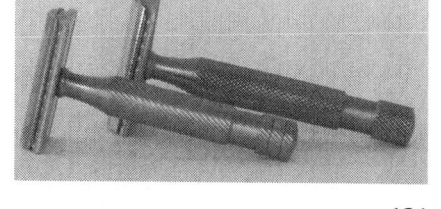

In this photo, the razor in front is an R1 on the Atlas handle; the one in back is the S1 slant on a Kronos handle.

The handles are extremely nice. The Kronos at 3.5" is an ideal length (for me) and the Atlas, though I love the engraved pattern, is a tad short for me at 3". I've not tried the Colossus. A longer Atlas handle may at some point be offered.

It's interesting how the Above the Tie razors convey the impression of being a precision machine even though only three pieces are involved[172]. Part of this is due to the precision of the machining and fit, and part is due to the design: the alignment studs in the cap are pins, and rather than using holes in the baseplate, the pins fit (precisely) into pits in the top of the baseplate so that the bottom of the baseplate is smooth metal (and, incidentally, so that you cannot install the baseplate upside down).

The Above the Tie web site is a complete on-line shaving store, offering various brands of shaving products—brushes, soaps, razors, and so on.

Barbe Bleu

Barbe Bleu is a new line of razors, sold on Amazon. I bought a black model, seemingly modeled on the Edwin Jagger design, and—like the Edwin Jagger—it was efficient and comfortable.

Barbe Bleu also offers a stainless DE razor, somewhat unusual in having no guard at all, which to me seems a dubious idea: a guard not only protects the man shaving, it also protects the blade's delicate cutting edge. Without a guard, the edge is totally exposed and vulnerable to damage. If the razor is placed on its side (supported by the end of the head), it can topple to land on its edge. (They offer a stand to hold the razor upright, which presents the edge to any hand that brushes by.) I do not recommend that model.

Edwin Jagger

In 2010 Edwin Jagger introduced a new head design developed by Neal Jagger and the Müller brothers of Mühle-Pinsel. Customer feedback on the new head has been excellent: it delivers a great shave and the new design is easier to clean than the head Edwin Jagger previously, the Merkur Classic head (which is still used by Merkur) plated to Edwin Jagger specifications.

With the new head, a novice occasionally makes the mistake of putting the razor back together with the baseplate upside down, which pretty much ruins the shave. Note in the photo that the three Edwin Jagger razors have the scalloped edge of the baseplate as the *top* side, facing the cap. The new head is shown on the razor in front, a DE87 model, which has a faux ivory handle. As you can see, the curved side of the baseplate is the bottom. The lined Chatsworth behind it and the Chatsworth with the faux ebony handle have the Merkur Classic head that Edwin Jagger

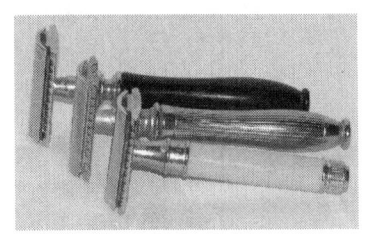

formerly used. That head is discussed in the Merkur section below.

Edwin Jagger razors come in a variety of designs and are solid performers worth considering[173]. The plating on most of the current models is heavy chrome, but gold plated versions of various models are also available. Edwin Jagger razors differ only in handle and price: the heads are all the same, and it is a comfortable and efficient razor.

The Chatsworth models in the photo are older versions that I've had for some years, hence the old head. The Chatsworth appeals to those who prefer a longer handle—either for regular shaving or, as for bicyclists and swimmers, for shaving their legs. As noted above, for 80% of shavers the smooth handles present no problem even if wet, but if you find the handle is slippery, brush your wet fingers across an alum block and your grip will be secure.

Merkur's Classic head was for many years the standard; I myself began shaving with a Merkur 34C. When I got an Edwin Jagger with the new head, it seemed fine—and then I had one of those "gradual awareness" experiences: over the course of several shaves I went from mild acceptance of the new razor to a realization that it really was a marked improvement—it just took me a while to notice. I had to "learn" the new razor (with any new razor there's a slight learning curve that may take one or several shaves), but as I become more accustomed to it, I became more enthusiastic about its performance.

The real eye-opener was an inadvertent blind comparison[174] of the Merkur Classic head and the new Edwin Jagger head (used also on Mühle razors): I was doing a two-razor shave, testing the smooth-handle situation, and I had assumed that both razors—an Elite Razor with a quartz handle and a Gerson (a rebranded Mühle Sophist) with a bone handle—had the Merkur Classic head (which Mühle, like Edwin Jagger, formerly used). I did the first pass with the Elite, and as soon as I began the second pass, I was surprised by the difference—and by how much better the Gerson felt: it turned out to have the new Edwin Jagger/ Mühle head design.

Elite Razor

Elite Razor is an artisan shop that uses existing razors (Merkur 34C, Merkur 38C, Merkur Progress, Edwin Jagger) and provides handles (and often matching brushes) of stone, semiprecious stone (e.g., gold-laced quartz, gold-laced onyx, lapis lazuli), wood, and other materials. He also sells handles and handle kits.

Fatip

Fatip makes all-brass razors that have some enthusiastic fans. I have an open-comb model, very efficient but (for me) uncomfortable, though

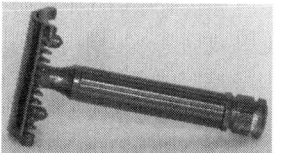

many like it. The razor has a very nice feel in the hand: solid heft, good balance. These razors are reasonably priced and will be durable.

Feather

Feather, a Japanese company that makes extremely sharp blades (which, of course, do not work for some in some razors: YMMV), also makes razors. Two are shown in the photo: the Feather AS-D1 (no longer made, in front) and its successor the AS-D2 (in back). Both are notable for quality (and price). They are

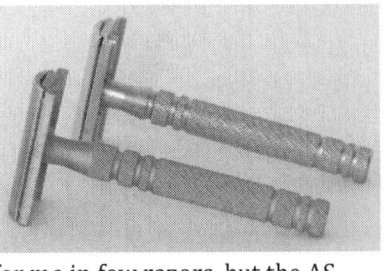

three-piece stainless-steel razors—simple designs executed with extreme precision and are quite similar in appearance. They are fine examples of a mild-aggressive razor: extremely comfortable—even gentle—on the face, but when used with a Feather blade, also extremely efficient, wiping the stubble away easily. Feather blades work well for me in few razors, but the AS-D1/D2 razors totally tame the blade (and don't seem to work so effectively with other brands of blades).

The AS-D2 makes a nice gift: not only is it a superb razor, it's well presented. An even more impressive (and expensive) Feather razor, the WS-D1S, is now available. It has a beautifully shaped handle of resinated wood, but is otherwise made of stainless steel—quite attractive, though I've not used it.

Feather also makes an inexpensive model, the Feather Popular, useful as a beginner razor. It is TTO lightweight razor with a plastic handle and shaves reasonably well. An all-metal version of the Feather Popular is sold as the Diamond Edge brand. I don't particularly recommend these for a beginner: they both are razors that one is going to want to replace. Those razors do feel somewhat flimsy.

iKon razors

Gregory Kahn has a small company in Thailand that has for almost a decade made stainless steel three-piece razors (and a couple of two-piece razors) in a variety of designs, both open comb and with a bar guard and—uniquely at the time—with an asymmetric design: open-comb on one side, bar guard on the other. I have found all iKon razors to be very comfortable and very efficient, and all the models I've tried (and I think I've tried them all) have been superb razors with wonderful feel, performance, and heft.

iKon razors are available with a Diamond-Like Carbon (DLC) coating on the head, or a B1 coating on head and handle. DLC is an extremely hard coating, often used for coating engine parts. It has a nice slip on the face. B1 seems similar to an anodized surface, very resistant to chipping. In the photo, the first row shows an iKon stainless open-comb on the left, the OSS asymmetric razor on the right. (The OSS has a bar guard on one side, an open comb on the other.) The second row shows to iKon Shavecraft models with aluminum heads: the #102 slant on the left, the #101 open comb on the right. In back is iKon's DLC-coated slant and the SE handle.

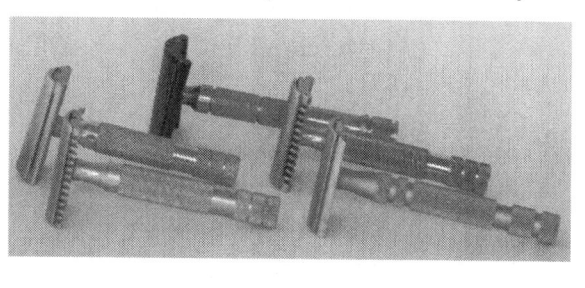

iKon makes three models of a stainless-steel slant razor: a plain head, a DLC-coated head, and a B1 head. The blade is twisted, typical of slants, so it cannot be held tightly in place by the alignment studs: the blade must have some room to move as it flexes. The shaver should load the cap first, pushing the blade into placed and then placing the baseplate over it and holding those together as the handle is tightened. (iKon offers a short video to show the loading technique[175]). The edge of the blade should be parallel to the edge of the cap. If one end protrudes, loosen the cap slightly and push back the protruding corner using your thumbnail or, more safely, a Q-Tip. Then retighten the cap. The same procedure can be used on other slants that twist the blade except for the Merkur 37C and 39C: those are two-piece razors, so you cannot hold baseplate and cap together as you tighten the razor.

iKon also makes the Shavecraft line, with heads of cast aluminum. The iKon Shavecraft #101 is an open-comb (the two sides look different when viewing the bottom of the baseplate, but I feel no difference in how they shave), and the #102 is a slant that does not twist the blade, the only modern slant of this design though some vintage razors (for example, Walbusch[176] and Mulcuto) used a similar approach. Both razors are very efficient and very comfortable and the #101 would be an ideal razor for a novice.

The #102 is asymmetric: the two sides slant in opposite directions. I thought this would be a problem, but (as often happens) experience contradicted expectations: the asymmetry makes no difference in feel or performance. In my opinion, the Shavecraft #101 and #102 are currently the acme of the iKon line in terms of performance and bang for the buck.

All the iKon razors are well-made and distinctly *comfortable* while still being extremely efficient. iKon often comes out with new models (and discontinues old models), so watch his Web site or follow his Facebook page.

My initial thought about the asymmetric design of the OSS was to use the open comb for the first pass and the straight-bar for the later passes. But as it turned out, both sides seemed to me completely comfortable and equally suited to the entire shave, including beginning and end, so I simply use it as a regular razor, using one side until it's full of lather, then switching to the other. I enjoy the slight change of feel during the shave, and the shave itself goes well. Some, however, do use the two sides for different passes.

The asymmetric-guard idea has now been adopted by other manufacturers and is seen in, for example, the Wolfman Razors WR1-DC.

Joris razors

Joris is a French make that offers top-of-the-line razors, some plated in palladium. The blade angle on the Joris heads seems to be markedly different from other razors I have. I found these razors quite harsh until I got the advice to use a much shallower angle of attack than the angle commonly used with other razors—that is, with the Joris, you 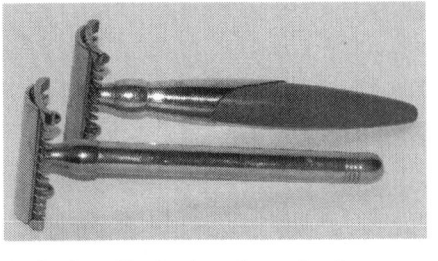 have more of the cap touching the face, with the handle farther from the face, than with most razors. This shallower angle of attack alleviates the harshness that results from a scraping rather than shaving action. These razors are efficient but uncomfortable.

Lord razors

Lord, an Egyptian company, makes a range of razor blades and also some razors. The three-piece Lord L6 razor is popular with beginners for much the same reasons as the Feather Popular: it's inexpensive and has a reasonably good head. The L6 has a (long) handle is made of soft aluminum, and the threads are easily stripped. Using a handle from some other razor for this razor is often a necessity rather than an option. I don't recommend this razor for that reason.

Merkur razors

Merkur, a German company allied with Dovo, makes many models of razors, and most vendors offer some Merkur razors. Though occasionally a problem may be encountered (typically, uneven exposure, with the razor exposing one edge of the blade more than the other), your dealer will replace any problematic razor with a new one. Merkur, in terms of the number of models on offer, is matched only by Edwin Jagger, but the lack of innovation by Merkur is an Achilles heel, particularly with many new and better designs coming to market from other makers, including many new razor makers.

Even so, Merkur is an overwhelming presence in the market and they may well enter a new period of innovation. (Their last innovation, the adjustable

TTO Vision 2000, did not wear well: bulky and highly sensitive to hard water, it makes a good first impression, but over time I find I have stopped using it.)

In my view the non-adjustable Merkur razors have been superseded by quite a few razors with better designs and better performance. I did begin with a Merkur (the 34C was the common beginner choice a decade ago), but I no longer recommend that model for a beginner because noticeably better options are available at lower prices. Merkur razors in general are efficient and comfortable. Indeed, the Merkur Progress is a wonderful razor. It seems to be a cost-engineered version of the vintage Apollo Mikron.

Some Merkur razors are available in either chrome- or gold-plated versions. There's no difference in performance, only in appearance. Merkur razors are normally shipped with Merkur blades, which work well for very few— but, as noted above, any new razor requires renewed blade exploration.

Merkur non-adjustable razors

Non-adjustable razors have a fixed blade angle and exposure. With no adjustment to consider (and tinker with), the novice shaver has one less thing to worry about—for example, if the shave is bad, the novice doesn't have to figure out whether it's his technique that's at fault or the setting of the adjustable razor (or both). Thus the best "starter razor" is non-adjustable. The Classic line of Merkur razors all have the same head geometry—only the handles differ. Thus they all shave the same, though the different handles do indeed give them a different feel.

34C & 37C

The 34C boasts solid construction, a thick handle, and a good blade exposure and angle so that it is efficient and reasonably comfortable. Nonetheless, some novices do find the 34C uncomfortable and prefer a more comfortable razor. The 34C is a two-piece razor, so you cannot swap out the handle. The 37C is essentially a slant version of the 34C: same handle and overall look.

23C

The Merkur 23C (also called the 180) serves as a beginning razor for many, but I note quite a few men who started with the 23C comment how much better they like their second razor (a vintage Gillette, for example, or an Edwin Jagger, or some other razor).

38C & 39C

The Merkur 38C has the Classic head, but a longer, heavier handle with a fine, deep, spiral engraving. Unfortunately, due to its weight, I found the razor difficult to hold with wet hands—it tended to twist because of the spiral engraving. Some shavers rest the end of the handle on the little finger to avoid the problem and love the razor, but I tried it twice, and both times I had to sell it. The 39C is the slant version of the same razor (with the same problem for me).

Merkur adjustable razors

Adjustable razors allow the shaver to change the angle and/or amount of blade exposed. I recommend you do not get an adjustable as your first safety razor for reasons stated above. Still, some novices do start with an adjustable and succeed.

The key to success with an adjustable razor is to start with the lowest setting—the setting that has the least blade exposure and the flattest razor angle. Then you advance the setting from shave to shave as needed to get a good shave. What you seek is the lowest setting that produces a good shave, *not* the highest setting you can stand. The settings usually start with "1" as the lowest setting, with higher numbers for longer, thicker, tougher stubble.

Despite this advice, a surprising number of new shavers, through misplaced pride and machismo, will start with the razor at its highest setting and get an amazing razor burn along with a harvest of cuts. Avoid that mistake.

Progress

The Progress adjustable is a two-piece razor, unusual in that the cap has only one correct orientation. A line stamped on one end of the cap must be placed above the triangle stamped on one end of the base. It's a delight to use, though the correct angle for this razor differs quite a bit from the HD angle. But whenever you pick up a new razor you have to learn the proper angle for it—this is called "getting used to it" and is much like getting a feel for how best to hold and cut with a new chef's knife.

The Progress is well designed—a hefty, chunky razor that feels good in the hand. It's a favorite of many shavers, though some complain of uneven blade exposure. One shaver noted a cure[177]: press down on the top (with your fingers hooked under the base, like a syringe) and then tighten the knob. This prevents blade slippage as the tightening occurs.

The photo shows a Progress and, beside it, the original adjustment knob. A replacement knob by iKon Razors is on the Progress. Since my Progress is gold-plated, I had the stainless knob gold-plated as well. Elite Razor makes Progress razors with handles and adjustment knob customized—made from semi-precious stone (lapis lazuli, gold-laced quartz, gold-laced onyx) or Damascus steel, and are sold by Bullgoose Shaving and Elite Razor.

In my opinion, the Progress is by far the best razor Merkur makes today and the only Merkur not superseded by other makes.

Futur

The Merkur Futur is a good safety razor, heavy and substantial. It is particularly aggressive, so by all means start at setting 1, and gradually work your way up until you get a satisfyingly close shave. For me, that was at 1.5, though I've now moved to 2.0. Some guys have started with the setting at 4 or even higher and then regretted it. I get the smoothest shave with the Futur when I carefully follow the procedure for all safety razors: to rest the cap (not the guard) on the skin being shaved. (Ignore the guard: it's there if needed.) Try different angles to find the one that works best.

Some have found the Futur's adjustment to be stiff. One shaver offers this advice[178]: "First remove the blade, then set the head to position 6. Now press the blade carriage and the bottom of the head together, hold against the spring pressure, and unscrew the handle with your other hand. Now that you have it completely stripped down, put some silicone grease on the threads and reassemble in the reverse order of the above. This still leaves the adjustment heavy due to the spring pressure but makes the action a great deal smoother."

The clip-on top is, I think, a clever design: if you've snapped the top in place, the blade is properly gripped. No need to wonder about how firmly you should screw shut the top. Others don't like the clip-on so much. If you are changing blades, it's highly advisable to do so with dry hands and a dry razor. Some have learned this the hard way—a slip can produce a nasty cut.

The Futur is available in a matte finish or a shiny finish in chrome or gold. The 80/20 split described earlier doubtless holds for the Futur: 80% will not find it slippery when wet; the other 20% can use the alum block trick.

Vision

The Merkur Vision (technically the "Vision 2000") is even more massive than the Futur. Some have reported problems with the Vision, apparently from hard-water deposits gumming up the mechanism inside the razor. Sometimes the problems are severe and prevent adjustment. If you encounter a problem, it's handy to have what amounts to a Vision user's manual[179], though it's obvious that the Vision was *not* designed for easy field-stripping. The best approach is prevention: making sure to clean the razor after each shave and, if you have hard water, soaking the razor periodically in a 1:4 vinegar water solution for an hour to dissolve deposits and then rinsing well. Because disassembly and reassembly of

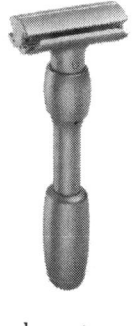

the Vision are difficult, an ultrasonic cleaner (described later) is extremely helpful. (If you have hard water, think twice about buying a Vision.)

The Vision is heavy and, using a good blade that suits you, you can clearly hear it cutting the stubble, a sound like the distant rampaging of an elephant through brush. If Merkur is analogous to Detroit (whose market was undercut by nimbler competitors with innovative designs), the Vision is the fully loaded SUV.

There are other Merkur models, but the above are representative of the line. I now resume with other manufacturers.

Los Angeles Shaving Soap Company

LASSC offers a premium, precision-machined stainless-steel razor, the BBS-1, made by Wolfman Razors (see below). It's very comfortable, very efficient, and somewhat expensive. It seems likely that LASSC will offer additional razors in the future. I'm hoping a slant will be next.

Maggard Razors

Maggard Razors is a full-line vendor that offers, among a wide variety of other shaving products (including straight razors), a line of modestly priced DE razors of good quality. Because the prices are modest and the razors in general are comfortable and efficient, they are quite deservedly popular with novices, and in addition Maggard offers good line of starter kits. The starter kits include the option of a Parker 26C as the razor, and I recommend that razor. But if you want a good razor at a modest price, the Maggard razors are definitely worth a look, since they are both comfortable and efficient. The head design is reminiscent of the Edwin Jagger.

Mühle

Mühle razors (like Mühle brushes and Mühle stands) are of excellent quality. They are less costly in the EU than in the US, thus ordering Mühle equipment from sites in the UK and EU makes sense, even with the shipping charges—and note that US purchasers do not pay VAT.

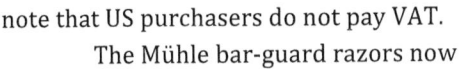

The Mühle bar-guard razors now use the same head design as Edwin Jagger razors, and that design is comfortable and efficient. The R41, designed along open-comb lines, is very efficient but, for me and for many, uncomfortable, verging on harsh. Some who have heavy beards like it because they appreciate the very efficient cutting action it brings, but I would recommend a slant as a better choice because it is much more comfortable and equally efficient.

Parker

The quality of Parker razors has improved in recent years, and I now recommend the Parker 24C (see photo) or 26C as an ideal first razor for beginners. (The two have different handles but the same head.) Though the razor is priced 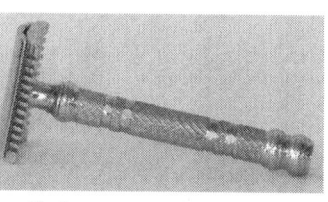 modestly (less than Edwin Jagger razors), they can easily be your permanent razor (unlike an inexpensive beginner razor such as the Lord L6). The 24C and 26C are very comfortable and very efficient. Other Parker razors, such as the 92R, are good, but I have not found another model that can match the performance of the 24C and 26C. The threads are somewhat off from the standard threading, so using a Parker handle with a non-Parker head or a Parker head on a non-Parker handle may not work so well—poor QC, I imagine.

Phoenix Artisan Accoutrements

Phoenix Artisan (for short) is sells a range of shaving products, and among those are a variety of modestly priced but good-quality razors. One is particularly an intriguing: a revival and slight redesign of the Grand Shave King vintage double-comb razor: the guard and the cap are both open-comb. It has an unusual

appearance, and it performs well, with an interesting feel on the face: the combed cap noticeably reduces the friction of the cap on the skin. The original was made by a Gillette competitor and was successful enough that Gillette purchased and then shut down the company. Look also at their other razors.

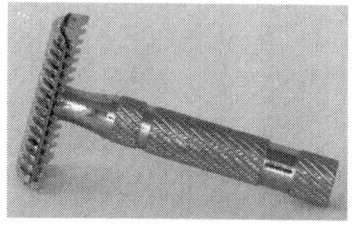

Pils

Pils, a German company, makes a line of shaving gear in a "modern-machine" aesthetic: unadorned machined surfaces.

Their stainless razor, for example, has only the word "PILS" stamped on the base of the handle; otherwise, not a letter or numeral on it: no manufacturer logo, no patent number, no model ID.

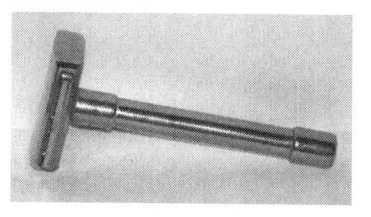

It is a good razor, beautifully made, and it is very comfortable and very efficient, thanks to the head design, which rounds sharply just above the blade's edge, thus stretching the skin just before the blade passes. It's a two-piece design, with the handle attached to the baseplate with a roller bearing so the handle can rotate easily, independent of the baseplate.

RazoRock

RazoRock razors, sold by Italian Barber, include two very nice designs: the Baby Smooth, an anodized aluminum razor (right-most in the photo) and the Stealth slant, made in both anodized aluminum (left-most) and stainless steel (in the middle in its stand). All three razors are precision machined, and all perform extremely well: very comfortable and very efficient. The

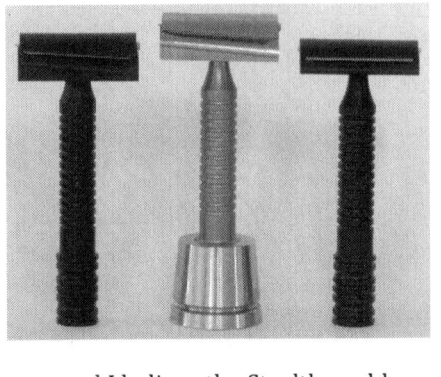

Baby Smooth would be an excellent first razor, and I believe the Stealth could even be used as a first razor—unusual for a slant. The ribbed handle is an unusual design but provides a secure grip even with wet hands, and the three razors are all very efficient and very comfortable. Aluminum is, of course, a lighter metal, which helps you keep the pressure light, since you control the (light) pressure directly (as you control blade angle when using a DE razor).

RiMei

The RiMei is a very inexpensive Chinese razor (less than $5) that actually does provide a comfortable and efficient shave. Because they tend to be shipped individually from China, it's not uncommon for individual razors wrapped only in a plastic bag to suffer some damage from being bent. Those shipped in a hard plastic case fare better. You can find them on Deal Extreme, eBay, and the like. Beware: some vendors show the RiMei and ship a different razor.

Standard

The Standard is a very comfortable and very efficient all-aluminum razor: smooth-cutting, close-shaving, and not inclined to nick. Looking at the side of the head, you can see how the tilt of the leading edge of the guard defines the beginning of a curve whose continuation matches the curve of the cap, with the blade's edge positioned just inside the envelope defined by the curve, which probably accounts for the razor's excellent performance. The blade gap for this razor is relatively large, a good illustration of the deficiencies of the blade gap as the defining metric. There's much more to razor performance than that (or any other) single number can convey. I found that using heavier handle (e.g., a stainless steel handle) improved the feel of the razor.

Weishi

Weishi makes razors of reasonable quality, sold also under the Micro Touch One and Van Der Hagen brands. Though they are very comfortable, they are also somewhat inefficient. A Weishi works best for a light beard—a beginning shaver, for example—but a man with a regular beard can use one effectively if the blade is sharp enough, so definitely do some blade exploration.

Wilkinson

Wilkinson is an old shaving brand and offers a very inexpensive starter razor, the Wilkinson Classic. It is made of metal and plastic and is the sort of razor sold in a plastic blister pack in pharmacies. It's a way to test the water, but generally one would want to upgrade soon to a better razor.

Wolfman Razors

Wolfman Razors is a Canadian single-man operation. He makes a line of premium razors precision machined from stainless steel. (He also makes precision parts for airplanes.) The razors are sold unbundled—head and handle separately—and he offers a variety of heads: bar-guard, open-comb, and an asymmetric head: bar-guard on one side and open-comb on the other. The solid stainless handles are extremely nice; instead of the usual diamond chequering,

they are textured in interesting ways: very grippy and also very attractive. I believe a slant will soon be forthcoming. All the razors are very comfortable and very efficient. Shown in the photo is the WR1-SB (front) and the LA Shaving Soap Company's BBS-1 (back), also made by Wolfman Razors.

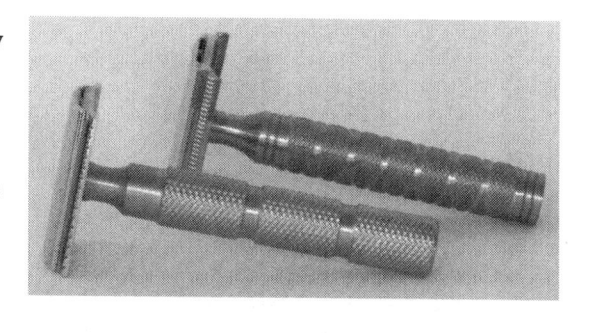

Vintage razors

There's great satisfaction in shaving with a vintage razor, particularly one that your father or grandfather or uncle used, and many vintage razors deliver an excellent shave. Vintage razors can be found from time to time at local flea markets and antique stores. Also, elderly relatives, garage sales, eBay, vendors specializing in restored razors, the Selling/Trading threads in shaving forums, and Reddit's /r/Shave_Bazaar are all good sources. If you go the vintage route, it's generally better to buy via the last two than through eBay. Sellers on the shaving forums know razors and sell razors that will work—many eBay sellers don't know razors and will unintentionally sell razors that are not shave-ready (missing parts, bent head or guard, etc.). On the other hand, you're more likely to find an underpriced treasure from a seller on eBay or at a garage sale who doesn't know razors. Examine carefully photos posted by an eBay seller. Look for misalignment and any signs of worn plating, often seen on the cap.

Gillette safety razors abound on eBay. BadgerandBlade has a good post with photos showing some common Gillette razors[180] you might encounter, and a reference site[181] gives detailed information on codes used for production dates.

Sometimes you will receive a vintage razor that is damaged or bent, so inspect carefully any that you buy before using them. This does not necessarily mean that the seller sold a defective razor: if the razor shipped to you is not properly packed (in a sturdy box, for example), it can be bent during shipment, so if the razor arrives in a padded envelope, inspect it carefully—it may require a little corrective bending. You can request shipment in a box to begin with.

As with most things in shaving, preferences in razors vary by shaver: what works well for one person will not suit another. Still, several vintage razors—the Super Speeds, the Fat Boy, and others—generally get high praise.

Occasionally, a used razor will arrive with a blade in place. *Do not use that blade*—you don't know where it's been. Start with a new blade, fresh out of the package. Also, vintage razors will occasionally arrive with a package of old blades. Don't use them: the edges will be rough due to oxidation. Use only new blades that you've purchased. Cleaning instructions are provided below, but some vendors provide shave-ready razors, cleaned and sterilized.

Gillette

Tech
Gillette made millions of the Tech model from 1939 through the 40's. It's a three-piece razor and, with a sharp blade (I use a Feather) it's very comfortable and very efficient. It's an excellent razor for a novice, and Techs are easily found (on eBay, for example) and generally inexpensive. I prefer the hollow fat handle to the solid ball-end handle, but of course you can use other handles as you wish.

Super Speed
The Super Speed is another razor often recommended for a beginner. It's a TTO (twist-to-open) razor: one piece with silo doors that open to admit a new blade. With the right blade it is comfortable and efficient. It was made in several models, the 1940's Super Speed being the first—and a very handsome razor indeed. That model, in gold plate instead of nickel plate, is called Milord. Later models had a flare tip, and the red-tipped model was intended for heavier beards. The British version, somewhat heavier, is the Rocket. They all work well.

Aristocrat
Gillette used the name "Aristocrat" for several different razors, including a gold-plated version of the Slim Handle adjustable described below, but my favorite is

the 1940s version: a gold TTO razor, comfortable and slightly more efficient than the Super Speed. That model is shown on the cover of this book.

The British Gillette Aristocrats look very different, with spiral engraving on the handle. They are handsome razors in a variety of models, all TTO and some with an open-comb guard. They are variously plated in rhodium, silver, and gold. (I had my silver Aristocrats replated in rhodium since silver tarnishes.) They are all efficient and very comfortable.

Fat Boy and Slim Handle

The Fat Boy and the Slim Handle are the first two adjustables Gillette made. The Fat Boy was version 1.0 and the Slim Handle version 2.0. The lowest setting is 1, the highest (most aggressive) is 9. Start at 3 and adjust the setting as needed to get the shave you want. Some like the Fat Boy, others prefer the Slim Handle. The head geometries differ, thus the correct shaving angles also differ. Some change the adjustment in the course of the shave, but I find a setting I like and keep it there. Currently, for me, the setting is "5."

On the Web you can find excellent disassembly instructions for the Fat Boy[182]. You occasionally see prototype versions of the Fat Boy: the Toggle, and also a model that has the adjustment dial at the bottom instead of the top of the handle. Those are rare and tend to be costly.

Super Adjustable

The Super Adjustable is the third and final version of the Gillette adjustables. It has a black resin handle and is available in a nickel-plated version and a gold-plated version, and with a long or short handle. This is a very nice razor indeed and is still available at a lower price (in general) than the Fat Boy and Slim Handle. Those with a metal baseplate are best—the very last version used a black plastic baseplate.

Lady Gillette

A long-handled version of the Super Speed designed for women. Like the Super Speed, it is a non-adjustable TTO design. The handle comes in pink, blue, or gold[183]. Although marketed to women, men also like the razor. Any long-handled DE razor would offer the same advantage for leg-shaving as the Lady Gillette. They are not hard to find and are often in excellent condition.

Wilkinson "Sticky"

The Wilkinson "Sticky" is an exceptionally attractive razor, and it won a number of design awards. In addition, it gives a terrific shave, similar in some respects to a good Super Speed shave. They come up on eBay every now and then and are subject to fierce bidding. The name refers to the smooth plastic handle which is not slippery even when it's wet, but this turns out to be generally true of smooth handles. The razor is very comfortable and, with a sharp blade, efficient.

Apollo Mikron

The Apollo Mikron is a German vintage razor that shows up on eBay infrequently. It is very like the Merkur Progress, but is slightly heavier and also more ornate. (The resemblance to the Progress is so marked that I suspect the

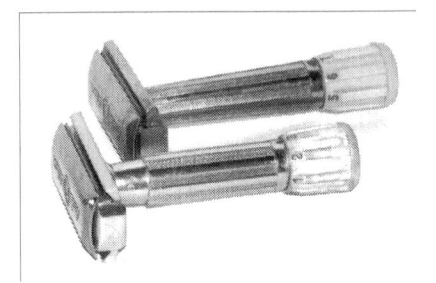

Progress may have been designed as a cost-engineered Mikron.) Pictured are the two I have; the one in back, with the full-tapered handle, seems to do a better job (and is better looking). The best way to acquire one is to post a "favorite search" on eBay for Apollo Mikron and to be sure the search includes both the US and the European (German, in particular) eBay sites.

Eclipse Red Ring

Bruce Everiss posted on his (photo-rich) shaving blog a short history of this razor[184], made in the UK. It has a small magnet in the base of the handle to pick

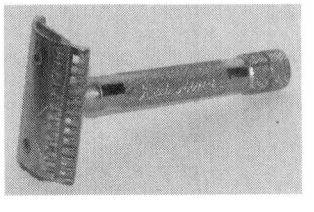

up blades, a nice touch. It's an open-comb design, but has a bar attached across the back of tips of the comb's teeth: this allows the open-comb action while offering excellent protection against bent or broken teeth. It's a very nice razor but extremely rare. It's very comfortable and very efficient.

Single-edge razors: Schick, GEM, and Mongoose

Three other razor options I should mention, because they're very nice razors: easy to use and offering a comfortable shave—and they seem to work well for those who tend to get razor bumps. They all use a *single-edged blade*, made of thicker steel than double-edged blades. These single-edged razors are the Schick Injector[185] and the GEM Heavy Flat Top[186] (both of which are vintage razors) and the Mongoose[187], in current production (though difficult to get because of high demand).

Schick razors come in various models[188]. I have a G8, a J1, and an M1, and all do a good job with regular Schick blades, still readily available. The key is to keep the (somewhat narrow) top of the head flat against the skin.

The GEM also has several models, but the GEM Heavy Flat Top (with a circled G on either side of the handle) seems to give a better shave (for me) than the more common GEM Micromatic. Moreover, the GEM Heavy is often available in excellent condition. The GEM razors are designed so that the blade is at the correct angle when the large flat head is held against the skin. This makes the razor good for head-shaving, since you can feel when the razor's flat against the skin even if you can't see it, and in that position the angle is correct.

Ted Pella Teflon-coated single-edged blades[189] work okay, but better are blades specifically made for shaving (Treet, PAL, and the GEM brands for the GEM, Schick or Personna Injector blades for the Schick). For the GEM, do **not** use hardware store blades made for utility knives: those are inadequate for shaving. Both the Schick (or "Schick-Eversharp") Injector and the GEM are easy to find on eBay and generally run less than Gillettes.

The Mongoose is an artisanal razor, like the Wolfman and others, and uses injector blades intended for shavettes. It is an extremely comfortable razor and has many fervent fans. It currently is in short supply, but that can change.

Favorite razors

I do have certain razors that are more enjoyable than others. Apollo Mikron, Eclipse Red Ring, Feather stainless premium razor, Gillette Super Adjustable and NEW and 1940s Aristocrat and Tech, the new slants (Above the Tie S1, Shavecraft #102, the iKon stainless slants, and the aluminum and the stainless RazoRock Stealths), the non-slant iKons, Above the Tie R1, LASSC BBS-1, and my Wolfman WR1-SB. My "desert island" razor is currently the #102.

I could add many more, but I tried (unsuccessfully) for a short list. Each razor seems to have its own personality, and I enjoy using them all. The Gillette vintage razors from the NEW to the Super Adjustable are particularly good.

Cleaning your razors

If you pick up an old razor (on eBay or at a flea market or the like), you will want to clean it before using it. Moreover, your own razors will also require cleaning from time to time as you use them—many, for example, clean the razor when changing the blade. If in cleaning your own razors you notice hard-water deposits or soap scum, try using citric acid to soften your shaving water.

Hard-water deposits can make a TTO razor hard to operate. A one- to two-hour soak in room-temperature vinegar water (1:4 solution) loosens hard-water deposits to free the action, and a drop or two of mineral oil will lubricate the razor. Do *not* use 3-in-1 oil: it will turn gummy and worsen the problem.

Some are concerned about biohazard issues with vintage razors and want to take extra precautions to sterilize them. Art of Manliness has a good article on restoring vintage razors[190]. Following is the procedure I recommend.

Step 1: First get rid of all encrustations and deposits (old soap scum, for example). There's no point in sterilization procedures if those are present. Open a TTO razor fully, and disassemble a three-piece razor. If the razor contains a blade, remove and safely discard it. If the razor is all-metal, you can soak it in room-temperature vinegar water (1:4) for an hour or two to dissolve or loosen hard-water deposits, then rinse well. Do **not** boil a razor in vinegar water: some razors use copper, which when boiled in an acidic solution will coat the razor with copper, turning a nickel plating yellowish.

After the soak, scrub the razor thoroughly with a toothbrush and a **nonabrasive** cleanser such as Scrubbing Bubbles or Bon Ami to remove any remaining deposits. A toothpick can help clear the grooves. Obviously, razors with handles of resin, bone, wood, or other such material will require greater care than an all-metal razor. Again: do not boil even all-metal razors in the vinegar-water, particularly a Gillette adjustable. In any event, boiling is not needed: this step is not disinfection, it's simply removing deposits on the razor.

Some recommend using lighter fluid, such as Ronsonol, and a soft cloth to clean razors. Lighter fluid melts soap scum and water stains, is non-abrasive, evaporates quickly, and doesn't affect the metal—but be careful with handles made of wood, resin, bone, and stone.

An ultrasonic cleaner[191] works extremely well provided you use an ultrasonic cleaning solution made for such cleaners. (Ad hoc improvised cleaning solutions of (for example) a little liquid detergent and household ammonia are sometimes used, but these are less effective.) Note that ultrasonic cleaners of modest price generally have the transducer attached to the stainless tank via an adhesive and thus the contents should be at room temperature: the heat from hot water combined with ultrasonic vibration can weaken the bond between transducers and tank.

Good-quality ultrasonic cleaners are now available at relatively low cost. Look for a cleaner that's at least 50 watts. (Many ultrasonic cleaners for consumer use are 35 watts.) I have a Kendal CD-4800, a 60-watt cleaner that I found on eBay by searching for "ultrasonic". Fill the tank and run a full cycle to expel dissolved gases. Then put your razors in for one or two cycles, depending on how much cleaning is required. Afterwards a little polish may be needed to remove minor discolorations on smooth surfaces—for example, the razor's cap. The end result is a very clean razor, inside and out. If you know or suspect the razor is exceptionally dirty, let it soak in hot water with dishwashing detergent for an hour before putting it into the cleaner.

An ultrasonic cleaner can be used to clean jewelry as well—except do not attempt to clean opals, pearls, emeralds, or any stone with a chip or crack: the ultrasonic cleaner can destroy those, but it will not harm metal. If you don't have an ultrasonic cleaner, ask a local jeweler if ultrasonic cleaning is available as a service.

Step 2: Once the razor is cleaned, sterilizing or disinfecting can proceed. The extent of your efforts is a YMMV issue. The focus is the head of the razor: the part that comes into contact with the skin, which may at some point be cut. However, note that even if blood does come into contact with the razor head, during a shave the razor's head is repeatedly rinsed (to remove lather as it accumulates), which makes it unlikely that any blood has been permanently deposited on the head.

Some will be satisfied at this point with rinsing and drying the razor. Some will want to rinse the razor or the razor head in rubbing alcohol (70% or higher). All-metal razors can withstand treatment (for example, boiling in plain water—*not* vinegar water) that would ruin a razor whose handle is resin, bone, wood, or other such material, but razors with those handles tend to be three-piece razors, so the head can be removed and sterilized alone.

Others with greater concerns may wish to let an all-metal razor (or the razor head from a three-piece razor: the only part of real concern) rest briefly in rubbing alcohol (though **not** for an extended period, which can discolor metal and ruin other materials—indeed, rubbing alcohol can ruin a resin handle immediately) or run it through a dishwasher's sterilizing cycle or use a commercial sterilizing liquid such as Barbicide. Using bleach, particularly at high concentrations, can destroy the razor totally. Pictured is a Gillette Fat Boy that sat in bleach for just 10 minutes[192]. Do not use bleach.

Some will simply not consider using a vintage razor under any circumstances, despite the fact that vintage razors are widely used with no problems reported. Certainly the risk from vintage razors seem much less than the risks associated with common hazardous sports—bicycling, for example—but each shaver must decide for himself his tolerance for risk.

I'm somewhat risk-tolerant to this sort of thing: I'm satisfied with the cleaning step and a rinse in alcohol, believing that the likelihood of a serious threat is low. I use many vintage razors regularly with no problems to date. However, you should note that I have no professional expertise in sterilizing procedures: if you have concerns (and *especially* if you have a weakened immune system), do further research.

Maas metal polish[193] can help bring a shine back to your razor, but use only a tiny amount. Using Maas with a toothbrush can clean the chequered handles quite well. After polishing the razor, be *sure* to wash off *all* the Maas before shaving: it burns newly shaved skin. The problem with any polish is that a polish is an abrasive, and the plating on most razors is thin: manufacturers did not design razors with the idea that they would be used for decades.

If you have a silver razor, it's best to remove tarnish chemically rather than abrasively. Use a heatproof bowl deep enough to allow the razor to be totally submerged. Line the bowl with a piece of aluminum foil, put the razor on the foil, and sprinkle generously with baking soda. Pour in boiling water, let stand for half an hour, and the silver will be tarnish-free. I eventually had my own silver razors replated in rhodium, roughly the same color but non-tarnishing since it's an inert metal (of the platinum family).

Barbicide can help in cleaning. Immerse the razor for less than ten minutes—more may damage the plating—and then rinse the razor in water or rubbing alcohol and let it air-dry.

If your razor is gold-plated, do not boil it. Let it soak for a long time in warm water, then cleaning it with Scrubbing Bubbles and a soft toothbrush. Boiling will remove the lacquer that protects the gold plating on some razors. The methods described above work well for routine cleaning, but a really good cleaning requires an ultrasonic cleaner, as described above.

Replating your razors

Gillette did not build their razors with an eye to long life: the expectation was that the buyer would replace the razor with a new model in a few years. So the original plating, being thin, was not very durable and easily would wear off in use—thus all the "brassing" seen on old razors. (Brassing occurs when the original plate, typically nickel, wears off to expose the underlying base metal, typically brass.) Replating can make an old razor look new.

Currently several companies offer razor replating services: RazorPlate, Razor Emporium, Reliable Electroplating, Sport Shaving, and West Coast Razors do replating; Restored Razors in the UK formerly was active but seems now to be inactive. You might also contact local jewelry stores to see whether they offer such a service or can refer you to a local replating service.

The photo above shows a Gillette Tech that has been replated by Restored Razors—"before" on the left, "after" on the right. The plating in this case is nickel, the same as the original plating. Even so, the value to a collector may be less with the replating—but of course, the original razor with its worn plating was also of little interest to a collector. (Hard to please, those collectors.) Even so, you could decrease the value of a rare razor by replating it, so take that into consideration.

I went through my own razor collection and picked out those that both would benefit from replating and for which I felt a special fondness: a Fat Boy, a Super Speed, an English Aristocrat #22, and a President, all made by Gillette, and I had them all replated in rhodium, a hard, lustrous silvery metal. Since these razors were replated with an inauthentic metal, collectors will not find the razors of value—but for the daily shaver, a freshly plated razor is much more pleasing than the worn original. And I had a Sheraton replated in rose gold.

The cost of replating varies with the plating metal chosen: nickel, black nickel, silver, rhodium, gold, rose gold, or perhaps part plated with one metal and part with another (for example, part plated in silver, part in gold; or part in nickel and part in black nickel). The process takes a while, mainly because of the prep required, so it might be a some time before your renewed razor is returned.

The time that can elapse between shipping your razor away for replating and opening the box on its return may well be longer than you expect. We're used to a shipping delay when we place an order on-line: the time to ship from vendor to us. But consider that replating involves considerable more time than just the shipping. Chris Evatt of RazorPlate.com describes the procedure:

1. Strip finish back to the bare brass to replate a fresh surface
2. Address surface irregularities to remove/reduce flaws
3. Clean in a heated ultrasonic machine
4. Polish brass to a mirror-like shine
5. Clean in a heated ultrasonic machine (again)
6. Dry-acid pickle (to activate the brass to better receive nickel plating)
7. Rinse in de-ionized water
8. Replate in nickel
9. Dry acid pickle (to activate the nickel to better receive other plating)
10. Rinse in de-ionized water
11. Plate in final plating (rose gold, rhodium, etc.)
12. Rinse in de-ionized water
13. Hand-wash razor with gentle detergent

14. Rinse
15. Sanitize razor with a dip in Barbicide
16. Rinse
17. Dry

Be prepared to wait some weeks if the replater is busy. In my opinion, the final result was worth the wait.

Two razor innovations I'd like to see

I have in mind two razor innovations I'd like to see. The first is to provide a sturdier cap for three-piece razors. Most mid-range razors nowadays are made of Zamak, usually plated with chrome (rather than nickel or gold like the brass razors of yesteryear). Chrome-plated Zamak razors fall short of plated brass razors in three ways. First, if the chrome plating is breached, Zamak corrodes rapidly in the presence of water, whereas in the old Gillette nickel- or gold-plated brass razors, wearing through the plating ("brassing") was more a cosmetic issue than destructive of the razor. Indeed, I assume that chrome is used for Zamak razors because it doesn't wear so easily as nickel or gold: If the Zamak is exposed, the razor dies.

Zamak has a second flaw: it is much more brittle than brass. Thus a dropped Zamak razor is much more apt to break (usually the cap's threaded stud breaking off in the handle) than a brass razor, which would bend rather than break—and probably could be bent back into shape.

And Zamak has a third problem: if you slightly overtighten the handle on a Zamak razor when you put in a new blade, the threaded stud's attachment to the cap is weakened, and eventually the stud simply parts from the cap when you tighten the handle. When that happens it feels as though no real stress is put on the stud, but the continued overtightening has weakened the joint so that when it eventually fails it simply comes apart easily. Zamak is not only more brittle than brass but also lacks the tensile strength of brass.

One innovation that would solve all three problems would be to make the razor's cap of plated brass or even stainless steel instead of Zamak. Baseplates are not subject to much stress or wear (the wear occurs on the threads), and so baseplates could still be made of plated Zamak without causing a problem. The breakage always seems to involve the cap and in particular the breaking off of the cap's threaded stud.

A second idea, more intriguing (and challenging) is to build some resonance into the razor's head—some sort of mini-soundbox that amplifies the faint cutting sound of the blade. A more audible razor would be appealing—and it's something a cartridge razor cannot offer, so it would be exclusive to the DE razor (as, indeed, are things like adjustable razors and slants).

152

The Merkur Futur, Vision, and Progress amplify to some degree the cutting sound, but it seems to be accidental rather than deliberate. With some thought and CAD work (perhaps with a luthier's help) it should be possible to design a razor's head so that the shaver can more easily hear the cutting sound, a sound he listens for in any case since it helps him find the best blade angle and is also very pleasant in a meditative way. So a sound-amplifying head would have both a practical use (making the angle easier to find) and an aesthetic use. And to sound a practical note, a sound-amplifying head requires no moving parts, just some clever design to create a cavity of the right size and shape. The amplification would be slight, but that's fine: just a little louder is enough.

I know: it's odd—but no odder than designing buildings so that the reflected sunlight erases shadows between them[194]. And it might be patentable.

I think prototypes could be created using a 3-D printer, in which case the designer can easily and quickly iterate design ideas—the technique known as rapid prototyping. Although 3-D printed razors would not be sturdy enough for real use, one could shave enough with such a razor to see how well it amplifies the cutting sound. Once the design is debugged, the prototype can serve as a manufacturing model. 3-D printers are now available at relatively low cost, and razors, being small, are a suitable size for small 3-D printers.

Of course, ideas are easy; implementation is difficult.

A modern-day barbershop shave

A traditional wetshaver often wants to experience a good, old-fashioned barbershop shave: luxuriously relaxing under the ministrations of a practiced professional. The image many men carry into such a shave is of loads of warm lather whipped up with a wonderful brush, a hot towel, and then the skillful application of a straight razor that leaves a perfectly smooth face, ending with the wonderful glide of an alum block and then a splash of aftershave.

However, modern-day health regulations and current practice have changed that picture. No brushes will be used, for example, and no alum block because the barber cannot use such items for multiple customers: health regulations forbid the practice to prevent infections. The lather comes instead from a lather machine, and an alum block is not to be seen.

And the hoped-for straight razor is more likely to be a shavette at best (which uses disposable blades, replaced after every shave, in another bow to health regulations) or, more likely, a multiblade-cartridge razor, though at least a fresh cartridge will be used for each shave: the customer doesn't have to endure shaves done with a two- or three-month old cartridge (as are often used at home).

One benefit of the multiblade cartridge razor is that it is easy to use and requires no training or learning or skill: anyone can use it from the start as well as they will ever use it. So as the shave progresses the customer naturally starts to think, "Why am I paying top dollar for this shave when the barber is using a razor that requires no skill whatsoever? I could do as good a job shaving myself at home."

And that's the sad bottom line: except in rare circumstances, a traditional wetshaver who uses a good brush, a good lather from a top-quality shaving soap or cream, and a good DE or straight razor is going to give himself a better and more luxurious shave than he would get in most modern-day barber's chairs.

There are exceptions: the shaves at the Geo. F. Trumper and Truefitt & Hill shops in London are still top-notch, according to reports I've read. But your local barber? or even the average big-city barber? Unlikely. The few shaving oases tend to be rare and located in places like New York, Chicago, and other major cities and in vacation destination cities such as Las Vegas, though occasionally one reads of a tiny barbershop in some strip-mall that still manages to provide a wonderful and luxurious shave despite the setting. But such are increasingly rare as the older generations of barbers depart the business.

Moreover, skills require continual practice to stay at their peak, the reason people facing heart surgery want a surgeon who does three a week rather than one a year. With so few men seeking a barbershop shave nowadays, the barber's skill at giving shaves grows rusty—and out come the multiblade-cartridge razors.

For most of us, the best shave is to be found locally is in our own bathroom and at our own hands, using traditional wetshaving equipment, methods, and supplies.

TEN

Shaving the stubble

USING a safety razor puts *you* in charge, and going from a cartridge razor to a safety razor is like going from an automatic transmission to a stick-shift: you can get better performance by being more in control, but you must learn to use it, practice your technique, and pay attention to what's going on.

One point before you actually pick up the razor and put blade to face: Some shavers have one or more moles in the shaving area, and some moles are shaped so they are often cut. If you have such a mole, I *highly* recommend that you get it removed. It's a simple procedure and a dermatologist can do it in an office visit. Not only does it make your shaving life better, it also removes a mole that, being on your face, is constantly exposed to sunlight.

Pressure

The first variable you must control is *pressure*. With a safety razor, you must **not** use pressure to try to get a closer shave: pressure must always be *light*, with the razor and the blade doing the work—exerting additional pressure will cause problems (cuts, razor burn, lack of joy, etc.). As described below, you get a closer shave with more passes, *not* more pressure.

Indeed, "pressure" conveys the wrong idea. What you are after is a *lack* of pressure. As noted earlier, use the same "pressure" you'd use if you had really terrible sunburn and the razor were an uncomfortably hot metal rod: still touch the skin, but barely. Or think of the razor as just barely grazing the skin, though still touching, as if you're using the razor to shave lather off a balloon. (Barbers once were tested with a balloon shave, using a straight razor for the task.)

To ensure light pressure, one shaver found that holding the very *tip*[195] of the razor handle with a two- or three-finger grip works well. This is an instructional grip, not intended for daily use, but try it to demonstrate to yourself how a razor with a sharp blade works well even with very light pressure. Try using *too little* pressure for a shave and see what happens.

The most common error for the novice shaver is incorrect pressure— and it is *never* having too light a pressure.

Using too much pressure can be a general problem, or it can be localized: on the right side of the face for right-handers, for example, or on the neck, often a problem area because of the various curves. Or too much pressure may happen only on the against-the-grain pass when the razor is upside down.

Symptoms of too much pressure are razor burn (face red and hot), small nicks, razor bumps, and skin irritation. If you think you may be using too much pressure, try "negative pressure": holding off some of the full weight of the razor (and negative pressure seems to be required for a heavy slant like the iKon stainless slants). A sharp blade will cut quite well so long as it's pulled at the correct angle through the stubble. *Never* try to achieve a clean shave in one pass.

I see two reasons for using too much pressure. First, getting a close shave with a multiblade cartridge requires pressure, so former cartridge shavers have a habit of pressing down. Indeed, some cartridge shavers, as the cartridge grows dull, are able to continue using it by exerting more pressure as they shave—a bad habit that causes serious problems when using a safety razor.

The second reason is that the shaver feels stubble when rinsing his face after the first pass and thinks he must not have used enough pressure. *Not so.* There *will* be stubble after the first pass—that's why you do multiple passes. The key is *progressive stubble reduction* over multiple passes: at least two, generally three, and sometimes four (see below). Each pass leaves less stubble.

In particular, reduce the stubble as much as possible before doing a pass against the grain: the shorter the stubble, the easier the pass against the grain.

Blade angle

Besides pressure, the other key variable in using the safety razor is *blade angle*. Try this: put the top of the razor's cap against your cheek, the handle perpendicular to the cheek and parallel to the floor. Gradually bring the handle down toward the face as you make a shaving stroke, pulling the handle to drag the head down your cheek. When the handle drops enough from perpendicular, the blade's edge will engage the stubble as you pull the razor. You'll feel and (in a silent bathroom) hear when that happens.

That's the angle (more or less). The idea is that the edge of the blade is *cutting through* the whiskers, *not* scraping over them. If the room is quiet, you can clearly hear when the razor starts cutting the whiskers. Think of the blade as being almost parallel to the skin, cutting the stubble at almost a right angle.

In the left photo, the razor is held at too shallow an angle, and the

blade is not cutting. In the center photo, the blade (bent over the hump of the platform) is close to parallel to the skin and is cutting through stubble. In the right photo, the handle is too low, so the blade is at too steep an angle and is scraping across the skin, producing razor burn.

Another image: think of the razor as a saw and the stubble as thin saplings. You don't want to dig the saw into the ground (your skin), and you want to saw through the saplings (stubble) more or less at right angles, close to the ground (skin).

As the skin on your face curves this way and that—over the jawline, around the chin, and so on—you continually adjust the razor's angle by moving the handle to keep the blade almost parallel to the skin being shaved.

Using short strokes enables you to focus on blade angle (and pressure) for the entire stroke—and for a short stroke the angle is likely to be constant. Try locking fingers and wrist, using your arm to move the razor: this makes it easier to maintain a constant angle. As you gain experience and skill, the strokes will naturally become longer, but when you start, short strokes are very helpful. It's similar to how you learn to play a passage on the violin or piano: at first you go slowly, note by note. But as you learn the passage through repeated practice, you can play it at speed and with expression. After much practice in shaving your face, you can take longer strokes, moving the handle as you go to keep the correct angle. This may take a few years: don't rush it. Slow and steady is best.

The correct cutting angle is different for different razors, and you determine the correct angle through feel and the sound the blade makes as you shave. Don't over-rely on feel: a double-edged blade is sharp enough so that you don't always feel any damage. Keep a close watch, and listen to the blade.

When I use my Gillette Super Speed, it's held flatter to the face than the Merkur Futur, for example. And with the Schick Injector and the Gem G-Bar, the cutting angle is when the razor's head is flat against the skin. You'll have to experiment to find the right cutting angle for each of your razors (just as you must experiment to find the best brand of blade for each razor). As a rule of thumb, hold the razor so that the edge of the cap, which lies just behind the cutting edge of the blade, stays in contact with the skin. Don't pay attention to the guard; the correct angle can be found by keeping the edge of the cap touching the skin. Think of the blade as sliding over a layer of lather, not quite touching the skin.

One shaver has pointed out[196] that the correct angle is extremely important. Use as little pressure as you like, but if the angle is too steep, the blade will dig in and cut. He said that none of the instructions on the Internet *emphasize* this point sufficiently. Consider it emphasized.

I had a tiny travel razor[197] with no handle: one holds it by the head. On shaving with it, I discovered that the tactile feedback from holding the head told me immediately if I stopped cutting and started scraping. One guy tried a similar approach[198] with a regular razor and found it helpful for getting the right feel.

So: hold the razor by the handle's tip to feel the proper pressure, and hold it by the head to feel the proper angle. (These grips are for instructional purposes only—in your normal, day-to-day shave you hold the handle close to the point of balance.)

Proper technique consists of using light pressure and maintaining the correct blade angle over your entire beard area, including the neck.

In summary: Don't focus your attention on the razor's guard—forget about it. A novice who focuses his attention on the guard will generally get too steep a blade angle, thus scraping his face and producing razor burn. The guard is there if it's needed, so you don't have to think about it.

Put your attention instead on the edge of the cap, where the blade is exposed. Keep the cap's edge on your skin, and the angle will take care of itself. If you put the very top of the cap on your skin, the handle sticks out at right angles and the blade's edge is above the skin. Lower the handle until the blade touches the skin. Then the edge of the cap (just behind the blade's cutting edge) will be touching the skin, but make sure it's not *pressing* the skin—that is, it should be in contact with the skin, but no more than that. (Imagine you're shaving lather off a balloon.) This combination—edge of cap touching the skin (for angle) but not enough to press into the skin (for pressure)—will minimize cuts and eliminate razor burn. If the cap is not in contact with the skin at all, the angle is too steep and razor burn and cuts are likely.

Men who have already established shaving habits using multiblade-cartridge razors will find that they unconsciously tend to hold the razor with the handle close to their face, as a cartridge razor requires. With a DE razor, this puts the guard on the face and the blade at a steep angle, scraping the skin and causing razor burn.

The correct angle with a DE razor puts the handle far from the face (to keep the cap's edge on the skin), which feels strange to someone accustomed to a cartridge razor, and often his muscle-memory will lower the handle (which puts the guard firmly on the face, increasing blade angle). The only way to avoid this is to pay careful and conscious attention as you learn.

In much the same way, muscle memory of the pressure required by cartridge razors leads novices to use excess pressure with a DE razor—again the cure is careful, conscious attention. Eventually, of course, new habits are established as the adaptive unconscious learns the new techniques and your conscious attention can relax somewhat.

The grip

Hold the razor at the point of balance. The handles of the Futur and the Vision have a definite waist, unlike most razor handles, and both are heavier than the typical razor. The waist is intended to show the center of balance and the right place for the grip. It's easier to control angle and pressure if you hold your razor at the point of balance.

When you grip the razor, your grip should be *light*, not tight—no more tightly than you would hold a small lizard, for example: tightly enough so that it cannot escape, but not so tightly that you harm it. (Much the same instructions are given to beginning fencers on how to hold the foil: enough for control, not so much as to cause tension and tiredness.) If your hand cramps, you are holding the razor too tightly.

The sound of shaving

Make sure your bathroom is quiet: turn off the fan, turn off the music, turn off any running water. When it's quiet, you can hear the sound of shaving. (The noise of running water is another reason that shaving in the shower is a bad idea.)

This is not some Zen idea (though the sound of the razor is certainly pleasant in a meditative way). By listening to the sound made by your blade and razor as you shave, you can tell how the shave is going: the sound of scraping your face (bad) is unlike the crisp sound of each whisker being cut (good).

Some razors—notably the Progress, the Futur, and the Vision—seem to hold the blade so that the sound is amplified and you can hear even more clearly the little drama taking place under the lather where blade meets the stubble, but with any razor you can hear the sound of shaving if your bathroom is quiet. That auditory feedback is valuable; use it wisely.

Here we go

Recall the grain directions over your entire beard, referring if necessary to the diagram you made in Chapter Six. If you're in a situation in which you have to carry your shave kit to the bathroom and back (as in a dormitory), I suggest you use a Rubbermaid or Tupperware container: use that to carry your kit to the bathroom, use the container while there to hold the water for your shave if you use citric acid to soften the water (so you don't have to clean out the sink), then at the end of the shave, rinse out and dry the container, put your kit back into it, and taken it to your room. (A barber towel is a very handy accessory in this situation.)

When you're ready to shave, do your prep—and take the time to do a thorough job and ensure the stubble is ready for the razor—pick up your razor, rinse the head under hot water (because cold metal against the cheek is unpleasant), murmur, "Light pressure, correct blade angle," and set to work on the first pass.

The mirror sometimes gets covered with condensation. To prevent this, spread some lather on the mirror, then wipe it clean. Or use a little liquid soap on the mirrors, spread it around with a paper towel or toilet paper, then wipe it clean. This prevents condensation easily, and the lather's right at hand.

Also, make sure the mirror is at the right height, so that you don't have to stand on tip-toe or hunch over to see yourself. Hunching over the sink to view yourself in a mirror that's too low will eventually cause back pain. If the mirror's at the wrong height and you can't move it, you can get a shaving mirror that you attach to the wall and then swing or pull out for use and push back against the wall when done. Usually these mirrors are two-sided: one side is a regular mirror and the other side is a magnifying mirror, which is occasionally useful.

Shaving patterns

The most common shaving pattern is a three-pass shave: first pass *with* the grain (WTG), second pass *across* the grain (XTG), final pass *against* the grain (ATG). Some do XTG at a slant and often include a second XTG pass on the opposite slant.

The ATG pass presents the most difficulty, and I suggest that initially you skip this pass, introducing it gradually as described below. One big exception: do **not** shave ATG in areas in which you tend to get in-growns. For men with curly beards, that area can be large. For maximum smoothness in those areas, do two XTG passes, in opposite directions.

Some men like a look that includes a lot of stubble, as though they had not shaved. For them, a single pass WTG can leave enough stubble so that it will be visible sooner. If that's the look you like, experiment with a single pass WTG.

I had assumed that the three-pass shave was favored by a large majority—75% to 80%. Just to check that assumption, I ran a poll on Shave Nook, and the pattern of responses was illuminating:

Some observations drawn from this particular sample:
- More than 25% do not shave ATG at all
- Only one person (1%) shaves using only ATG
- Almost 20% do dual XTG passes (both directions)
- About 10% do a four-pass shave
- Only 43% do a "traditional" 3-pass shave

The responses to the poll are summarized in the graph on the next page.

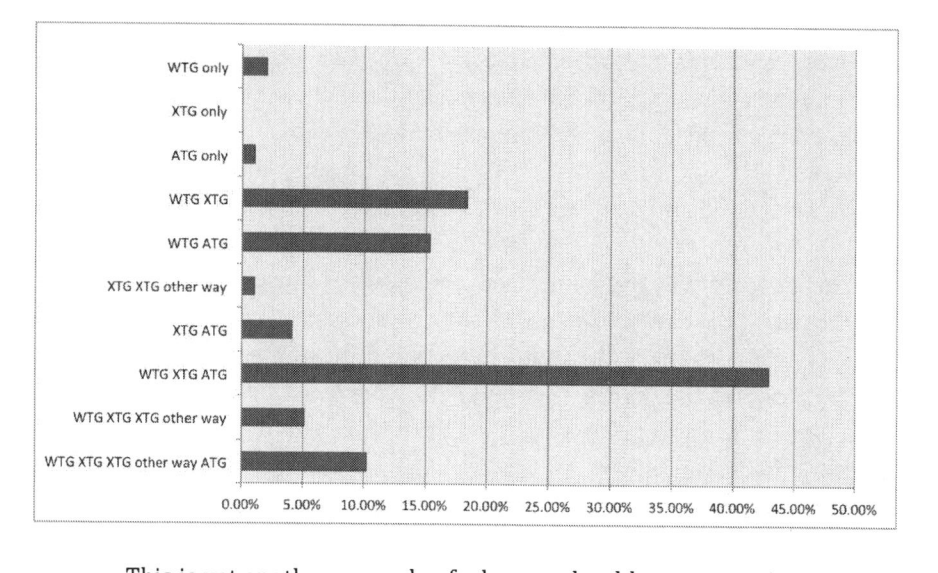

This is yet another example of why one should test suppositions: 43% instead of the 75%-80% I expected. While this is clearly not a scientific survey, I don't see any systematic bias—that is, men who shave in a particular pattern are not selectively hindered or favored in responding to the poll.

Of course, different circumstances might suggest a different shave pattern. For example, if you shaved in the morning using the common three-pass shave and then you want to freshen up for an evening function, you might well do just two passes—XTG and ATG—or perhaps even a single pass ATG (though I am always inclined to avoid ATG until I know the stubble's been reduced as much as possible.)

First pass: With the grain

Again: use short strokes, light pressure, and keep the correct blade angle for the entire stroke. Pay close attention to what you're doing and what results, and your technique (and results) will improve from shave to shave as you gain experience. Paying close attention engages your adaptive unconscious, which does the actual learning.

Of course, as with all advice regarding shaving, experiment: try shorter and longer strokes, and see how they work for you. The long, sweeping strokes possible with a pivot-headed cartridge razor will not work so well with the non-pivoting safety razor until you've gain considerable experience and mastered the pressure and the sequence of handle movements that your face requires.

Stretching the skin where you're shaving can help lift the whiskers, and taut skin is less likely to be cut. Stretch the skin against the grain to raise the stubble for cutting, or you can contort your face by grimacing or puffing out your cheeks. Experiment with different techniques to find those that work for you.

Brush your wet fingers over an alum block (discussed later) to grip the skin, or use a damp washcloth in your stretching hand. (Generally, for the skin around your mouth, grimacing is enough.) The skin under the chin is easily stretched by lifting your chin.

The upper lip is tricky because the nose is not removable. Fortunately, though, the nose is flexible, so with your free hand, you can push or pull the nose to one side or upward to give your razor more room to work. You also can shave under the nose—the philtrum area—by shaving down from either side at a slant.

To stretch the skin of my upper lip, I simply draw my lip down over my teeth. Some push their tongue between the front teeth and the lip.

The Adam's apple presents a problem for some men. One technique is to pull the skin to the side, where it's flatter: simply grip some neck skin between your fingers and pull to the side. Another trick is to swallow and hold the swallow—that flattens the Adam's apple long enough for you to shave it. As you shave your neck, pay especially close attention to blade angle and pressure and to the grain. The neck presents a tricky area in shaving.

Another place difficult for many is the jawline. On some men, the jawline is a rather sharp curve, easily navigated with a multiblade cartridge because of its pivoting head, but with the safety razor you yourself must manage the angle changes to keep the blade almost parallel to the skin being shaved: a DE razor is a "manual transmission," not "automatic." When the skin curves, you must move the handle to keep the head properly aligned. At the jawline this generally means large handle movement. Short strokes help—in a short distance, the skin curvature is less apt to change drastically. You also can use the same trick as for the Adam's apple: pull the skin on the curve to a flatter place and shave it there.

The safety razor has two sides, and in shaving you flip back and forth, using both edges of the double-edged blade. After the razor's head has accumulated lather from a few strokes, flip it to the "clean side" until that also is filled with lather, then rinse and repeat. I normally rinse only at the end of a pass.

When you rinse your face after the first pass, you'll feel stubble. That's fine. You will be doing another pass, and each pass further reduces the stubble, with the end result a smooth face. Do **not** increase pressure in an attempt to remove stubble faster: you'll remove a thin layer of skin along with the stubble.

Second pass: Across the grain

Once you complete the first (WTG) pass, rinse your face and re-lather. (Lather is always applied to a wet beard.) The second pass is across the grain (XTG), and this further reduces the stubble. The XTG pass is particularly useful for reducing the tough stubble on the upper lip. In fact, I go *both* directions XTG on my upper lip and on my chin. The stubble there is particularly tough, and I want to minimize it as much as possible before doing the against-the-grain pass; the double-XTG pass makes the ATG pass much easier. I don't relather between the two XTG passes there, but you should try it with relathering and without relathering to see which works best for you. Always experiment: you will then develop a technique that matches your unique shaving requirements.

Again: light pressure, correct blade angle, and short strokes, with your attention focused on what you're doing.

Rinse, and—when you first start shaving with a safety razor—that's it. If you want further stubble reduction, you can re-lather after rinsing and do another XTG pass, going the other direction, but when you first start using the safety razor, *don't shave ATG*, for two reasons. First, until you master blade angle and pressure, ATG is likely to cause cuts and/or skin irritation. Second, in the ATG pass, you hold the razor upside down, and more practice is needed to keep pressure and angle correct in that maneuver.

Third pass: Against the grain

When you are ready to shave ATG: rinse your beard before that pass and feel the stubble. The stubble should be almost gone—and if you're using a very efficient razor and good technique, it will in fact be completely gone in some few areas. But if you feel a lot of stubble still remaining, apply lather and do another XTG pass the other way—still using very light pressure. Before the ATG pass, you want the stubble minimized as much as possible.

If you are prone to getting razor bumps or in-growns in some areas, do **not** do an ATG pass in those areas. For smoothness in those areas you can shave a second XTG pass, in the opposite direction from the first.

When you first begin shaving ATG, re-lather your wet beard after the XTG pass and do an ATG pass *only on your cheeks and sideburn area*. That area is easiest and will give you good practice without getting into the difficult curves and challenges of chin, jaw, neck, etc. After a few shaves, when you're happy with ATG on your cheeks and are comfortable with the ATG razor position, add your chin as well, then your upper lip, and finally your neck and under the jaw. Remember to keep a correct blade angle for the skin you're shaving, as the skin curves this way and that, and remember to use light pressure. Again: short strokes allow you to focus on angle and pressure for the entire stroke.

For a thorough shave, try a **four-pass shave**: WTG, XTG on a slant, XTG on the other slant, and ATG. You can modify the basic four-pass method[199] to suit the lineaments of your own face. The benefit of this method is how much it reduces the stubble so the final, ATG pass is quite comfortable.

Going for a clean, close shave in one pass results in using too much pressure, a guarantee of razor burn and cuts—progressive reduction through multiple passes is the key.

I usually do a **three-pass shave**: WTG, XTG (ear-toward-nose), and ATG. As I mentioned, one small patch at the heel of my right jaw grows horizontally toward my chin, so with my usual three passes that particular patch never got a pass against the grain. So now my XTG pass includes one little backward (nose to ear) pass over that spot. And my ATG pass on my right cheek, near the mouth, tilts to match the grain pattern of my beard.

For me, as for most men, the beard on chin and upper lip is particularly tough, which is why I do XTG both directions in those places—again, to reduce the stubble as much as possible before the ATG pass. I also lather them first in each pass and shave them last, so the stubble has as much time under the lather as possible. Again: **no** ATG pass where you tend to get in-growns.

A polishing pass [optional]

Once you've completed the ATG pass, you can finish the shave with a polishing pass to remove the last traces of roughness. (I seldom do a polishing pass because, with long experience, good prep, a good razor, and a blade good for me in that razor, it's simply not needed.) Do *not* do a polishing pass where you get razor bumps—in such areas you want to avoid shaving too closely. Three ways of doing a polishing pass are a water pass, an oil pass, and a pre-shave pass.

The water pass

The water pass works well as a natural extension of the final (ATG) pass, especially if during the ATG pass you're using your non-razor hand to stretch the skin. After finishing that ATG pass, rub your face with your wet left hand (assuming you're right handed—with the non-razor hand, in any case).

When you find a rough patch, use "blade buffing" to remove it: keeping the proper angle and light pressure while doing extremely short ATG strokes, on the order of 1/4" or less, not lifting the blade as you move it back and forth. One shaver described the motion as if you were trying to scribble in a small section of your beard with a pencil. Blade buffing is one of the advanced shaving techniques[200] that experienced shavers use in the final passes.

Another advanced shaving technique, the J-hook, often works well on the neck. One shaver reported that he used the J-hook (a final-pass technique, remember), both clockwise and counterclockwise, and got a much smoother result with no irritation. Again: experiment.

The water from your hand as you feel for roughness, together with the residue of the lather, provides lubricity, and because you are shaving with only water and whatever tiny bit of lather remains, the pass is will remove even very short stubble.

If too little lather residue is left on your face, squeeze the bristles of your shaving brush with the fingers of your non-dominant hand. Then as you feel for rough spots, you will apply a bit of lather to your face. The non-dominant hand does double duty, both feeling for roughness and stretching the skin as needed, and if it's already been doing that through the third pass, the transition to the water pass is seamless.

The oil pass

In Method shaving (described at the end of the chapter), the final pass is a "touch-up" using their Hydrolast Cutting Balm, a combination of oils and essential oils. The Cutting Balm pass works extremely well, so it's a natural step to try other oils.

The idea is this: after you finish your regular shave—for me, a three-pass shave (with, across, and finally against the grain, lathering before each pass)—rinse well, apply a few drops of oil to the palm of your left hand (assuming you hold your razor in your right), rub it over your **wet** beard, and then do a "polishing" pass, feeling with your left hand for rough spots, then buffing those with the razor against the grain.

Rinse, dry your face with a towel (which removes most of the oil, with the oil remaining acting as a skin conditioner), and apply aftershave of choice. If you want to use an alum block as described below, use it after that final rinse.

My current "complete" shave:

1. Wash beard with a high-glycerin soap such as MR GLO or Whole Foods 365 glycerin soap.
2. Partially rinse with a splash. Lather. Pass 1 (WTG).
3. Splash rinse. Lather. Pass 2 (XTG), both directions on lips and chin.
4. Splash rinse. Lather. Pass 3 (ATG).
5. Rinse well. If you do a polishing pass, do it here. I skip that, but sometimes glide the alum bar over face and let sit a moment.
6. Rinse well. Towel dry. Rinse brush, razor, put away to dry.
7. Apply aftershave.

Commercial shave oils

I have experimented with several different oils, trying them as a pre-shave, as a lather substitute, and for a polishing pass at the end of the shave. I tried a variety of commercial oils, all of which identify themselves as "pre-shave" oil or as a lather substitute. When I tried them as pre-shave oils, using the 3-week test, none improved my shave. (They might for you: experiment.) As a lather substitute, they were not nearly so good as lather and also made it hard to see easily where I had shaved and where I had not—plus they tend to gum up the razor since the oil, unlike lather, is not readily rinsed off with water.

Art of Shaving shave oil is generally judged by those who have tried it as being much too thick and gummy and altogether unsatisfactory, so I skipped that one. True to YMMV, however, some shavers say they do like this oil.

Hydrolast Cutting Balm[201] is but one component of the Method shave system (described below), but it can be used on its own. It's a "proprietary blend of vegetal oils, proprietary blend of essential oils." This was the origin of the oil pass idea, thanks to Charles Roberts of Method shave fame. It's very nice: light fragrance, light oil, and does a great job.

Total Shaving Solution[202]: This oil is *very* mentholated, so it should appeal to menthol fans. Very slick, light, and does the job.

All Natural Shaving Oil[203]: Often called Pacific Shaving Oil since it's made by Pacific Shaving Company. This oil seems to have some emulsifiers which make it mix with the water, but it still provides an excellent surface for the oil pass. Though it lists menthol among the ingredients, the menthol is subdued.

King of Shaves Kinexium ST Shaving Oil[204]: This one easily wins the prize for packaging: a little flip-top lid that hinges open, a press button that produces exactly the right amount. It does a good job, but the fragrance is somewhat off-putting—to me, it's like machine-oil.

Gessato Pre-Shave Oil[205]: This oil is light and clear and has no discernible fragrance, a benefit. Does a very nice job, but is somewhat pricey.

Oils from the supermarket

You can also use oils you find at the supermarket. All of those listed below are non-comedogenic oils[206]—that is, oils that have a very low probability of clogging pores. However, some people are more apt to get clogged pores than others, so you should (as always) be guided by your own experience.

All of the oils listed below have well established histories of cosmetic use and don't go rancid (as would, say, flaxseed oil). They all are listed as being good for the skin. And except for jojoba oil, they all are good oils for cooking or salads, so they certainly don't have to be reserved exclusively for shaving—the oil pass requires very little oil, in any event, so you'll have plenty of oil left over for other uses. I recommend against using mineral oil (or products based on mineral oil) on your skin. Mineral oil is a petroleum derivative; it's good for oiling wood blocks to protect them, not so good for your skin.

- Almond oil
- Avocado oil
- Grapeseed oil (good used just by itself)

- Jojoba oil (good used just by itself)
- Olive oil (good used just by itself)

You can make a mix or use a single oil, and you can add an essential oil for fragrance. It's important to add only *one* (1) drop of the essential oil and then try the mix—you can always add another drop, but removing a drop is difficult.

You can readily find plastic dispensers in natural[207] or cobalt blue[208] or other colors. The "treatment pump" top (available in white or black) works just right to dispense a drop or two per push: exactly the right top for this application. If you buy one of the commercial oils in a larger container, you might want to decant an ounce into one of these little bottles with the treatment pump to use in travel (or at home).

Baby massage oils generally have good ingredients—babies frequently put their fingers and toes into their mouths, so these oils are made with harmless edible ingredients—but always read the label carefully. A search on "baby massage oil" will find a wide selection for your consideration. Look for organic natural ingredients and try one of those.

You can let the shave oil container sit in warm water while you shave so that it's comfortably warm when it's applied after the final pass.

Pre-shaves for a polishing pass

The commercial oils used for the polishing pass are mostly identified as "pre-shave" oils. And, as you might suspect, you can use other pre-shaves for a polishing pass: Proraso Pre- and Post-Shave Cream, PREP, or Crema 3P.

A different razor for each pass

Bruce Everiss came up with the idea, mentioned earlier, of using the most appropriate razor for each pass: the three-razor method (assuming that, like most shavers, your typical shave consists of three passes). For example:

First pass (WTG): Bulk removal: Slant razor
Second pass (XTG): Smoothing the face: Edwin Jagger DE8x
Third pass (ATG): Polishing pass: A Super Speed or Tech

Obviously, the blade also can be chosen with an eye to the nature of the particular task each pass must perform (and, as noted earlier, a blade can perform differently in different razors).

The three-razor technique is much simpler than it may at first seem. Most shavers who have multiple razors keep several razors in rotation, already loaded with blades and ready for use. The shaver simply takes the appropriate razor, shaves one pass with it, rinses it, places it back on the shelf or in the rack, and picks up the appropriate razor for the next pass. With the razors loaded and ready to go, changing razors between passes is totally trivial, especially since you already rinse the razor between passes. The only added task is to set down the razor just used and pick up the razor for the next pass.

Another situation in which a change in razor might be useful is described in the Slant Bar section: when you have a spot (at the corner of your mouth, for example) that feels rough after shaving, even though you took care to shave against the grain at that spot and could feel no stubble remaining when you check. Yet later in the day the little rough patch still is present.

Very thin whiskers, when cut short and fully wetted, are imperceptible to the touch (because then they are so soft), and a regular razor, pushing the blade straight at them, simply pushes them over without cutting them (because then they're so flexible that they bend readily under the pressure of the cutting edge, lacking the rigidity to stand upright and be cut).

If you have stubble of this sort, use a slant for the polishing pass there. The slanted blade slices through the stubble rather than pushing at it, and thus the slant will cut even soft, thin whiskers before they can bend. Or you can use the slant for the entire shave. Choosing the appropriate razor for the task/pass at hand is worth a try, assuming you have a collection of razors with different shaving characteristics.

Method Shaving

Charles Roberts of EnchanteOnline.com developed a method of shaving that some shavers really like. He uses some special supplies, and recommends the Merkur HD razor and a sharp blade. The special supplies consist of:

- The Shavemaster brush—or any large, fan-type brush
- An olive-oil soap, originally "The Cube" but now rounds
- A shaving paste used with the soap to produce the lather
- "Activator," a product to help in lather production
- Cutting balm, discussed above
- Skin tonic and conditioner

A good introduction to Method shaving is provided by three videos made by Mantic59[209]. The supplies listed are available online[210].

Because in Method shaving the lather depends on the proportions of soap, shaving paste, and Activator, it tends to vary somewhat from session to session, at least until you become skilled in creating the mix. The Shavemaster brush is large and works well to generate a lather from soap—if you have large hands, you're likely to be particularly appreciative of the brush. But, as noted, you can use any large brush.

ELEVEN

The post-shave routine

AFTER you finish your shave, rinse your razor in hot water and leave it out to dry. If you're using a carbon-steel blade, or if you have hard water, or if you have acne or get razor bumps, rinse the razor head in high-percentage rubbing alcohol (91% or higher), which drives out the water and then immediately evaporates, leaving the blade dry and without hard-water deposits.

There's no need to remove the blade or even to loosen the razor's grip on the blade. Minimize handling the blade: remove it only to discard it. Lay the razor on its side out of sight and out of reach of any toddlers. A razor stand is unnecessary.

Rinse out your brush—first with warm water until the lather's gone, then (with natural-bristle brushes) with cold water. Shake it well, dry it on a towel if you want, then stand it on its base in the open to dry. A brush stand is not necessary.

After you put the razor and brush away, rinse your face first with warm water and then with cold—quite refreshing.

The alum block

After the cold-water rinse and prior to using an aftershave, definitely try using an alum block. It's extraordinarily refreshing, but something that (like coffee) appeals primarily to adults: the sensation is a tingling and sometimes a slight stinging. It will stop weepers from bleeding, but that is not its purpose.

The alum block is a mild antiseptic and has proved highly beneficial for those who suffer from acne or other skin problems. A common comment from a new wetshaver is that once an alum block becomes a regular post-shave routine, skin blemishes in the beard area simply stop occurring. And, of course, one gets good feedback on shaving technique: a better shave results in less sting.

One good-sized alum block should last for a year or two (unless you drop it on a hard floor). If you do drop it, you can melt the pieces and pour that into a mold (made from non-stick aluminum foil) to make a new block.

According to Shavex: "The Alum Block (for shaving and deodorant purposes) is usually Potash Alum. Potash Alum doesn't sting so much as Ammonium Alum, but some companies do use Ammonium Alum as a shaving block." Potassium alum (another name for potash alum) is used in some deodorant crystal sticks, and for some reason these are often priced much less than alum blocks sold to shavers. Naturally Fresh makes a deodorant crystal of potassium alum with aloe vera. (Some deodorant crystals are made with Ammonium Alum, so be sure to check—though "mineral crystal" may be the only information.) The Wikipedia article on alum[211] provides more information.

RazoRock is a potassium alum block in stick form, packaged in a travel container and specifically intended for aftershave use.

Whether you use the block daily, weekly, or not at all will depend on how your skin reacts. Most find that an alum block works fine and with no problems, some must use it sparingly, and a few must avoid it altogether. If the alum block causes your skin to turn red and hot for a few minutes after you use it, you may be one of the unlucky few. Some have reported that the alum block seems to interact with Nivea aftershave balm to produce irritation.

As with so many things in shaving: try using the alum block for a week, then skip it a week, then use it another week. Then decide whether it works for you based on your own experience. You might want to do this experiment early on, and again after you've developed your shaving skills—say, after six months.

Glide the alum block over your freshly shaved part of your face while your face is still wet from the cold-water rinse. (No need to wet the block unless the indoor humidity is quite low, as in very cold weather: the water remaining on your face is usually ample.) Do not press—*glide* the block, don't push it. The action is non-abrasive: the block simply slides lightly over your wet, freshly shaved face. Then let the block air-dry. I use a wooden ladder-style soap rack: it's best not to let wet alum rest on or near metal because it's reactive and wet alum will in time corrode metal. Store it dry. If you let it rest on a smooth countertop to dry, alum can develop sharp edges: it dissolves slightly, then when it dries, the edge that forms against the countertop is sharp.

In hot weather, try keeping the alum bar in the freezer, bringing it out just before you shave: the frigid bar gliding over your wet, freshly shaved skin is a wonderful sensation. (Keeping aftershave splashes in the fridge during hot weather offers a similar post-shave pleasure. Balms and milks will probably not work: too thick.)

I have read instances in which some have inexplicably attempted to use a styptic pencil as though it were an alum block, rubbing the side of the pencil on the face. This is misguided. The styptic pencil is not the same substance; it's usually aluminum sulfate anhydrous or titanium dioxide. Get a real alum block.

The alum block has multiple uses. One woman notes[212] that the alum block seems to take care of pimples—she just washes her face with water and then glides the alum block over her wet face and follows that with Thayers Rose Petal Witch Hazel. The result: no pimples, and no residual powder from the alum block. (She reports that it also stops the stinging on bug bites.) Also, those with skin blemishes may want to use the alum block even on non-shave days.

An alum block helps to get a secure grip (on wet, soapy skin or the razor): just run your wet fingertips over the block.

When I use an alum block, I leave my alum-blocked face wet while I rinse my brush—first with hot water, then with cold—then shake it well and put it out dry. (My brushes dry standing in the open on their base.) Then I police the sink area, putting things away and using a sponge to wipe up splashed water.

After cleaning up the shave equipment and around the sink, which takes a couple of minutes, I rinse the alum from my face (it's important to rinse after using an alum block: otherwise the alum dries the skin), dry my face, and apply an aftershave. And that's it: the shave is complete.

Some see that aluminum in the chemical formula and become concerned. First, note that sodium and chlorine are both present in sodium chloride (table salt), and though both individually are dangerous, the compound is not only safe but in fact essential for health. Second, aluminum is simply not the danger that it was once thought to be[213].

Styptics

The alum block is primarily a skin treatment, as noted above, though it will stop bleeding from weepers. But to staunch a nick, a styptic is much better than an alum block (though powdered alum can serve as a styptic: dip your fingertip in the powder and press onto nick to stop bleeding).

If I have a nick or cut, I use My Nik Is Sealed[214], a liquid styptic in a roll-on applicator. It works like a charm, *much* better than a styptic pencil, and it doesn't leave white deposits on your face as a styptic pencil does. I find that this product has very little sting—for me: individuals vary in their response to styptic. Other forms of liquid styptic are Pacific Shaving Company's Nick Stick (though it doesn't work quite as well as MNIS) and Proraso's Styptic Gel[215]. The least expensive liquid styptic, is KDS-Lab Liquid Styptic[216], which you apply using a Q-Tip. In my own experience My Nik Is Sealed works best of the lot.

Aftershaves

The shaving products previously mentioned—shaving brushes, shaving soaps and creams, double-edged blades, safety razors—have a somewhat limited (though rapidly growing) market: men who have discovered the benefits of traditional wetshaving. The marketing dollars that create a constant string of new variations, and the advertising dollars that work to convince ~~gullible victims~~ potential customers of the wondrous benefits of the latest variation—even when it's only changing the color of the plastic in the razor's handle—are markedly absent for traditional wetshaving.

But now we reach aftershaves—products sold to *every* shaver—so here you will find incredible variety. Badger & Blade has a lengthy review[217] that covers just some of the products available, sorted by skin type (dry, normal, combination, and oily). And Mantic59 devotes one of his excellent shaving videos specifically to aftershaves[218].

Generally speaking, you can choose among an aftershave splash (bracing) or a balm (soothing) or a gel (moisturizing). The splash can be alcohol-based or witch-hazel-based (generally with a little (10%) alcohol content). An aftershave "milk" is a balm's idea of a splash: thicker than a splash, thinner than a balm, alcohol-free, and moisturizing. Some shavers have found that their skin (particularly in cold weather) simply can't take high-alcohol aftershaves.[219]

Many kinds of gel are available: Gillette gels, and also Anherb from India, Tabiano from Italy, Arko from Turkey, and Taylor of Old Bond Street from the UK. For razor burn, aloe vera gel works well (as does plain jojoba oil); read the ingredients to see how pure it is. You can find 100% pure, but you might want it to include some things (such as vitamin C) that help preserve it.

Thayers Witch Hazel is available at drugstores and health food stores and comes in a variety of fragrances[220], none of which linger. (Thayers occasionally offers a sampler pack of their various witch hazels.) There's also a Thayers Witch Hazel Aftershave[221], a bit more bracing and an excellent aftershave if you're traveling or if you're a night shaver: it has no fragrance. (It's a 4-oz. bottle, but if you fly, you'll be checking your shaving things anyway: blades.) Some guys add a few drops of tea-tree oil to their witch-hazel to make an even more restorative aftershave—worth considering if you're fighting some skin conditions. Dickerson's witch hazel is commonly available, but has what some consider an offensive odor. A little fragrance or drop of tea-tree oil helps.

I've read high praise for Eucerin Face Lotion SPF 30 (or Eucerin Body Lotion SPF 15) used as an aftershave balm. I've also read high praise for Nancy Boy Body Lotion as an aftershave balm (and Nancy Boy shaving creams are wonderful).

Some aftershaves that I've tried and especially liked: Klar Seifen Klassik, TOBS Mr. Taylor's, Shave Shop, and Sandalwood (though note that Sandalwood in general seems to trigger sensitivities fairly often), Dominica Bay Rum (and bay rum is a traditional aftershave with a long history[222]), Pashana, Geo. F. Trumper's

Spanish Leather and West Indian Extract of Limes (with a wonderfully intense fresh lime fragrance), and the various types of Floïd aftershave. Pinaud Clubman has a nice old-timey fragrance. Some continue to swear by Old Spice, Mennen Skin Bracer, Barbasol, or Aqua Velva, which can be found at your local drugstore. Some aftershaves are preparations specifically made to treat razor bumps. These are discussed in the next chapter.

The artisanal soap makers— Barrister & Mann, Ginger's Garden, Honeybee Soaps, Mickey Lee Soapworks, Phoenix Artisan Accoutrements, Saint Charles Shave, Shave Place, Stirling Soap Company, and others—also make aftershave splashes, lotions, balms, and milks that are well worth trying. I have a large collection of Saint Charles Shave aftershave splashes: excellent and quite different from commercial products. Krampert's Finest Bay Rum is a terrific bay rum aftershave splash that is also moisturizing. I didn't think I'd like Mickey Lee Soapworks Italian Stallion aftershave milk just from reading the description, but I got a sample and it turned out that I love it. Descriptions can be misleading, so do try samples when you can.

Bathhouse Soapery makes a very interesting alcohol-free aftershave splash with these ingredients:

> Organic Aloe Leaf Juice, Organic Lavender, Organic Bilberry Extract, Organic Sugar Cane Extract, Organic Sugar Maple Extract, Organic Orange Fruit Extract, Organic Lemon Extract, Organic Cranberry Extract, Phenoxyethanol, Malic Acid (from apples), Tartaric Acid (from grapes), Glycolic Acid, Lactic Acid, Vegetable Glycerin, Black Willowbark Extract, Tetrasodium EDTA, Citric Acid

The use of acidic ingredients is probably to help restore the acid mantle that normally protects the skin. As noted earlier, shaving soaps are somewhat alkaline, the better to wet the stubble by breaching the cuticle sheath. A slightly acidic aftershave will neutralize any residual alkalinity. (This is my own theory.) The alum block also is slightly acidic—pH around 5—so that too would help. Latha aftershave has a formula quite similar to that used by Bathhouse Soapery: the first eight ingredients are the same and are listed in the same order.

Appleton Barber Supply offers a great variety of aftershaves, including many old-time favorites. Booster's aftershave splashes[223] from Canada are modestly priced and very nice.

If you want a balm as an aftershave treatment, look (at your drugstore, for example) for Neutrogena Razor Defense lotion, Triple Defense cream, or Nivea Men Sensitive Post Shave Balm. Experiment with applying those balms while your beard is still wet following the final rinse. Barclay Crocker offers a very nice aftershave balm. L'Occitane Cade aftershave balm includes shea butter and works well for moisturizing your skin. A very nice balm is Shea Moisture Three-Butters Balm (avocado, mango, and shea butter).

Both Taylor of Old Bond Street's Luxury Herbal Aftershave Cream and the Geo. F. Trumper Skin Foods (Coral (rose), Sandalwood, or Lime) are quite good aftershave balms. Proraso's pre- and post-shave cream[224] works well as an aftershave balm. Some particularly good balms are Primalan (almond-oil based), Alt-Innsbruck (which also has a very nice aftershave splash), and Institut Karité 25% shea butter balm. Only a pea-sized amount is needed, so the bottle lasts a long time. When looking at prices, also look at the amount you get: all three of those last mentioned are around $30, but the first two are in 100ml bottles and the Institut Karité is in a 250ml bottle: 2.5 times as much for the same price.

A blog reader offered his recipe for aftershave balm. He makes only a small amount since it does not include a preservative.

1. Mix equal parts of witch hazel (he uses a high-quality witch hazel from a supplies shop) and Aloe Vera gel (which is very good for razor burn). Try 50 ml (1/4 cup) each. Mix with a mixer or blender to blend well.
2. Add a little glycerin (you can try with and without to see how you like the glycerin): 5-10 ml (1-2 tsp)
3. Add a little Lime essential oil (or Lavender essential oil or whatever you prefer) for fragrance
4. Add a little water to thin it if you want. Or you can leave it as a gel and dip it from a tub with your fingers.

He uses an eggbeater to mix the ingredients—though a whisk would probably work as well. The ingredients must be mixed well. It's the gel in the Aloe Vera gel that makes it balm-like—water is added just to thin it if you want to keep it in a bottle instead of a tub. Very little is required.

In adding the essential oil, add just one drop, mix, let sit, and see how you like it. If not enough, add one more drop—it's very easy to add too much, so caution is advised. You might want to experiment using one of the Thayers witch-hazel-and-aloe-vera toners (no alcohol) or astringents (a little alcohol) as the base for your homemade aftershave.

Both Learning Herbs and Straight Razor Place have good recipes for intriguing DIY aftershave splashes[225]. HowToGrowAMoustache.com (later reborn as Phoenix Artisan Accoutrements) has an interesting recipe for an aftershave Bay Rum Butter[226] that sounds especially good for winter, when the air is cold and dry; I believe it might also work as a pre-shave application.

Another reader, David from Miami FL, offers this version:

1 oz witch hazel
1 oz aloe vera gel

1/8 tsp of menthol crystals, roughly crushed
1/2 tsp isopropyl alcohol to dissolve the menthol
3 drops lavender essential oil
1/4 tsp glycerin (not more: too much glycerin feels odd)

Let the menthol dissolve in the alcohol. While it's dissolving, mix everything else together in a small plastic bottle, shaking vigorously. After the crystals dissolve (about an hour), add the liquid to the mixture and shake vigorously once more and let it sit overnight.

Next morning, you have colored balm that smells of mentholated lavender. Put a small amount (around an eighth of a teaspoon) in your palm, rub palms together, and rub on your face. It has a strong menthol, cooling feeling. (You can alter the amount of menthol as you wish.) After an initial drydown, your face is left feeling very clean with very little residue. The small amount of glycerin provides just enough moisturizing, but again you can alter the amount to suit yourself.

You can vary the menthol level according to the amount of menthol crystals used: 1/4 teaspoon is *strongly* mentholated, and I would not use more. You can in fact eliminate the menthol altogether.

An even easier DIY witch-hazel-based aftershave is described in a comment on Amazon[227]: Buy a bottle of Thayers Alcohol-Free Unscented Witch Hazel Toner with Aloe Vera, which has a very faint fragrance (undetectable to many). Remove a little from the bottle (or decant some into a smaller bottle) and add a little of an expensive aftershave or cologne or eau de toilette. Shake it well, let it sit overnight, and you'll have a pleasant aftershave that is quite affordable—probably much more affordable than the cologne you use.

The example given in the Amazon comment is to add 1 oz of Czeck & Speake "Cuba" cologne ($128 for 3.4 ounces, or $38 per ounce) to get 12 ounces of the mix for a total cost of $3.80 per ounce—just 10% of the cost of a bottle of "Cuba." (The cost of the mix is $38 for the ounce of Czeck & Speake and $8 for the bottle of Thayers, a total of $46 for 12 ounces of homemade aftershave: $3.80 per ounce). You can, of course, split the 12 ounces of Thayers into three 4-oz bottles and add a different fragrance to each, giving you a choice of three different aftershaves. If you're making up only four ounces, you would not use a full ounce of the high-priced cologne—try using 1/3 of an ounce, which is two teaspoons.

If you get into making your own aftershaves or fragrances, take a look at CreatingPerfume.com, which offers things like perfumer's alcohol. For example, you could add some of this alcohol to your aftershave made from Thayers witch hazel to get an aftershave more like a traditional splash.

The particular fragrance of the aftershave is important because, unlike the fragrance of the pre-shave soap and the shaving soap or shaving cream, the aftershave fragrance will linger. I don't attempt to describe the fragrances of the various aftershaves because my nose is illiterate, as it were. (A man with a highly educated nose is profiled in Chandler Burr's informative and fascinating book *The Emperor of Scent: A Story of Perfume, Obsession, and the Last Mystery of the Senses*[228]—highly recommended.) As observed earlier, anyone's nose will over time become habituated to a fragrance, which can lead to using too much fragrance (because you smell it less as you become accustomed to it). Be careful of this if you use the same fragrance daily.

Aftershaves and colognes in retail stores have a high markup. Look at on-line discounters such as FragranceNet.com or check for bargains on eBay. Note, however, that sometimes fragrances purchased via eBay have not been stored properly and thus do not represent the true fragrance.

Some information on the relative fragrance strength of various dilutions of perfumes can be useful. From Wikipedia[229]:

> Perfume types reflect the concentration of aromatic compounds in a solvent, which in fine fragrance is typically ethanol or a mix of water and ethanol. Various sources differ considerably in the definitions of perfume types. The concentration by percent/volume of perfume oil is as follows:
>
> - Perfume extract (Extrait): 15-40% (IFRA: typical 20%) aromatic compounds
> - Eau de Parfum (EdP), Parfum de Toilette (PdT): 10-20% (typical ~15%) aromatic compounds. Sometimes listed as "eau de perfume" or "millésime".
> - Eau de Toilette (EdT): 5-15% (typical ~10%) aromatic compounds
> - Eau de Cologne (EdC): Chypre citrus-type perfumes with 3-8% (typical ~5%) aromatic compounds
> - Splash and Aftershave: 1-3% aromatic compounds
>
> Perfume oils are often diluted with a solvent, though this is not always the case, and its necessity is disputed. By far the most common solvent for perfume oil dilution is ethanol or a mixture of ethanol and water. Perfume oil can also be diluted by means of neutral-smelling oils such as fractionated coconut oil, or liquid waxes such as jojoba oil.

If you discover that an aftershave you like (such as New York, by Parfums de Nicolaï) is no longer available but the corresponding Eau de Toilette is still on offer (and New York EDT is available), you could buy that and dilute it with a little water and/or alcohol to make an aftershave (or simply use a very small amount, perhaps while your face is still wet after the final rinse). I routinely used EDTs as aftershave without diluting: I spray a small amount into my palm, rub my palms together, then rub my face. It works fine and I don't find the fragrance overpowering. (I use only a little.)

TWELVE

Skin problems

SOME shavers suffer specific skin problems such as acne, razor bumps, and/or ingrown whiskers. Weather can trigger other skin issues—for example, shavers in cold climates know well what winter's cold dry air (and the warm, even drier air inside buildings) does to their skin, and shavers with curly beards may find that in humid weather they get more in-growns.

This chapter addresses those problems, but only up to a point. Never assume that medical advice from a layperson is accurate. Indeed, some lay people warn that vaccines cause autism, a notion clearly (and repeatedly) disproven by much evidence.

Dermatologists go to school for years because there's much to know, and they do continuing study because new treatments and drugs regularly appear. What you learn in this section is not a final answer and may not even apply to your situation.

What I will explain are some suggestions from men who have tried various regimens and describe what worked for them. It may or may not work for you because your skin, your general condition, your environment, and/or your problem may not correspond to their situation and their remedies. The same holds true for products mentioned: they work for some, but that doesn't mean that they will necessarily work for you: YMMV, as you recall.

For any of these conditions, however, shaving with a multiblade cartridge is a bad idea, even though multiblade cartridges are highly recommended by companies that make and sell them. But multiblade cartridges, with their tug-and-cut action and the pressure needed to make them work, irritate the skin (bad for acne) and tug out the whisker before cutting it (bad for razor bumps and ingrown whiskers). Single-blade shaving—either with a safety razor using a single- or double-edged blade, or with a straight razor—is much kinder to your skin once you have learned proper shaving prep and technique.

Acne

Acne is a skin problem that results from different causes, typically one (or a combination) of the following conditions:

- Excess sebum (an oily substance produced by certain cells)
- Rapid production of bacteria which live on the sebum
- Skin cells shedding too quickly
- Inflammation resulting from the above

Acne can be mild, moderate, or severe. Mild acne can be treated at home, but moderate or severe acne is best treated with the care of a dermatologist. To see improvement once treatment begins may take as long as 4-8 weeks.

Note that your dermatologist may not be well-informed about shaving options and might, for example, recommend a multi-blade cartridge, even though that type of razor is strongly contraindicated if you have acne (or razor bumps or any tendency to have ingrown hair where you shave).

Treatment of mild acne focuses on three things:

1. Avoiding skin irritation—avoid harsh scrubs, aggressive cleaning, rough brushes, strong soaps, and shaving with multiblade cartridges.
2. Keeping skin clean by gentle washing with a mild soap.
3. Applying preparations designed to treat acne.
4. Adhering to a diet that reduces acne

Over-the-counter acne creams often contain benzoyl peroxide or salicylic acid. Benzoyl peroxide kills the bacteria that cause acne. Its principal side effect is excessive dryness of the skin, so don't use more than directed. Benzoyl peroxide also can bleach hair, sheets, towels, and clothing: be careful.

Salicylic acid helps correct abnormal skin shedding and helps unclog pores, but has no effect on sebum production or bacteria. Salicylic acid may be irritating to your skin, so you may be unable to use it—the general rule is always to avoid skin irritation.

Sulfur-based compounds work well for some (although there's some research[230] that shows that acne returns with increased severity after using sulfur-based compounds). In addition to over-the-counter treatments, prescription medicines are available through your doctor or dermatologist.

There's more information at Acne.net, and Acne.org[231] describes a good regimen. In terms of shaving, that regimen requires some extension.

1. When you wash your face, do it gently, using only your hands and a mild soap or cleanser. Do not use a washcloth or scrubber. Cetaphil cleanser is recommended by many dermatologists. In particular, you should treat gently those areas that you shave, since shaving itself is highly exfoliating: using scrubs where you shave is overkill.
2. Use a fresh towel for each shave. You can buy thin, 100% lint-free cotton barber towels (aka bar towels) for about $11/dozen. Huck towels for surgical use are also good. Towels are microbe incubators, so this is important[232].

3. Use a fresh pillowcase each night. You can buy inexpensive pillowcases from hotel supply vendors.

4. Use a mild, unscented shaving soap or shaving cream, and a soft shaving brush rather than a "scrubby" one. The Plisson synthetic or the Omega S-Series synthetics, for example, are quite soft and gentle, yet efficient, or you can try a silvertip badger shaving brush.

5. Swish the head of the razor in high-proof rubbing alcohol before and after each shave. Use a squat wide-mouth jar that formerly held a food product; those lids open/close with one-quarter turn. (You have to keep the alcohol in a closed container or it evaporates quickly.)

6. Use very light pressure when shaving and maintain a good blade angle. If you cut a pimple, apply a topical antiseptic to the cut.

7. You may find that you cannot use a shaving oil, even those having low comedogenicity[233]. If an oil makes the acne worse, give it up—or skip it in the first place: a good lather should be enough, though washing your skin with a high-glycerin soap before applying lather may help.

8. After the shave, try using an alum bar, which is a mild antiseptic. Glide the bar gently over your skin after the cold-water rinse, let it sit for a minute, then rinse and pat your skin dry with a towel. Do not rub; use very light pressure. (You might add this step each time you wash your face.) Acne suffers frequently report that using the alum bar helps a lot, and others have reported that alum has also helped Seborrhoeic dermatitis. Obviously if the alum block turns your skin red and hot for some minutes after use, it's unfortunately not for you. (You can test alum on the crease of your elbow joint before using it on your face, and I recommend that.)

9. Aftershaves or tonics containing alcohol may be too drying or irritating when used in combination with acne treatments. You can try them to see whether they work for you; if they do not, use witch hazel or a witch-hazel-based aftershave, or a balm or aftershave milk.

10. Tea-tree oil has helped some with their acne. Dr. Bronner makes a tea-tree soap, and you can try adding a couple of drops of tea-tree oil to witch hazel to use as an aftershave to see if it helps.

11. Wait until your skin is dry before applying any acne treatments.

More detailed instructions, including timings and amounts, are available at the AcneNet and AcneOrg sites, which also offer products to help with the acne. And Wicked_Edge has a useful reference post on acne and shaving[234].

The Mayo Clinic has a detailed series of articles[235] on acne, including information on causes and risk factors, when you should seek medical advice, and guidance on treatment, prevention, and self-care.

The book *Anticancer: A New Way of Life*[236] has this interesting passage:

> When [Loren Cordain, PhD] was told that certain population groups whose way of life is very different from ours had no experience of acne (which is caused by an inflammation of the epidermis, among other mechanisms), he wanted to find out how this could occur... Cordain accompanied a team of dermatologists to examine the skin of 1,200 adolescents cut off from the rest of the world in the Kitavan Islands of New Guinea, and 130 Ache Indians living in isolation in Paraguay. In these two groups they found no trace whatsoever of acne. In their article in Archives of Dermatology, the researchers attributed their amazing discovery to the adolescents' nutrition. The diets of these contemporary sheltered groups resemble those of our distant ancestors: no refined sugar or white flour, thus no peaks of insulin or IGF in the blood.
>
> In Australia, researchers convinced Western adolescents to try a diet restricting sugar and white flour for three months. In a few weeks, their insulin and IGF levels diminished. So did their acne.

Recently there have been important new findings on sugar's role[237]. And many have found that a low-carbohydrate, high-fat diet that avoids dairy products (for example, a Paleo diet) can dramatically improve acne[238].

In a low-carb high-fat diet, maintain the protein intake at normal levels, replacing calories formerly obtained from carbohydrates with calories from fat. The recommended daily protein intake for men is 56g; for women, 46g (pregnant women need 71g); for teen-age boys, 52g; for teen-age girls, 46g. These are general guidelines; requirements may vary by weight and activity.

Razor bumps and ingrown whiskers

Razor bumps are caused when hair cut close to the skin curls as it grows and either curls under the skin without emerging or curls into the skin next to where it emerged. Either event irritates the skin, causing inflammation. In some cases, infection follows, which causes a sore and drainage. Men who are African, Celtic, Mediterranean, Nordic, Semitic, or from other peoples who have naturally coarse and tightly curling hair often get 'razor bumps.'

The technical name is *Pseudofolliculitis Barbae*: "*pseudo*" (false) + "*follicle*" (hair) + "*itis*" (inflammation) + "*barbae*" (of the beard), often abbreviated as PFB. If the site becomes infected, "*pseudo*" no longer applies and the condition is called *Folliculitis Barbae* or "barber's rash."

Causes

The usual cause of PFB is shaving too closely. A multiblade cartridge, with its tug-and-cut action, is particularly bad: by tugging the whisker before it's cut, the cutting point is too close to the skin and can even be slightly beneath the skin's surface after the whisker pops back into place. But even a double-edged safety razor can deliver too close a shave, which leads to razor bumps. Electric razors, like multiblade cartridges, are bad for men prone to PFB.

Shaving against the grain is a bad idea for the parts of your beard where you tend to get PFB or in-growns, and stretching the skin as you shave there is equally bad. Both techniques are aimed at getting a closer shave, one source of the problem.

Another cause of PFB is irritation and damage to the skin from using a dull blade, or using a sharp blade with bad technique, or shaving after inadequate prep. All those should be avoided.

A common cause of infection is *Staphylococcus aureus* bacteria. The bacteria normally resides benignly in the nasal passages, but shaving can sometimes introduce it to hair follicles on the face. Once the hair follicle is infected, the result is redness, itching, and even small, pus-filled blisters. This is something that varies by individual—I've never had this problem, but some shavers are prone to such infection. Rinsing the razor in rubbing alcohol before and after the shave can help, as can using a fresh towel for every shave as described above in the section on acne.

Cures

If you now have razor bumps, stop shaving for a few days or a week—let the whiskers lengthen, and with a sterile needle release any whiskers caught in the skin or beneath the skin. If you have infected sites, apply an antibiotic and let the sites heal. Benzoyl peroxide can help, but apply it sparingly since it can be irritating. It's a good idea to see your doctor or a dermatologist, who can help with the diagnosis and prescribe appropriate medication.

Prevention

First is how you shave; second are products designed to prevent razor bumps.

Prep

Make sure that your preparation is thorough and excellent. You want the whiskers fully wetted so they will be more easily cut and less likely to be sharp at the cutting point. Shave after you shower. Use a softening conditioner on your beard in the shower. Use ample warm water to soften whiskers before shaving.

Wash your beard at the sink, using a good high-glycerin pre-shave soap such as Musgo Real Glyce Lime Oil soap or Whole Foods 365 brand glycerin soap. Rinse and, leaving your beard wet, apply a wet, hot towel or washcloth to your beard for 3-5 minutes. You can apply lather or Geo. F. Trumper's Coral Skin Food to your wet beard before the hot towel/washcloth if you find that this increases the wetting action of the towel. Place the hot wet towel over your lathered beard. Make sure this prep includes the shaving area of your neck as well as your face.

After removing the towel, rinse your beard with hot water, and then use a technique suggested by Themba[239] on the ShaveMyFace forum. He suggests using an Innomed Lice Comb[240]. (Moore Unique also makes a tool[241] for lifting the beard.) The comb is quite fine. As you comb against the grain, use firm but comfortable pressure and a shallow angle (as if shaving with the comb). This lifts the stubble and removes in-growns and dead skin.

Then make a good (thick, wet, dense) lather from a good shaving soap or shaving cream, and brush it on your wet and combed beard against the grain.

Tools

Men who suffer from razor bumps say that the best razor to use is a straight razor. If you don't want to go that route, a single-edged razor—the Schick Injector or a GEM razor, both readily available on eBay, or the Mongoose—is, they say, just about as good. A double-edge razor also works well provided that you do not attempt to shave too closely. The Bump Fighter Razor[242] with its special Bump Guard blades is also recommended by some: it is specifically designed to prevent shaving too closely.

Use a new blade for each shave (if your blade is inexpensive) or else sterilize the blade before you begin each shave by rinsing it in a sterilizing solution. You can use rubbing alcohol (91% or higher) or a sterilizing product such as Ritual Razor Rinse or Barbicide[243]. The blade must be sharp: discard blades at the first sign of tugging at the whiskers rather than cutting effortlessly.

Shaving

Consider shaving on alternate days, if that's possible for you. Shave bumpy areas last so the lather has more time to soften the stubble.

Don't stretch your skin while shaving places that get razor bumps. Stretching your skin while you shave increases the chance that a whisker will 'snap back' to below skin level when it's cut.

Shave with the grain and possibly across the grain, but never against the grain in areas prone to razor bumps—do not try for a totally smooth (close) shave in those areas. (You can shave against the grain in places where you never have razor bumps.)

If you cut a bump, apply an antibiotic to prevent infection. Use an alum bar after the shave, since it's a mild antiseptic. Just glide it over your skin after the cold-water rinse. Let it sit for minute—perhaps while you tidy up the shaving area—then rinse well with water, pat dry, and apply your shaving balm or aftershave or razor bump treatment. Rinse your beard area after the alum has had a chance to do its work. If using the alum doesn't seem to agree with your skin, stop using it. (Adverse reactions to an alum bar are rare, but given the variation among shavers, there's a possibility it can happen for some.)

Products

A number of over-the-counter products are specifically meant to prevent razor bumps, and through your doctor or dermatologist, you can get prescription medicines for the condition, such as eflornithine hydrochloride 13.9%, sold under the trade name Vaniqa. It's designed to remove facial hair for women, but it's apparently proven effective in controlling and treating razor bumps as well.

Following is a list of over-the-counter products. These—like most things in shaving—work for some, not for others. Posting questions in the shaving forums about any particular product will get you information from those who have used it. It would be a good idea to do a forum search before posting the question, though, since you may well find the product has been discussed. You will probably get a variety of answers, so ultimately you decide.

Common products[244] (links at the endnote) that are used to combat razor bumps include the following:

Bump Fighter products (in particular the razor)

Bump Patrol

Dermagen Skin Revival System

Elicina Biological Treatment

Follique Treatment

High Time Bump Stopper Products

Moore Unique Skin Care

Impeccable Aftershave

Prince Reigns gel

Smart Shave Products

Tend Skin (you can make a version of Tend Skin at home[245])

Other skin issues

Eczema is a skin inflammation that has a number of causes; for some, certain fragrances used in shampoo and conditioner[246] will trigger the condition. If your skin suffers from dryness and recurring skin rashes characterized by redness, skin edema (swelling), itching and dryness, crusting, flaking, blistering, cracking, oozing, or bleeding, you may have one or another type of eczema, and you should see a dermatologist.

Winter's cold, windy weather and hot, dry air indoors can adversely affect a shaver's skin. Look for moisturizing products to help your skin: For shaving soaps, consider Mitchell Wool-Fat Shaving Soap or a shea-butter soap from Strop Shoppe, Shaver Heaven, or other good artisanal soapmaker. Insitut Karité shaving soap contains 25% shea butter and produces an excellent lather.

Similarly, seek out moisturizing shaving creams. Saint Charles Shave offers a shea-butter shaving cream, or use Nancy Boy Shaving Cream—the Nancy Boy products in general are quite good for your skin. Institut Karité also makes shea butter shaving creams (20% and 25%). Mickey Lee Soapworks offers a number of aftershave milks (a thinner version of a balm) that work well.

For an aftershave, try Nancy Boy Body Moisturizer (heavier and cheaper than their face moisturizer and works quite well). Also, Shea Moisture Three Butters Lotion works well; it uses avocado, mango, and shea butters. Cade aftershave balm by l'Occitane has a high shea-butter content. Primalan, an almond-oil based aftershave balm, and Alt-Innsbruck pre- and post-shave balm are both very good aftershave balms that come in 100ml containers; for about the same price, Institut Karité has a 25% shea butter aftershave balm in a 250ml container. You need only a pea-sized amount of these balms. Eucerin Daily Protection Body Lotion (SPF 15) or Face Lotion (SPF 30) would also be good, though in winter if you're very far from the equator at all, the SPF is irrelevant: the winter sun is weak.

Also you might try a tiny amount of The Shave Den's Pre-Shave Balm as a dry-air aftershave treatment. Note its ingredients: Shea Butter, Lanolin, Jojoba Oil, Avocado Oil, Sweet Almond Oil, Vitamin E, and fragrance (sandalwood and oakmoss). I live in a very temperate climate and have little recent experience with dry air, summer or winter.

You can also use plain grapeseed oil or jojoba oil as a balm.

Mickey Lee Soapworks, Saint Charles Shave, The Shave Den Store, Shave Place, and Barclay Crocker all offer soothing and moisturizing aftershave lotions and balms. You can email or call them to ask about the specific problem you're facing and get their informed opinions on the best approaches and products for you. In addition to any advice you get, pay attention to your own direct experience and see what in practice works best with your skin. Skin types vary widely, and it is not possible to give specific advice, so (once again) experimentation and close observation of results will be your best guide to what works for you.

THIRTEEN

Recommendations for a beginner

SEVERAL vendors—Maggard Razors, Italian Barber, Whipped Dog, Men Essentials, and others—offer beginner kits, often with some choice as to brush (get one of the Omega S-Series brushes if it's on offer) and razor (get a Parker 24C or 26C if available) and blades (as you know, you cannot know in advance which brands of blades will work best for you: try a few and stick with the best of those for a couple of months).

Should you find that DE shaving does not work out for you (highly unlikely, and since true lather will improve even shaves using a cartridge razor, the soap and shaving brush are solid purchases), you can readily find buyers for the equipment and supplies in the Buying/Selling threads of shaving forums or on reddit/r/shave_bazaar. Indeed, you might be able to get some of your equipment from the same place—along with advice (sometimes inconsistent advice, though offered with sincere intentions).

Hair conditioner instead of lather?

Some have found that they can use hair conditioner in place of shaving soap or shaving cream: they wash with soap and water, then rinse and apply the hair conditioner. After each pass, rinse and apply hair conditioner again before the next pass. Hair conditioner is often used for body shaving—for example, shaving the legs—but that is most often done because the shaver has not tried a true lather and does not realize how much better it is—the same reason that some continue using canned foam with a DE razor (or use a multiblade cartridge).

If it works for you, you won't need a shaving brush, shaving soap, or shaving cream—so it may be worth a try. "Not working" means either some skin reaction to the hair conditioner and/or razor burn (red, burning skin) because the hair conditioner is not providing enough protection from the blade.

I did try it, and at first it seemed fine. But then I had a difficult time seeing where I had shaved (the hair conditioner makes a thin and transparent layer), and I did get a fierce razor burn. So I returned to the traditional shaving cream or soap. I rate hair conditioner at best an emergency substitute for shaving soap or cream, and then for just one shave. Razor burn is unpleasant.

Leisureguy's idea of a beginner shaving kit

A novice can split his transition from using canned foam and multiblade cartridges to traditional DE wetshaving into two steps, buying separately what is needed in each step. This has the budget advantage of breaking start-up costs into two purchases, perhaps a month apart.

Step 1 is *prep*: everything before you pick up the razor:

- **Pre-shave soap**: I like MR GLO, but Whole Foods 365 brand glycerin soap also works well; or try any other high-glycerin soap. No soap works well in hard water, so try distilled water if you're unsure of how soft your water is: that will show you if your water is hard. If it is, use citric acid to soften your shaving water (see the Water section).
- **Brush**: Omega S-Series synthetic brush. Good but inexpensive, it also makes a good travel/gym brush. Be careful: do not buy the Omega Syntex brush; it uses coarse white-nylon bristles and is not very good.
- **Shaving soap or shaving cream**: Try a variety of samples from Garry's Sample Shop or Maggard Razors and/or order samples from the artisanal soapmakers listed earlier. The best bang for the buck in shaving cream is J.M. Fraser, and TOBS Avocado has proved good for beginners. In soaps, you have a wider range of choices. Any of the previously listed artisanal soaps would be good. Arko (shave stick) is also popular and inexpensive. Read the ingredients and descriptions and get samples or tubs of those that strike your interest.

In Step 1 your focus is on learning good prep: wash your beard with pre-shave soap at the sink using your hands and rinse partially with a splash. Then make a good lather and take your time working it into your beard. You may find the pre-shave soap lacks lubricity and/or it's difficult to get a good lather from shaving soap. If so, that may be due to hard water. Try the distilled water shave described previously. The difference can be astonishing. If the water is hard, use citric acid as described in the section on Water.

Also determine the grain of your beard and start doing two passes, still using your multiblade-cartridge razor. Try using very light pressure. Do one pass with the grain and one pass across the grain, applying lather before each pass.

Step 2 is *shaving and aftershave*: the rest of the shave:

- **Razor**: Although the Lord L6 or Feather Popular are inexpensive, they are (in effect) throwaway razors: you will eventually want to replace either. Moreover, the L6 is prone to breakage because of the flimsy and soft aluminum handle. Those razors are also too light to use the pressure of the razor alone. On the other hand, they do allow you to try DE shaving at low cost. Still, I *strongly* recommend the Parker 24C (or 26C: same head, different handle), a razor that is both very comfortable and very efficient. It's a lifetime razor at a reasonable price. The fact that it's an open-comb razor is irrelevant in this context. If you prefer a vintage razor, the Gillette NEW (from 1930) or the Gillette Tech (with a sharp blade) can also serve you well.

Other good options, in approximate order by price: one of the Maggard Razors; an Edwin Jagger (they all have the same head); or the RazoRock Baby Smooth razor (the best performing but the most expensive as well, and not always available).

- **Blade sampler pack**: Buy a large pack with a good variety of blades. Initially try no more than four brands, then stick with the best of those for two-three months so your technique can settle. At that point, explore the other brands by trying a new brand of blade every 4 weeks. If it's better, it becomes your new daily blade; otherwise, return to the best so far for another 4 weeks. You may want to include brands available in local stores, though those are costly. When you discover a transcendent blade that takes your shave to a new level of excellence, continue to explore, trying a new brand every two months.
- **Styptic**: I recommend My Nik Is Sealed or other liquid styptic. You will inevitably get a few nicks as you learn, and a liquid styptic staunches the bleeding more effectively than a styptic pencil.
- **Alum block**: The alum block as a post-shave skin treatment is pleasant and also seems effective against acne and some other skin conditions. It also offers a non-slip grip if you brush your wet fingers over it, on the one hand for your razor, on the other hand for gripping wet soapy skin to stretch it. You use a styptic only when you have a nick; you use an alum block after every shave. Note that some men have a skin reaction to alum: their skin turns red and hot for a few minutes after using it. I suggest you test the alum by wetting it and rubbing it in the crease of your elbow and letting it sit for 10-20 minutes. Better that your arm turns red for a while than your face.
- **Aftershave**: You can continue with your current aftershave, or experiment with a witch hazel (I recommend one of the Thayers line) or witch-hazel-based aftershaves that you either or purchase of make as described earlier, or try an aftershave splash or balm or milk. Krampert's Finest Bay Rum is a classic fragrance and quite good. Buy samples when you can—and most artisanal vendors sell samples.

You already know prep from Step 1, so in Step 2 your focus is learn to use the razor. Read carefully the technique description and instructions earlier in this book. By properly focusing your attention—and being careful to use light pressure—you can achieve a reasonably good result even with the first shave. Do just two passes: with the grain, rinse, relather, and across the grain. Your skill will improve from shave to shave if you pay attention and experiment carefully—trying different directions of cutting, for example: sometimes going at a slant (for under the nose and, for me, under the forward part of my jaw).

Recall the importance of keeping the edge of the cap in contact with the skin, which puts the razor's handle away from your face, and be careful to keep the pressure light. This will require much conscious attention at first, but eventually—and surprisingly soon—the adaptive unconscious learns the new practices so that intense conscious attention is no longer required.

All of the above, Step 1 and Step 2, costs about the same as the price of 30 Fusion disposable cartridges.

For both equipment and supplies look in the Buying/Selling sections of the shaving forums and reddit/r/shave_bazaar. You often can find bargains there. Post a "WTB" (Want To Buy) if you're looking for a specific item.

Your second razor

In time you will want a second razor (and—who knows?—perhaps a third and fourth). I *strongly* recommend that your second razor be a slant. The slant is recommended as your *second* razor because it requires a light touch and a sure hand, so it's best if you're experienced with a safety razor before using it. The reasons for this recommendation I discuss in detail in the section on slant razors.

Whatever razor you get as a second razor, you should accept that you will have to "learn" it, much as you learned to shave with your first DE razor, though of course the learning time for the second razor is much shorter—sometimes a single shave will serve, sometimes it's a week or more before nicks stop altogether. Generally it takes somewhere around 3-4 shaves. If it's not working, take a break and return later. You may find that your layoff enabled your previous experience to take hold, and on trying the razor again after a break, it works much better.

Understand, too, that a new razor may well have a different head geometry, which is why you have to learn it. One result of a different head geometry is that you'll have to experiment some with the angle: the new razor may require a shallower angle, for example. Tune the angle by listening to the cutting. You should also do some renewed blade exploration as well: the brand of blades that was best in your first razor may not be best (or even good) in a new razor. Judicious experimentation is always a good idea.

I believe that learning the second razor will be easier and go faster if you shave exclusively with the new razor until you once again are getting smooth, nick-free shaves with no razor burn, though taking a break can help if you have consistent difficulties at the start. Once you learn the new razor, you can switch back and forth between your new and old razor easily, your adaptive unconscious making any technique adjustments required.

Whether to collect

Earlier I wrote that shaving is not, per se, a hobby, however pleasurable it may be. Bicycling to work is also pleasurable; like shaving, it provides health and financial benefits compared to common alternatives, but getting to and from work on a bicycle would not be what most would call a "hobby"—although bicycling can indeed become a hobby.

And although most shavers begin DE shaving to save money—"The blades are so cheap! Look at much money I'll be saving in just a year!"—it would be disingenuous not to recognize that many find that shaving does indeed become a hobby, one of the "collecting" genus. When this happens the shaver begins building collections—of razors, brushes, shaving soaps or creams, aftershaves, or any combination. While the supplies will ultimately be used (though it's surprisingly easy to amass a 25-year supply of shaving soap), a large collection of razors and brushes (and shelves on which to display them) can quickly run into money. (This is especially true for straight razors.)

Think about whether you desire—or can afford—to go into collecting. There's much to be said for viewing a razor and a brush as one views a hand-drill and a hammer: specialized tools to do a specific job. You pick one good razor, one good brush, and get on with it. You may want to upgrade the razor—for example, start with a Lord L6 and when the handle breaks, replace it with a Parker 24C, and perhaps ultimately get a premium razor: Above the Tie, or an iKon Shavecraft, or a Standard, or a Wolfman, selling off or giving away each razor as it is replaced, and follow a similar route for the brush. Perhaps you might want a small number of razors—a vintage razor, a slant, and a modern razor—and avoid any further accumulation

One possible drawback to a minimalist approach is that when you have a single-item set (one each of brush, soap, razor, and aftershave), you never make a morning choice of what to use for your shave and thus can fall into doing the shave on autopilot, with no mindful awareness of the experience, thus missing a significant benefit of the shave. And a two-item set (two of each of the components) is not much better: it's easy to slip into mindlessly toggling between each pair of items: on even days this one, on odd days the other. It's with *three* of each that choice really enters the picture. (And three is often the number at which something interesting happens. Consider, for example, billiards. Using only a cue ball is not a game at all, and adding a second ball doesn't help: making the cue ball hit the other ball is too easy. But add a third ball and try to make the cue ball hit *both* the other balls, and you have a game. Include the requirement that the cue ball must strike a cushion three times before the shot is complete, and you have a game for a lifetime.)

So one sensible limit is a three-item set: three each of razors, brushes, soaps, and aftershaves. Each morning, then, you make conscious choices to begin your shave, which engages you in the shave, fighting the auto-pilot tendency.

Of course, those three items could be the beginning of a slippery slope. It does make sense, however, to have different razors of very different types for different jobs: for example, a slant for removing heavy stubble easily, another modern razor for variety, and perhaps a vintage razor. And you might want a regular brush for home and also a travel brush, perhaps a Wee Scot, or the Omega 11047, or one of the Mühle travel brushes.

However, a larger collection can take on a life of its own, with the tail wagging the dog: the collection continually pushing the collector to extend it. The open secret about collections is that inevitably the owner will have to leave the collection: any collection at some point must find a new home, and a large collection can be a burden and a challenge to dismantle. As in most of this book, I am writing from my direct personal experience, which included downsizing for a move to a smaller place. And if you personally don't dismantle the collection, it's left as a task for someone else who may view it as so much trash.

I suggest that you establish rigorous limits to collection size: a few different razors and an equal number of brushes can offer a good variety that's nonetheless consistent with seeing razor and brush as useful tools, just as you might own a range of hammers—a tack hammer, a framing hammer, a ball-peen hammer, a mallet, and a sledgehammer—and still view (and use) the hammers as (pounding) tools rather than collectible artifacts.

If you truly want to collect *something*, consider collecting individual razor blades in their colorful paper wrappers. Some such collections are quite impressive[247]. Blades (and their wrappers) come in a great variety—as you can see in your sampler pack—and offer a relatively inexpensive collecting venue. Moreover, razor blades use little space and are easy to store and transport, perhaps mounted in photograph albums with the plastic-wrapped pages.

I won't address supplies: those you can figure out (and use up). Although it's not actually collecting, I do suggest you try at least a shaving soap and a shaving cream, and it's worthwhile to get shaving soap both in a tub and as a shave stick: if you don't explore some of the options, you will not learn what

190

your own preferences are: expectations are often belied by experience, so in general you cannot know whether you will like something until after you've tried it a few times. But be careful even here: it's easier than you think to acquire a five- or ten-year supply of shaving soaps and creams[248].

With aftershaves, I think it's easier. You might want a few, of different types: a light fresh aftershave, a more musky aftershave, and perhaps a floral and a citrus... Well, maybe it's not so easy. But beware of getting too many. One good thing about shaving soaps, creams, and aftershaves: they're naturals for gifts, and with a little judicious hinting at the right times of the year, you can easily achieve a good selection.

Here are some suggestions regarding razors and brushes, which tend to be the big-ticket items: First, think about setting limits if you're inclined to collect, limiting either quantity or price or both. For example, if your interest is vintage Gillettes, you might decide that you will not spend more than $20 on a razor. This makes the hunt more difficult and a find more exciting. Or if your interest is brushes, you might decide that you will buy only old brushes for under $10 with the idea that you'll restore them, replacing the knot—probably a good idea in any case, since frequently the knot on old brushes is ratty and also difficult to sterilize if that's a concern. A nice sequence showing a brush restoration in detail can be seen on Wicked Edge[249].

Another approach might be to acquire one single representative of each type of razor or brush. For razors, perhaps a three-piece, a TTO, and an adjustable. Or you could go for six razors: those three types in open-comb design and in straight-bar design. I, of course, believe that any set of razors should include a slant: it's an interesting razor, unique in its cutting action, and for most men it shaves extremely well. And speaking of unique razors, it's tempting to add an asymmetric razor to the mix: an unusual and intriguing design.

Another possibility is to focus on (say) the Gillette Super Speeds or the Gillette adjustables. Though either collection may have more different razors than you at first would think, at least you are focused on a single type of razor.

For brushes, I suggest you get one brush of each type—badger, boar, horse, and synthetic—to experience their differences (thus discovering your own preferences) and get an idea of the range. If you get another brush of a type, you get rid of the one of that type you already had.

Some unusual brush(es) might be included—for example, the tiny brushes: a Wee Scot (badger), an Omega 11047 (badger+boar), a small horsehair brush (several are available from GiftsAndCare.com), and a small boar brush. Small badger brushes, though uncommon, are made by other manufacturers as well: Omega makes one, and Plisson once did.

For both razors and brushes you can find stunning examples of custom craftsmanship. For example, Robert Quinn of Elite Razor and Rod Neep of Pens of the Forest and offer some remarkable razors and brushes. Just as artisanal soaps have greatly increased in number (and in quality) in response to growing demand, so have artisanal shaving brushes, some of which are exceptionally attractive. Brent's Brushes, Brushguy.com, and Wolf Whiskers are just three of a growing number. The brushes are unique—truly collector's items—but that's the drawback: how do you decide when to stop? That's the danger. Moreover, fine items such as these tend to be expensive.

The idea of a "collection" is that it is *not* simply a bunch of stuff, but rather a bunch of stuff with a definite structure that reflects a specific plan. Approaching your purchases with a plan that you've developed after some thought will help you know what you're not interested in (because it doesn't fit your collecting plan), and it also helps you to know when your collection is complete (if such a thing is possible).

In serious cases in which you do have concerns about the money and time being spent, it's best to try to discover the underlying psychological forces that drive you to collect. This can be done through one's own introspection combined with keeping a journal of your thoughts and findings (cf. *A Life of One's Own*, mentioned earlier), but a therapist can also help a lot. It can be a problem akin to addiction and it's better to confront the issue than to ignore it.

On the other hand, if you're comfortable with collecting, take a look at ShaveWorld.org, a site devoted collecting shaving memorabilia.

FOURTEEN

The most common problems

PROBLEMS you encounter in shaving usually—though not always—fall into one of the following areas. If you have some problem in your shave that doesn't seem related to the causes listed below, the shaving forums (see Appendix) are a good source of informed (albeit sometimes inconsistent: YMMV) advice. And problems often are solved by judicious experimentation once you realize it *is* a problem.

Hard Water

Hard water is a "hidden" problem because most shavers using hard water never consider water quality, and assume that their problems in making lather are due to their lack of skill. If a high-glycerin pre-shave soap doesn't add lubricity and produce a better shave, and if when you shower you get "squeaky clean" (the "squeak" being due to friction from soap scum adhering to your skin), and particularly if you find white mineral deposits around faucets, hard water is the prime suspect. A distilled-water shave is easy to do and will show whether hard water *is* the problem, so if a pre-shave soap doesn't help your shave and/or getting a good lather is difficult, get some distilled/"purified" water and try it. If the shave is markedly better, use distilled water regularly or add a pinch of citric acid to a sink half-filled with tap water to soften it as described earlier.

Another common source of lather problems, particularly from soaps, is that the brush has not been loaded with enough soap. If your lather is mediocre, before trying distilled water (especially if the pre-shave soap does in fact produce lubricity on your skin), make sure you're fully loading the brush. Brush the puck of soap *at length, briskly,* and *firmly* for 15-25 seconds (or until all large bubbles are gone and you see only fine-grained lather). Thus you continue brushing even after lather has started to form on the puck. Your initial focus is to load the brush fully with soap—you can work up the lather more on your beard (or in a bowl or on your palm), perhaps there adding a little water if it's needed (if the lather seems too dry). With practice, you can load the brush quickly: my regular loading time is 10 seconds.

Insufficient Prep

Your beard must be fully wetted to soften. Shave after showering, wash beard again at the sink with a pre-shave soap, and apply a good lather—dense and holding a substantial amount of water—to your wet beard. Take your time working the lather into the stubble before the first pass; the lather applied for later passes can simply be applied without much ado, but before the first pass, work the lather into the stubble, giving it time to do its job. You might also a hot towel. Do **not** neglect prep of your neck shaving area.

One sign of insufficient preparation—and, in particular, of a lather that's too dry and/or a lathering process that's too brief—is that the blade seems dull, pulling and tugging at the beard instead of cutting smoothly and easily. It may be, of course, that the blade *is* dull, particularly if you've been putting off changing it. Or, if it's a new brand, it may be either a dud blade or a brand that doesn't work for you (or both, of course).

But if you have a brand of blade that's been working well for you, and suddenly it doesn't seem to be cutting, suspect the prep. Make sure the lather's wet enough, and spend a good amount of time with the brush, working the lather over and into your beard. Lather your chin and upper lip (the toughest part of your beard) first before each pass and shave them last so that those whiskers have more time to soak in the lather and thus soften.

Wrong Blade for You

Blade selection is crucial. Novices focus on the razor, but the razor is just a device for holding the blade and presenting the edge at the correct angle to the stubble. Different people require different blades. Get a sampler pack so you can find the best blade for you. This step is absolutely essential if you want close and comfortable shaves. Do not skip it. And you *cannot* rely on recommendations from other shavers: one man's pebble is another man's pearl, and vice versa.

This idea is enormously difficult to grasp—if you have a terrible shave with a blade, it's hard to believe that others would actually *like* the blade, and if you have a wonderful shave, you want to recommend the blade to everyone. And yet it's true that *every* brand of blade has those who love it and those who hate it. Until you try the blade, you don't know into which group you fall.

Incorrect Blade Angle

Blade angle is absolutely critical. The blade should be *almost* parallel to the skin being shaved, so that the blade's edge strikes the stubble almost at a right angle as the blade slides over your skin. Generally speaking, keep the cap's edge—just behind the blade's edge—in contact with your skin. Focus on that and forget about the guard bar. Think of the blade as gliding along parallel to the skin, riding on a thin layer of lather. The sound the blade makes in cutting the stubble is helpful in tuning the angle.

Where the skin has a lot of curves (for example, jawline, neck, chin), you have to maneuver the razor a fair amount to keep the blade angle correct because the safety razor, unlike the cartridge razor, does not pivot. Making short strokes helps you stay focused on blade angle. Even with light pressure, if the angle's wrong, you'll nick or cut yourself.

Too Much Pressure

Shaving with a cartridge either requires or encourages pressure, so exerting too much pressure is a habit that cartridge shavers must unlearn.

Often the weight of the razor by itself is enough to cut the stubble—and for some razors, the weight of the razor is too much, so the razor must be supported in the hand. (The iKon stainless slants are like this.) Hold the razor by the balance point on the handle to better control the pressure. When you rinse after the first pass, you'll feel stubble. This does **not** mean you should use more pressure—eliminate stubble by progressively reducing it over 2, 3, or 4 passes.

Oddly, a very light razor, such as a bakelite razor the RazoRock Baby Smooth, might encourage too much pressure. An efficient razor does a good job even if the razor is barely brushing the skin, so on using a very light razor some will unconsciously apply more pressure so that they can *feel* pressure, and that can easily be too much. You want the razor just barely *touching* the skin. A DE razor requires—and allows—you to control blade angle directly, and the same applies to pressure: control it, and keep it light. Your face will thank you.

Ignoring Your Beard's Grain

It's vital that you know the direction of your beard's growth, since the sequence of passes is first *with* the grain, then *across* the grain, and then (if stubble is sufficiently reduced and you don't have to be concerned about razor bumps) *against* the grain. (If too much stubble remains for a comfortable against-the-grain pass, first shave across the grain the other way.)

Generally, the beard on your face will grow downward—but not always. I have a couple of patches where it grows more or less sideways. The grain on the neck can be anything, even whiskers growing in whorls, which is why good prep of the neck shaving area is so important. To find the grain, wait 12-24 hours after you've shaved, then rub your face and neck. The direction that's roughest is against the grain. You'll find the "roughest" direction is different on different parts of your face and neck. Use the interactive diagram[250] to map your grain.

Bathroom Too Loud

If your bathroom is not quiet—if, for example, water is running or the fan is on or you're listening to music—then you cannot hear the sounds of shaving. Shaving deaf, as it were, is like flying blind: it doesn't work well. You need auditory feedback to fine-tune the blade angle. Moreover, one benefit of shaving is the mindfulness meditation that close focus on what is happening can produce. Music is a distraction. It may be difficult at first, if you are used to distraction, to do without it, but with practice you will find that the act of shaving is satisfying in itself, with only the quiet sounds of water, the brush, and the razor.

Setting an Adjustable Razor Too High

Some novices inexplicably dial their adjustable razor to the most aggressive settings—4, 5, or 6 on the Futur or Progress, or 8 or 9 on the Gillette Adjustable—and then find themselves staring in the mirror at their lacerated face. With adjustables, start with a *low* setting (1 on Futur or Progress, 2 or 3 on Gillette Adjustable), and advance the setting only as you must in order to get a good shave. As soon as you get a good shave, stop there. You want the lowest setting that works, not the highest setting you can stand. It's not a contest with a prize awarded for a high setting. Quite the contrary.

Razor repeatedly becomes clogged

If the razor doesn't rinse well and clogs with lather and stubble, take a look at the lather. If the lather is too thick and doesn't rinse away easily, the problem is likely due to hard water (which produces a sticky scum when mixed with soap) or too thick a lather (too much soap for the amount of water) or both. It may also be caused by too liberal a use of a pre-shave oil, since oils don't rinse easily away.

The solutions to the hard-water problem (generally, using distilled water or softening the shaving water with citric acid) are discussed in the section on Water. For too thick a lather, experiment by loading the brush for a shorter time and/or working more water into the lather. You might want to start with a dryish lather—that is, deliberately use little water to load the brush—and then work in small amounts of water, little by little, until the lather is obviously too wet, feeling the lather as you go. Along the way, you should discover a lather that is slick and rinses easily away, but is still thick enough to be used as a lather. That becomes your target lather. With some experimentation and practice, using soft(ened) water, you can create lather that does the job and also rinses easily away, not clogging the razor.

You will have a learning curve, as you transition from cognitive understanding to practiced skill, but you at least know what you're trying for.

FIFTEEN

Where to get more information

NOW that you're at the end of this introductory book, you may well want to know more. Take a look at the on-line article "Exploring the Science of Shaving"[251] from the February 1957 issue of *Science and Mechanics*. The advice in the sidebar, "10 Minutes to a Good Shave," offers an alternative to the procedure described in this book; experiment and test them. A write-up on MSNBC[252] on how to get a perfect shave covers some of same points discussed in this book.

The series of videos[253] by Mantic59 offers an introduction to and demonstration of many of the topics covered above. Betelgeux of Wicked_Edge also regularly posts shaving videos on his YouTube channel theshockwav. Geofatboy[254] and Michael Freedberg[255] also make good shaving videos.

The wetshaving forums and Reddit's Wicked_Edge subreddit[256] are good sources of information on new products and also offer invaluable advice to novices. You can post your own questions and receive in return a range of views and advice, which is all to the good: shaving solutions vary quite a bit from person to person, so knowing a range of solutions is useful. You must, of course, test proposed solutions to see whether someone else's solution works for you.

One particular benefit of using the forums is that, when you describe a problem you're facing, you will often get responses from men who have faced (and solved) the identical problem, so you can profit from their direct experience. You will get better help if you provide a good description so that the advice you get is useful. Include at least the following:

- The brush you're using (brand and also the type of bristles)
- Which brand of shaving soap or shaving cream you use
- Whether you are have hard or soft water (or that you don't know)
- Your prep procedure—whether you shave after showering, what pre-shave treatment(s) you do (if any), whether you use a hot towel
- The make and model of your razor
- The brand of blade and whether you have tried other brands

- The sequence of your passes and which passes you do (with, across, against the grain) and whether you've mapped your beard's grain
- The kind of problem you're having (nicks? rash? bumps?) and when it appears (during shave? right afterwards? an hour after? next day?)
- Where you live (which country and which state/province) to help with vendor recommendations—knowing which state or province also gives an insight into whether the water is likely to be hard

The reason for most of these is evident. The blade information is to determine whether you're simply using the brand that came with the razor (for example, Merkur blades), or whether you've done some exploration. By providing that information, you'll get much more helpful answers. If you don't provide the information, you will be asked for it anyway, so giving it at the start smooths the process.

Do not overlook the learning you gain by answering questions from newbies and offering help to them based on your own experience. In explaining things you will perforce examine your own experience and get a deeper understanding of what you're doing, why you're doing it, and the results you get. Indeed, your first explanation is generally explaining to yourself, but by repeated efforts to explain, you notice more and learn better what your own technique is and how better to explain it: as in shaving, practice improves performance.

It's worth noting that some forums have a strong tribal ethic, and that their rules and guidelines include rigorously enforced *unwritten* rules. These will, of course, be unknown to the new participant. For example, I was banned for life from one forum for a post in which I recommended a product and made the mistake—unknown to me, and not covered in the written rules—of linking to three different vendors: one in Canada and two in the US[257]. It would also take three links for a vendor in the US, one in Canada, and one in the UK, but the (unwritten) rule was that at most one vendor link is allowed in a post. Because I had linked to three vendors, I was immediately banned from the forum for life.

One of the vendors to whom I linked had been banned from the forum, which I did not know. I did know that some did not want to buy from that vendor, thus the second US link. There apparently was another unwritten (and thus secret) rule that you were not allowed to link to a banned vendor, but the forum doesn't state which vendors are banned and which are safe for links. A violation apparently results in being banned for life.

As you can see, in a new forum you should first simply read posts and observe. Be *very* careful what you post, since some of the most stringently enforced and draconian rules can be unpublished: the moderators will spring those on you if you run afoul of them, but no warning signs are posted. (I don't understand this, but I do observe it, so be careful out there.)

198

Some manufacturers of shaving products offer samples (free or at low cost), which are quite useful. A sample is more than enough to test the fragrance and to see whether you have any special sensitivity or allergic reactions to the product. On ShaveMyFace you can find a comprehensive list[258] of sources of samples, and the Appendix lists sources that offer a good selection of samples (and will consider requests).

Ultimately, the best source of information to improve your shave is likely to be your own experience, experiments, observations, and reflection. For example, if you are wondering whether your lather is sufficiently wet—or too wet—the best course is to experiment. Try using less water, then using more water, and see how it works for you.

If you are wondering whether a particular pre-shave you have really works, or whether it works better if you apply it before each pass, experiment. Shave a week with it, followed by a week without. Try a week of using it only before the first pass, followed by a week of using it before every pass. If a week's too long, try just two days.

Thoughtful experimentation and close observation of outcomes are, in shaving as in science and life in general, the most reliable source of knowledge.

Go now and experiment.

Appendix

Links are also available at **tinyurl.com/leisureguyfe** in clickable form.

Forums

Badger & Blade – badgerandblade.com
Lady Shavers – reddit.com/r/ladyshavers
Paste and Cut - paste-and-cut.com.au
RazorAndStone – razorandstone.com
Sharpologist list of forums - sharpologist.com/shaving-forums
Shave Bazaar (buy/sell/trade) – reddit.com/r/shave_bazaar
ShaveMyFace –shavemyface.com
Shave Nook – shavenook.com
Straight Razor Place –straightrazorplace.com
The Shave Den – theshaveden.com
The Shaving Room – theshavingroom.co.uk/forum
Wet Shavers – reddit.com/r/wet_shavers
Wicked Edge - reddit.com/r/wicked_edge

Reference

Betelgeux shaving videos - youtube.com/user/theshockwav
Bruce on Shaving – bruceonshaving.com (many photos)
Geofatboy shaving videos – youtube.com/user/geofatboy
Gillette collectors reference – razorarchive.com
Gillette date codes – gillettedatecodes.com
Gillette razors v. blades myth debunked – tinyurl.com/3cjbgtj
Gillette Rockets (British Super Speed) - tinyurl.com/78qzjlr
Mantic59 shaving videos – youtube.com/user/mantic59
Michael Freedberg shaving videos – youtube.com/user/mfreedberg
Mr-Razor.com – mr-razor.com (German site, with English option)
Schick Injectors – tinyurl.com/27vor9
Sharpologist – sharpologist.com
Shaving 101 – shaving101.com
Shaving information – shaveinfo.com

Product samples

The following offer samples of shaving soaps, shaving creams, aftershaves, and the like:

> Alllatheredup.weebly.com
> Maggardrazors.com
> Samples.manmachine.co (UK)
> Sampleshop.blogspot.com
> Tinyurl.com/2gwu8c – big list of samples sources

Blade Sampler Packs

Vendors selling blade sampler packs as of this edition are:

> BullGoose Shaving Supplies (in the US)
> Connaught Shaving (in the UK)
> Details for Men (in the US)
> Em's Shave Place (in the US)
> Fendrihan (in Canada)
> Italian Barber (in Canada)
> Kinetic Blue (in Australia)
> Razor Blades & More (in the US)
> Razors Direct (in the US)
> Royal Shave (in the US)
> The Shave Den (in the US)
> Shave Nation (in the US)
> Shave Shed (in Australia)
> Shaving.ie (in Ireland)
> Shoebox Shaveshop (in the US)
> Straight Razor Designs (in the US)
> Tryablade.com (in US, offers $4 flat-rate shipping worldwide)
> West Coast Shaving (in the US)
> Via Amazon.com: tinyurl.com/ycq3fb7
> Via eBay.com: tinyurl.com/6azkz5s

Vendors

Following is a list of on-line vendors for the wetshaving community. This list is a partial list, since the rapid growth of DE shaving continually brings new vendors on-line, but the list can serve as a starting place.

Australia--

Note: For Australians, sometimes it costs less to order from Connaught Shaving (UK) or Shaving.ie (Ireland), even with shipping costs.

HimAge – himage.com.au – option of looking at products by fragrance
Kinetic Blue – kineticblue.com.au – men's grooming and shaving supplies
Men's Biz – mensbiz.com.au – broad line of shaving supplies
Occams – occa.ms - artisanal products including shaving cream
Otoko Organics – otoko.com.au – extremely interesting shaving soap
Pureman – pureman.com.au – men's grooming and shaving supplies
Shaver Hut – shaverhut.com.au – men's grooming and shaving supplies
The Shave Shed – theshaveshed.com.au – 60-day return policy
Shaver City – shavercity.com.au – good line of shaving supplies including cutthroat razors (aka straight razors)
Shaver Heaven – shaverheaven.com.au – artisanal vegan soaps, also available from some vendors in Canada, US, and UK
The Razor Shop – therazorshop.com – an eclectic little shop: razors, brushes, shaving supplies, pressure cookers, etc.

Canada--
Atkinson's – tinyurl.com/qc8jlfh - Plisson brushes; store in Vancouver
Classic Edge – classicedge.ca – good selection of straight razors and DEs along with shaving supplies
The Copper Hat – thecopperhat.ca – good range of shaving supplies, interesting brushes; store in Victoria
Fendrihan – fendrihan.com – good range of shaving products, along with leather goods, writing implements, and knives
Italian Barber – italianbarber.com – RazoRock products, including the Baby Smooth and Stealth razors; starter kits; broad range of shaving supplies; routinely ships to the US
Kent of Inglewood – kentofinglewood.com
Mark of a Gentleman - markofagentleman.com – good range of shaving supplies
Men Essentials – menessentials.ca – broad range of products; store in Toronto
Moss Scuttle – sarabonnymanpottery.com – the original modern scuttle
Shaving Style – shavingstyle.com – straight razors, DEs, and shaving supplies
Soapy Bathman – soapybathman.ca – artisanal soaps
Wolfman Razors – wolfmanrazors.com – premium stainless razors and handles

France--
Plisson – blaireauxplisson.com/en/ - exquisite shaving brushes

Germany--------------------------------------
Shavemac – shavemac.com – excellent brushes along with German shaving equipment and supplies.
Wiborg – wiborgshavingbrushes.com – superb shaving brushes

Ireland--

Shaving.ie – shaving.ie – broad range of products, routinely ships internationally at low rates

Italy--

Tcheon Fung Sing - tfssoap.com – extremely nice artisanal soaps, available from some US vendors

Netherlands--

Shave and More – shaveandmore.com – broad range of shaving products
Total-Shave.nl – tinyurl.com/7y949t3 – URL for English-language storefront

Portugal--

The Portugal Online Shop – theportugalonlineshop.com – Claus Porto products (Musgo Real, Ach. Brito, and others), brushes. Ships readily to US.
Vintage Scent – vintagescent.com – Semogue brushes and interesting shaving supplies. Ships readily to US.

Singapore--

Double-Edge Shaving Place – doubleedgeshavingplace.com – good range of shaving supplies

Spain--

Gifts and Care – giftsandcare.com – excellent selection of good horsehair shaving brushes and shaving stuff. Shipping to US is inexpensive.
UFO Razor Handles – uforazorhandles.com – excellent handles when available

Turkey--

BestShave.net – bestshave.net – inexpensive supplies

U.K.--

Caveman Grooming – cavemangrooming.co.uk
Connaught Shaving – connaughtshaving.com – ships internationally
The English Shaving Company - theenglishshavingcompany.com – home of Edwin Jagger
Executive Shaving Company – executive-shaving.co.uk – very broad range of shaving products and instructional guides
Fredricssons – fredricssons.co.uk – artisanal shaving soaps
Gallant & Klein – gallantandklein.co.uk – limited range but good quality
G.B. Kent & Sons – kentbrushes.com – excellent shaving brushes
The Gentlemen's Groom Room – thegentlemansgroomroom.com – broad range of shaving products
The Gentlemen's Shop - gentlemans-shop.com – good range of shaving supplies
The Groomed Man – thegroomedman.co.uk – broad range of shaving products

The Invisible Edge – theinvisibleedge.co.uk – straight razors

Man Machine Sample Shop – samples.manmachine.co – product samples

Nanny's Silly Soap Company – nannyssillysoap.com – artisanal soaps

New Forest Brushes – newforestbrushes.blogspot.com – artisanal brushes

Niven & Joshua – nivenandjoshua.com - good range of shaving supplies

Pens of the Forest – pensoftheforest.co.uk/shaving – artisanal shaving brushes, handles

Safety Razors – safetyrazors.co.uk – good range of shaving products

Shave Lounge – shavelounge.co.uk – broad range of shaving products

Shaving Station – shavingstation.co.uk – good selection of artisanal soaps

Shaving Time Company – shavingtime.co.uk - good selection of artisanal soaps

The Strop Shop – strop-shop.co.uk – straight razors

The Traditional Shaving Company – traditionalshaving.co.uk – broad range of shaving products

Wickham – w-soap.co.uk – artisanal soaps, 5" puck; sold in the US as Huntlee

U.S.--

Above the Tie – abovethetie.com - premium stainless razors, shaving supplies

All Lathered Up - alllatheredup.weebly.com – good range of samples of various mainline shaving products

Al's Shaving Products – alsshaving.com - artisanal shaving creams, soaps, aftershaves

Appleton Barber Supply – tinyurl.com/7xy3j5u – inexpensive aftershaves, barber towels, etc.

BadgerBrush.net – badgerbrush.net – DIY supplies for brushes and razors, along with handcrafted brushes and razors

Barclay Crocker – barclaycrocker.com – preshaves, soaps, creams, aftershaves

Barrister & Mann - barristerandmann.com – artisanal soaps, aftershaves, etc.

Bathhouse Soapery – bathhousesoap.com – artisanal soaps, good aftershave

Best Grooming Tools - bestgroomingtools.com – broad range of shaving supplies

Blankety Blanks - tinyurl.com/rbwjd - artisanal brushes and DIY brushes

BM Vintage Shaving – bmvintageshaving.com – good range of shaving supplies

Bramble Berry – brambleberry.com – Soapmaking supplies, including DIY Melt & Pour Base for shaving soap

Brent's Brushes - brentmjohnson.net/brushes – artisanal shaving brushes

Brushguy.com – brushguy.com – artisanal shaving brushes

BullGoose Shaving Supplies – bullgooseshaving.com – artisanal soaps, horsehair brushes, and other shaving supplies

Catie's Bubbles – catiesbubbles.com – excellent artisanal soaps

Chiseled Face Groomatorium – chiseledface.com – artisanal soaps and aftershaves

Classic Shaving – classicshaving.com – excellent range of shaving supplies, including straight razors

Cold River Soap Works – coldriversoapworks.com – artisanal soaps

Crabtree & Evelyn - tinyurl.com/7n4xlgn – limited range of shaving supplies

Dapper Dragon – dapperdragon.com – artisanal shaving soaps

Dirty Bird Pottery – dirtybirdpottery.com – scuttles and brush warmers

eBarbershop – ebarbershop.com – barber supply, shaving products

eBay - tinyurl.com/2hj626 – link is for safety razors

Elite Razor – eliterazor.com – beautiful custom razors and brushes

Enchante Online - enchanteonline.com – home of Method Shaving, good range of products

Garry's Sample Shop – sampleshop.blogspot.com – samples of soaps, etc.

The Gentlemens Refinery – thegr.com – superb preshave, shaving creams, aftershaves

Ginger's Garden – tinyurl.com/85duy8w – Handmade "shaving-cream soap" that lathers abundantly, and also good aftershaves

The Golden Nib – thegoldennib.com – DIY supplies for brushes and razors

Green Mountain Soap - gmsoap.com – artisanal shaving soaps

The Handlebar Supply Company - thehandlebarsupply.com – excellent range of shaving products; has a brick-and-mortar store

Highland Mens Care – highlandmenscare.com – good range of shaving products

The Holy Black Trading Co. - theholyblack.com – artisanal soaps, aftershaves, brushes

Honeybee Soaps – honeybeesoaps.net – artisanal shaving soaps

Ian Tang's Shaving Workshop - tinyurl.com/3pxa52w – Frank Shaving brushes

iKon Razors – ikonrazors.com – very comfortable and very efficient high-quality razors—my current favorites are the iKon Shavecraft #101 and #102.

Kell's Original – kellsoriginal.com – artisan soaps

LA Shaving Soap Company - lashavingsoap.com – artisanal soaps, starter kit, premium stainless razor (made by Wolfman Razors)

Lee's Razors – leesrazors.com – excellent range of shaving stuff

Lijun Brush - tinyurl.com/8xcv7dn – Inexpensive shaving brushes

Maggard Razors – maggardrazors.com – good selection of artisanal soaps including their own, good line of their own DE razors, starter kits, full range of shaving supplies, many samples available; has a brick-and-mortar store

Mama Bear - mamabearssoaps.com – artisanal soaps

Men Essentials – menessentials.com – broad range of products

Mickey Lee Soapworks – mickeyleesoapworks.com – artisanal shaving soaps and aftershave milks. Drunken Goat and Bee Witched are well worth a try.

Mike's Natural Soaps - mikesnaturalsoaps.com – excellent (and very thirsty) artisanal shaving soaps

Mystic Water Soap for Men – mystic4men.com – artisanal soaps

Nancy Boy - nancyboy.com – excellent shaving creams and skin care

Penchetta Pen & Knife – penchetta.com - 480-575-0729 – Primarily custom and DIY brushes and razors, also shaving stuff

Phoenix Artisan Accoutrements – phoenixartisanaccoutrements.com - artisanal soaps and aftershaves, double-open-comb and other razors, broad range of shaving supplies

Q Brothers – qbrothers.com – the on-line shaving store of Merz Apothecary in Chicago, with its own brick-and-mortar store

QED – qedusa.com – good range of shaving products

Queen Charlotte Soaps, LLC - queencharlottesoaps.com – artisanal shaving soaps

Razor Blades and More – razorbladesandmore.com – broad range of shaving supplies

Razor Emporium – razoremporium.com – shaving supplies, secondhand razors, restoration services

Razor Plate – razorplate.com – razor restoration and replating services

Razors Direct – razorsdirect.com

Reef Point – reefpointsoaps.com – artisanal shaving soaps

Reliable Electroplating - reliableelectroplating.com – replating services

Retrorazor – retrorazor.com – good site for novice and aspiring DE shavers

Royal Shave – royalshave.com – excellent range of shaving products

Rubinov's Barber Supply - rubinovs.com – shaving products; also has a brick-and-mortar store in Phoenix AZ

Saint Charles Shave - saintcharlesshave.com – artisanal aftershaves, eau de toilettes, shaving soaps and creams.

Shannon's Soaps – shannonssoaps.com – artisanal shaving soaps and others

The Shave Den Shop – theshavedenshop.com – artisanal shaving soaps and creams, aftershaves, colognes, and the like. Extra menthol on request.

Shave Nation – shavenation.com – good range of products; also has videos

Shave Place – shaveplace.com and shaveinfo.com – good range of products, artisanal soap

Shave Revolution – shaverevolution.com – good selection of artisanal soaps, along with a range of other shaving stuff

Shave Select - shaveselect.com – good range of shaving supplies, instruction

The Shaver Shop – shavershop.com – custom shave sets, general shaving supplies

ShaveTools – shavetools.com – broad range of shaving products

ShavingStyle – shavingstyle.com – broad range of shaving products

Shoebox Shaveshop –shoeboxshaveshop.com – excellent range of products

Smallflower – smallflower.com/men - the on-line site of the brick-and-mortar Merz Apothecary in Chicago

Soap Commander – soapcommander.com – artisanal shaving soaps and aftershaves

Soap Smooth – soapsmooth.com – artisanal shaving soap; formerly Seifenglatt

Sport Shaving – sportshaving.com – restored razors and restoration and replating services

Stirling Soap Company - stirlingsoap.com – artisanal soaps with distinct fragrances, aftershaves

Straight Razor Designs – straightrazordesigns.com – excellent straight razors

Strop Shoppe – stropshoppe.com – Excellent artisanal shaving soaps made by a biochemist

The Superior Shave – thesuperiorshave.com – good range of shaving products

Superlather – superlather.com – good US source for European products

Through the Fire Fine Craft – ttffcraft.com – artisanal shaving soaps and aftershaves

Tiki Bar Soap – tikibarsoap.com – artisanal soaps

Vintage Blades LLC - vintagebladesllc.com - straight razors, DEs, and supplies

Weber Razors – weberrazors.com – at one time razors, now only handles

West Coast Razors – westcoastrazors.com – limited range of supplies, restored razors, restoration and replating services

West Coast Shaving – westcoastshaving.com – excellent range of products; has a brick-and-mortar store.

Western Razor – westernrazor.com - new razor maker

Whipped Dog – whippeddog.com – DIY and pre-made brushes, restored straight razors.

WhollyKaw – whollykaw.com – vegan artisanal soaps

Wolf Whiskers – wolfwhiskers.com – artisanal shaving brushes

[1] As an experiment, record for a while each time you are surprised, pleasantly or unpleasantly, by something. Each surprise is evidence that your expectations did not match by your experience. If the list is long, then the practice of making decisions based on expectations is clearly questionable.

[2] Dan Gilbert: TED talk on happiness: See tinyurl.com/l7ghu5s
TED talk on why we make bad decisions: See tinyurl.com/q5voa8k
A report of some of Gilbert's research: See tinyurl.com/llug2am

[3] *Getting to Yes*: Inexpensive used copies at tinyurl.com/kg78mx5

[4] *Managing Management Time*: Inexpensive used copies at tinyurl.com/n2ytsuy
See also his classic 1974 *Harvard Business Review* article "Who's Got the Monkey" at tinyurl.com/3eou7ua

[5] *Mindset*: See tinyurl.com/pdm5on2 – strongly recommended for parents

[6] *The Lantern Bearers*: tinyurl.com/m8fvfdw for full text—and read the entire essay. (You'll see why when you do.)

[7] Epicurus: See tinyurl.com/7kafxfj and (of course) the Wikipedia entry.

[8] Mihály Csíkszentmihályi: See tinyurl.com/a5f4s. Each person can find activities appropriate for him or her that will promote flow: rock climbing, painting or drawing, gardening, cooking, playing a musical instrument, and the like. Csíkszentmihályi defined the term in his studies and in the fascinating book that emerged from them, *Flow: The Psychology of Optimal Experience* (tinyurl.com/ywzrea for inexpensive copies).

[9] Sharpologist article "Shaving-Tool Innovation and the Weber Razor": See tinyurl.com/6u98nm8 – and see also a *Harvard Business Review* blog post (and also the comments) on Gillette strategy in India: tinyurl.com/bn77ohy

[10] Using a razor cartridge long after it has become dull leads to using too much pressure in an effort to get it to cut—and that's very hard on one's skin. Those who do use cartridges should not try to stretch the life of the cartridge. Instead, when the cartridge starts to feel dull, replace it. Gillette claims a cartridge will last 5 weeks; I would guess that for most the cartridge doesn't last much longer than two weeks. I suggest you test it: start using a cartridge, and once a week switch it out for one shave with a new cartridge. If the new one is not noticeably better, switch the old one back in and use it another week. At some point you'll notice that the new cartridge really does feel and work better. For example, suppose at the 4th test (four weeks in), you find the new cartridge provides a much better shave (enjoyment and result). So from then on, replace the cartridge after the 3rd week of use.

11 Tug-and-cut action of multiblade cartridge in close-up video: See tinyurl.com/o6b38gz Has good points on hydrating beard before shaving.

12 A skeptical take on "progress": See tinyurl.com/mmm7xol

13 Obsidian razor macrophotograph: See tinyurl.com/7uu93hm

14 Obsidian razor shave: See tinyurl.com/6mzcz9y and tinyurl.com/7j9nmcq

15 Miracle shaving device (the DE razor described using marketing-speak): See tinyurl.com/7r4qs3n

16 Barber towels: See tinyurl.com/pw83bev Surgical huck towels also work well and are available from Amazon. Also, check Ikea guest towels.

17 Skin care: See tinyurl.com/2pttmv

18 Gillette statement of cartridge life: See tinyurl.com/72dqnjk

19 Joanna Field/Marion Milner secondhand copies: For *A Life of One's Own*, see tinyurl.com/mjdss3b and for *On Not Being Able to Paint*, see tinyurl.com/ltbhkga

20 Ellen J. Langer describes well mindfulness and its benefits in her book *Mindfulness*. See tinyurl.com/lxmvc4s for inexpensive secondhand copies.

21 Prefer electric shock to sitting alone with one's thoughts: See tinyurl.com/n7wntr5 for press release; tinyurl.com/og5gmo7 for news story. See also tinyurl.com/ncaecv4

22 My recipe for Breakfast Bites: See tinyurl.com/o4c8oom

23 Rituals do work: See tinyurl.com/lrd2f2z

24 Cognitive dissonance: See tinyurl.com/boyuz

25 Ben Franklin was familiar with the effect if not the term. He decided to win over an opponent in the Pennsylvania state legislature:

> I did not ... aim at gaining his favour by paying any servile respect to him but, after some time, took this other method. Having heard that he had in his library a certain very scarce and curious book I wrote a note to him expressing my desire of perusing that book and requesting he would do me the favour of lending it to me for a few days. He sent it immediately and I returned it in about a week with another note expressing strongly my sense of the favour. When we next met in the House he spoke to me (which he had never done before), and with great civility; and he ever after manifested a readiness to serve me on all occasions, so that we became great friends and our friendship continued to his death. This is another instance of the truth of an old maxim I had learned, which says, "He that has once done you a kindness will be more ready to do you another than he whom you yourself has obliged."

In terms of modern psychology, the opponent observed himself doing a favor for Franklin, a favor that Franklin framed as a great favor, and reduced his cognitive dissonance by deciding that he must like Franklin after all.

[26] Pride—feeling self-worth and self-respect—increases a person's support of the common good: See tinyurl.com/ozkb93t

[27] Life changes resulting from new self-regard: See tinyurl.com/9yuyrev

[28] Other personal-renewal notes: See tinyurl.com/7qko4ja and tinyurl.com/78y3z6f

[29] Products that require effort and skill help one regain the locus of control: See tinyurl.com/n9mgb4l

[30] Locus of control: See tinyurl.com/p4ea939

[31] The pleasures of preparing for a party: See tinyurl.com/mzvwg8t

[32] See, for example, the posts on baking, illustrated with step-by-step photos, at KorenaInTheKitchen.com.

[33] The Ikea effect: See tinyurl.com/pj2wy8n

[34] Health benefits of daily shave: See tinyurl.com/oo7y3ta

[35] William James on Habit: See tinyurl.com/lt53yhm

[36] "Worth" as a function of wealth: The idea that the "worth" of something is relative to a person's ability to pay is seen clearly in the "day-fine" idea used in Scandinavian countries. (See tinyurl.com/p2zewk7) Fines are not a fixed amount but are based on earnings. Thus a (highly paid) Nokia executive in Finland was fined $103,000 for going 45mph in a 30mph zone. The fine for a day laborer for the same offense would be more on the order of $150. The two fines are equal, however, in terms of the offender's ability to pay. Thus a razor that appeals equally to two men may be worth its price to one and not to the other, depending on their financial circumstances.

[37] Kamasori razors: See tinyurl.com/7mekms5

[38] Gillette did not invent safety razor: See tinyurl.com/kwrcgzp

[39] Links for used straight razors:
Edson Razors: See tinyurl.com/kubaeqj
Gemstone Customs: See tinyurl.com/kf5r7ow
Maggard Razors: See tinyurl.com/lzw65qm
Straight Razor Place classifieds: See tinyurl.com/mz6sh34
Strazors.com
WhippedDog.com

[40] *The Art of the Straight-Razor Shave*: See tinyurl.com/ys9y5h (PDF) and tinyurl.com/6ptzfr9 (book)

[41] *Straight Razor Shaving*: See tinyurl.com/7w7pz9s (PDF) and see also the discussion in this thread: tinyurl.com/83b8h99

[42] Shavette: For a good introduction to the shavette, see tinyurl.com/kjx4q9s

[43] Wilkinson technology: See tinyurl.com/qgdc3x8

[44] Intellectual-property law: See "How Intellectual Property Destroyed Men's Shaving" at tinyurl.com/c7dgbte

[45] Gillette strategy in India: tinyurl.com/bn77ohy

[46] *Changing for Good*: See tinyurl.com/cslde8e

[47] For my thoughts on the motivation that enables people to enjoy engaging in learning, where difficulties, awkwardness, and a general sense of cluelessness abound, see tinyurl.com/q4zltgw

[48] Shy/bold in animals: See tinyurl.com/l4toh6t

[49] Brain benefit of willingness to explore: See tinyurl.com/m9layv2

[50] Explorer/settler brain chemistry: See tinyurl.com/cdlofqv

[51] Report on revisiting Mach 3: See tinyurl.com/kwayf8o

[52] "What was I thinking?": See tinyurl.com/2a4rm3

[53] Returning to cartridges: See tinyurl.com/7mjs8ec

[54] Women using DE razors: See www.reddit.com/r/ladyshavers

[55] Cultural ebb and flow of body shaving: See tinyurl.com/nkhlv5n

[56] eBay safety razors: See tinyurl.com/qbytwoj

[57] For a wonderful account of the first-time experience, read what brderj and DEsquire say: See tinyurl.com/2aln4w

[58] Awareness of difference the Edwin Jagger made: See tinyurl.com/7grj9ks

[59] Surprises along the way: See this thread: tinyurl.com/k8wuxcg

[60] *Decision Traps* - For inexpensive secondhand copies: See tinyurl.com/ogt26cp Russo and Schoemaker later wrote another book, which seems to be a substantial revision and expansion of *Decision Traps*, with a somewhat pointed subtitle: *Winning Decisions: Getting It Right the First Time*. See tinyurl.com/laegvrr for inexpensive secondhand copies. Both books are excellent and well worth reading if you make decisions important to you.

[61] *Predictably Irrational*: secondhand copies: See tinyurl.com/ckydhpm

[62] Making a brush: See tinyurl.com/l2zay3r

[63] Restoring old brush: A series showing one brush restoration:
Part 1: See tinyurl.com/7lr7xd3
Part 2: See tinyurl.com/6q9wrvb
Part 3: See tinyurl.com/6tf3jy5

[64] Wire-bending tool: See tinyurl.com/4455xy7

[65] Videos by Mantic59: See youtube.com/user/mantic59

[66] Videos by geofatboy: See youtube.com/user/geofatboy

[67] Videos by Freedberg: See youtube.com/user/mfreedberg

[68] Videos by betelgeux (theshockwav): See tinyurl.com/6tqdmyt

[69] Slant solving neck problems: See tinyurl.com/ku5kbtv

[70] Mantic59's Advanced Shaving Techniques video: See tinyurl.com/2tzyeu

[71] Interactive beard-map diagram: See tinyurl.com/7waok6b

[72] Luca Turn and fragrances: See tinyurl.com/kja45sw and also tinyurl.com/maruayz Both books highly recommended.

[73] Photosensitivity: See tinyurl.com/7nnvgqw

[74] Potentially harmful cosmetic ingredients: See tinyurl.com/25jy9rq and tinyurl.com/6teu7x8 for two lists; a search for "harmful cosmetics ingredients" will produce a plethora of lists—use your own judgment to determine the reliability of any particular list. Note also that skin types vary considerably, including in how they react to cosmetics.

[75] Comment on difference between good and mediocre shaving soap: See tinyurl.com/p2oracz and tinyurl.com/q6hjlgd

[76] Hair conditioners: See tinyurl.com/ytfhfn

[77] Why to use a shower filter: See tinyurl.com/qgtprg7

[78] Plated brass shower filter: See tinyurl.com/obd5ofz

[79] High-velocity aerating low-flow showerhead: See tinyurl.com/mv7s6m2

[80] Ach. Brito Glyce Lime Glycerin soap: See tinyurl.com/pz2ezyw

[81] Pre-shave soaps article: See tinyurl.com/7amxgov

[82] Emu oil therapeutic benefits: See tinyurl.com/p2olx5r

[83] 100% glycerin: See tinyurl.com/7b8qe6p

[84] Pre-shave oil recipes: See thread at tinyurl.com/cx9czp2

[85] indiexsunrise shave oil recipe: See tinyurl.com/ceogrnq

[86] Softens the beard: What happens to the whisker in the presence of lather, water, and moist heat is complex, with "soften" being the common colloquial shorthand for the results of the process; see tinyurl.com/7jzfs2l I will use the word "soften" to describe how the beard becomes more amenable to cutting even if at a technical and microscope level the word is not accurate.

[87] Hydrosol: Herbal distillates are aqueous solutions or colloidal suspensions of essential oils usually obtained by steam distillation from aromatic plants or herbs. They are used as flavorings, in medicine and skin care. Herbal distillates go by many names: hydrosols, floral waters, hydrolates, herbal waters, toilet waters, aqua vitae, essential water. See tinyurl.com/829uony

[88] Barbasol history and how it paid for an island: See tinyurl.com/lmttk36

[89] Loading brush and working up lather in 40 seconds: See tinyurl.com/pl9q2x3 Experiment with working the lather into the beard for a longer time before the first pass, especially if you've not done a pre-shave beard wash.

[90] Somewhat drier: See tinyurl.com/23cop2

[91] Good brushless shaving creams: See tinyurl.com/lj2wdzt

[92] Synthetic bristles: See tinyurl.com/22r92w
Edwin Jagger synthetic brushes: See tinyurl.com/oj6ourc
Mühle synthetic brushes: See tinyurl.com/6uaqxwp

[93] Soft brush quickly making good lather: See tinyurl.com/mm6okdb

[94] Developments in synthetic brushes: See the excellent Sharpologist article at tinyurl.com/k44qvzb, which has links to more information.

[95] Horsehair brush anthrax scare: See tinyurl.com/26hwnp8

[96] Omega boar family: See tinyurl.com/7ca4leq

[97] Guide to boar brushes: See tinyurl.com/28kp67r

[98] Several grades: See tinyurl.com/23vwkc

[99] Made by hand: See tinyurl.com/2y4wev

[100] Clear differences: See tinyurl.com/yow8zh

[101] Simpson brushes: See tinyurl.com/ndeoyq9 and tinyurl.com/n6hcq3n

[102] Gary Young on the Wee Scot: See tinyurl.com/6roacgv

[103] Rod Neep artisanal shaving brushes: See tinyurl.com/72j3fc4

[104] Bruce Everiss review of New Forest brushes: See tinyurl.com/3reovy9

[105] Rooney brushes: See tinyurl.com/ncnfna4 and tinyurl.com/obwfqu4

[106] Emilion, Victorian, and Thäter with hooked tips: See tinyurl.com/7b6v3me

[107] Gary Young on hooked bristles: See tinyurl.com/7p4vyrv

[108] Andrew's close-up photos of hooked tips: See tinyurl.com/7tpr4p9

[109] Simpson measurements: See tinyurl.com/24kuln

[110] Omega brushes: See tinyurl.com/oblfxx7

[111] Omega brush measurements: See tinyurl.com/2c6pad

[112] Kent brushes: See tinyurl.com/jvme969 - The BK4 is the best all-round size.

[113] Bruce Everiss review of Morris & Forndran brushes: See tinyurl.com/3rxewcj

[114] Wooden-handled brushes: See tinyurl.com/22prko

[115] Shaving brush innovations: See tinyurl.com/22xrfs

[116] Leisureguy 10-second-brush-loading video: See tinyurl.com/mm6okdb

[117] Mühle travel brush: See tinyurl.com/mtl8y4p

[118] Shaving bags: For Eagle Creek, see tinyurl.com/oojm9gs; for eBags, see tinyurl.com/oht654p

[119] Hair shaft: See tinyurl.com/3elobn and photos at tinyurl.com/lbnyflz

[120] Stand no help in drying brush: See tinyurl.com/mz43y37 for a convincing demonstration, and photos at tinyurl.com/k43xrdn

[121] Brush cleaning: See tinyurl.com/yvmfr6

[122] Gold Dachs Shaving Brush cleaner: See tinyurl.com/3yrlw7p

[123] M.A.C. brush cleaner: See tinyurl.com/8y8trf9

[124] Moss Scuttle: See tinyurl.com/6pw9gc

[125] Georgetown Pottery: See tinyurl.com/74h43ux

[126] Dirty Bird Pottery: See tinyurl.com/3s2twxf

[127] Rival Little Dipper lathering bowl: See tinyurl.com/7qfzjzq

[128] Benefits of cold-water shave: See redd.it/1hbklv, redd.it/2rnz3n, and redd.it/2rs260

[129] Testing water hardness: See tinyurl.com/qabs6y8 for more information.

[130] Improvement from softening water with citric acid: See tinyurl.com/n7lf2q4 and tinyurl.com/p2oracz and tinyurl.com/na43jde

[131] Quality of good shaving soap: See tinyurl.com/mqp8ydn

[132] Water softener technology and options: See tinyurl.com/o4sfrvd

[133] Surprising improvement from distilled water: See tinyurl.com/79ab5e6

[134] Hard-water regions: See tinyurl.com/6qfu8bu

[135] Sunbeam Hot Shot: See tinyurl.com/yqxzng

[136] Pump bottle for distilled water: See tinyurl.com/kc624es

[137] Interview with Al Raz, who makes Al's Shaving cream: See tinyurl.com/la4wnp3

[138] J.M. Fraser's shaving cream: See tinyurl.com/ma5zhlh

[139] High praise: See tinyurl.com/2zp35v

[140] Nancy Boy shaving cream: See tinyurl.com/6r82q4o

[141] An illustrated guide: See tinyurl.com/29zlku

[142] Bruce Everiss review of Otoko soap: See tinyurl.com/3epaps4 and for a more detailed review and a description of how the soap is special, see tinyurl.com/ltzmfev

[143] Essence of Scotland shaving soaps: available from The Gentleman's Groom Room (UK) and Razor Emporium (US).

[144] Bramble Berry melt-and-pour shaving soap base: See tinyurl.com/7zbuxee
Also a Wicked_Edge thread: See tinyurl.com/7cakwdw
Another recipe, at About.com: See tinyurl.com/lxpw7w

[145] More information: See tinyurl.com/2cbkvo

[146] This excellent tutorial: See tinyurl.com/pylqk

[147] Video of loading and lathering MWF: See tinyurl.com/mm6okdb

[148] Another video, loading and lathering Col. Conk: See tinyurl.com/ndj9ahj In this video you'll see my familial tremor—one reason (in addition to cost and learning new skills and risk) that I don't shave with a straight razor.

[149] Photos of the part of the collection that's in my bathroom: See tinyurl.com/ocumnx7 You'll note that the shelves of soap are pretty close together.

[150] To make a shaving stick from any glycerin-based shaving soap: (This will *not* work with triple-milled soaps.) Get a shaving stick container (e.g., from tinyurl.com/cc8ggc). Put the glycerin soap in a Pyrex measuring cup, and put that in a pan of hot water. Heat the pan of water to 150ºF, then turn off the burner and wait for the soap to melt. You may have to reheat the water, but don't go over 150ºF. While waiting for the soap to melt, turn the pusher of the container so that it's at the bottom. Do not lubricate the container—and in particular, do **not** use silicone grease—it will waterproof your brush and kill the lather. When the soap has melted, pour it into the container and let it cool. Voilà! Your own shaving stick. If it does not advance easily out of the container, put it briefly in the freezer, then try again.

[151] Superlather video: See tinyurl.com/2a2z7t

[152] StraightRazorPlace superlather tutorial: See tinyurl.com/7jqzm4u

[153] Gillette myth of giving away razors to sell blades: See tinyurl.com/3cjbgtj

[154] Different shavers respond differently to the same brand of blade: See tinyurl.com/mrl6w64

[155] Blade reviews with photos: See tinyurl.com/lpz5lf

[156] Feather Blade Safe: See tinyurl.com/2ddz2k

[157] Pacific Handy Cutters blade bank: See tinyurl.com/7vtayuz

[158] If you're willing to undertake learning to use a straight razor, check out StraightRazorPlace.com and also *The Art of the Straight-Razor Shave,* by Chris Moss—see tinyurl.com/2c4zuz for the book, tinyurl.com/ys9y5h for PDF—and the introduction to straight-razor shaving by Larry of WhippedDog.com—see tinyurl.com/7w7pz9s

For straight razors—sharpened, honed, and ready to shave—and accessories and advice, see Straight Razor Designs (see vendor list above).

For an excellent introduction to straights (with diagrams), see tinyurl.com/ybwjkt6 at StraightRazorPlace.com.

[159] Three types of razors: tinyurl.com/yqxeah

[160] Three-piece razors use two different thread pitches: 10-32 (US) and M5x.8 (Metric). If the handle is tapped to M5, practically any head will work with it, but this may not be true when trying to use a 10-32 handle (such as used on

all vintage Gillettes) on an M5 head. The pitches are very similar, but M5 is ever so slightly larger. However, not all manufacturers maintain close tolerances on their threads, so sometimes a handle from one razor will not fit the head from another. Parker razor threading is often incompatible with other makes: I could not use a Stealth handle with a Parker 24C head, although the 24C handle fits the 24C head just fine. (Stealth razors are machined with very close tolerances, so the problem is not due to the Stealth.) It seems that Parker's threading has drifted somewhat from the standard threading. I have not encountered the problem with other brands.

161 Razor handles from Pens of the Forest: See tinyurl.com/7w4tgy5

162 Edwin Jagger razor head: See tinyurl.com/cfsfcog

163 Slant Bar history: See tinyurl.com/6obtzkz

164 First slant patent: See tinyurl.com/mfdwfmf

165 Slant works well: See tinyurl.com/8yldz4t

166 Gillette slide: See tinyurl.com/2tzyeu

167 Mandolines: Search Amazon on "mandoline"; most have a slanted blade.

168 Why the burst of activity in slants: See tinyurl.com/k5kvyjm

169 Pot metal: See tinyurl.com/7v5ukj

170 Sintering : See tinyurl.com/a3n5s

171 Bruce Everiss and the three razor shave: See (in sequence) tinyurl.com/7woayos and tinyurl.com/7ner5zw and tinyurl.com/2fhcsne

172 Above the Tie's 3-part precision machine: See tinyurl.com/nz6yxdp for my musings on how they manage this.

173 Edwin Jagger razors: See tinyurl.com/kpuhn8j

174 Inadvertent blind comparison: See tinyurl.com/7grj9ks

175 Loading an iKon slant video: See tinyurl.com/kne9bzb

176 Close-up of a vintage Walbusch: See tinyurl.com/owq3ygg The Walbusch looks somewhat different from the #102, but that is because the Walbusch has a rectangular rather than slanted silhouette: extra material at one end of the cap to make the cap's top horizontal rather than slanted, and extra material at the other end of the base to make the base's bottom horizontal rather than slanted. If you mentally strip off the extraneous (non-functional) material, you get the same shape as the #102.

177 Loading Progress: See tinyurl.com/24cgdb

178 This advice (Futur): See tinyurl.com/2dsrxe

179 Vision user's manual: See tinyurl.com/2b4h5t; general instructions for care of Merkur razors: See tinyurl.com/pz8d2ko

[180] Common Gillette razors: See tinyurl.com/2zq4yh
Also see these Super Speeds: tinyurl.com/393qsb6

[181] Dates of Gillette razors: See gillettedatecodes.com

[182] Fat Boy disassembly instructions: See tinyurl.com/3dy8k6

[183] Lady Gillette photos: See tinyurl.com/3m5ldg

[184] Bruce Everiss review of Eclipse Red Ring: See tinyurl.com/3orgqps

[185] Schick Injector: See tinyurl.com/ygf3mn

[186] GEM Heavy Flat-Top: See tinyurl.com/26mh3z

[187] Mongoose Razor: See facebook.com/MongooseRazors

[188] Schick various models: See tinyurl.com/27vor9

[189] Pella single-edged blades: See tinyurl.com/k6ld8es

[190] Art of Manliness on restoring razors: See tinyurl.com/25cf8zq

[191] Ultrasonic cleaning: See tinyurl.com/dkm7hx

[192] Bleached Fat Boy: Post at tinyurl.com/n3drzl5; photo at tinyurl.com/lx6snxx

[193] Maas metal polish: See tinyurl.com/mqb8ugt

[194] Shadow-erasing building design: See tinyurl.com/lddh9b2

[195] Holding the tip: See tinyurl.com/2955zd

[196] Pointed out angle: See tinyurl.com/yuz6p4

[197] Tiny travel razor: See tinyurl.com/yuuwxn

[198] A similar approach: See tinyurl.com/29sstk

[199] The basic 4-pass method: See tinyurl.com/2akgaq

[200] Advanced shaving techniques: See tinyurl.com/2y9ovh

[201] Hydrolast Finishing Balm: See tinyurl.com/3ktec2

[202] Total Shaving Solution: See www.totalshave.com

[203] All Natural Shaving Oil: See pacificshaving.com

[204] Kinexium ST Shaving Oil: See tinyurl.com/llulsxl

[205] Gessato Pre-Shave Oil: See tinyurl.com/lv2n57l

[206] Non-comedogenic chart: See tinyurl.com/555esn and tinyurl.com/q26u2pp

[207] Natural 1 oz bottle: See tinyurl.com/ourcwvz

[208] Cobalt blue 1 oz bottle: See tinyurl.com/nzuyq48

[209] First Method video: See tinyurl.com/4llmby

[210] Method shaving supplies: See tinyurl.com/3ktec2

[211] Wikipedia article on alum: See tinyurl.com/3dfw2qz

[212] One woman notes: See tinyurl.com/yqx6vk

[213] Aluminum not hazardous: See tinyurl.com/otyolw and also this PDF: tinyurl.com/7vjoevx

[214] Cheapest price I've found for My Nik Is Sealed: See tinyurl.com/7zhg3op

[215] Proraso Styptic Gel: See tinyurl.com/7ecx6vs

216 KDS Lab Liquid Styptic: See tinyurl.com/mjxcl6u

217 Lengthy review: See tinyurl.com/35ekgm

218 Mantic59 video on aftershaves: See tinyurl.com/3f9vmtx

219 Skin problems with aftershave: See tinyurl.com/nmrcn3

220 Variety of fragrances: See tinyurl.com/y8kw3o

221 Thayers Aftershave: See tinyurl.com/2c3vnd

222 The story of bay rum: See tinyurl.com/bayrum

223 Booster aftershaves: See tinyurl.com/qfo6ysa

224 Proraso pre- and post-shave cream: See tinyurl.com/k3lafun

225 Learning Herbs aftershave recipe: See tinyurl.com/pftx4s9
   Aftershave recipes at Straight Razor Place: See tinyurl.com/og3rkkx
   And a bonus bay-rum aftershave recipe: See tinyurl.com/nzwomvo

226 HTGAM Bay Rum Butter: See tinyurl.com/m5d6nhz

227 DIY witch-hazel-based aftershave: See tinyurl.com/pq4h2hr

228 *The Emperor of Scent*: For inexpensive copies, see tinyurl.com/6red2p7

229 Wikipedia perfume article: See tinyurl.com/hmrda

230 Sulfur-based compounds: See tinyurl.com/lfmgpjo

231 Acne.org: See www.acne.org See also these posts for additional tips that may
   be of help: tinyurl.com/6etgup and tinyurl.com/nstb5mk

232 Good shaving towels: Do a search on "barber towels" or "bar towels" or
   "surgical towels" (See ebay.com/bhp/barber-towel, Appleton Barber Supply
   at tinyurl.com/pw83bev, and tinyurl.com/pw667gq).

233 Low comedogenicity: See tinyurl.com/crl2u4y

234 Wicked_Edge acne reference post: See tinyurl.com/84lb6gs

235 Mayo Clinic articles: See tinyurl.com/oes3akb

236 *Anticancer: A New Way of Life*: See tinyurl.com/rdhruc

237 Findings on sugar: See tinyurl.com/3g8y22z for informative article in *NY
   Times* and tinyurl.com/3fp83sb for an extremely informative talk.

238 Low-carb, high-fat diet: See tinyurl.com/jwu3mwx for an example of how it
   can help; for an introduction to a low-carb, high fat diet see
   www.dietdoctor.com/lchf and also tinyurl.com/nukuldr; in these diets, you
   might want to skip the dairy if you are using the diet to minimize acne. For
   more information, including why doctors got it wrong, see
   tinyurl.com/kbbtx7w

239 Themba's technique: See the threads at tinyurl.com/yr5lz6 and
   tinyurl.com/5qbqpj (scroll down at both links)

240 Innomed Lice Comb: Easily found with a Google search

241 Moore Unique Razor Bump Tool: See tinyurl.com/mqgj7aa

242 Bump Fighter Razor: See tinyurl.com/59lm8f

243 Barbicide: tinyurl.com/4pvmou

244 Bump Fighter: See tinyurl.com/bvxyop5

Bump Patrol: See tinyurl.com/3rt6hu

Dermagen Skin Revival System: See dermagen.info

Elicina Biological Treatment: See elicina.us

Follique treatment: See follicareresearch.com/Men.php

High Time Bump Stopper Products: See tinyurl.com/d3ouatk

Moore Unique Products: See tinyurl.com/blwgclg

Impeccable Aftershave: See tinyurl.com/3uugej

Prince Reigns Gel: See tinyurl.com/4buq27

Smart Shave Products: See smartshave.com

Tend Skin: See tendskin.com

245 Homemade version of Tend Skin: See tinyurl.com/p32ru4r

246 Eczema from shampoo: See tinyurl.com/lpxygf

247 Razor-blade collection: See tinyurl.com/kce3pd3

248 Storage of soaps: For nice shelves, check out www.zipcabs.com

249 Brush restoration:

Part 1 – Photo at tinyurl.com/7449ff8, thread at tinyurl.com/7lr7xd3

Part 2 – Photo at tinyurl.com/88h98eu, thread at tinyurl.com/6q9wrvb

Part 3 – Photo at tinyurl.com/7q5ez7h, thread at tinyurl.com/6tf3jy5

250 Interactive diagram: See tinyurl.com/7waok6b

251 "Exploring the Science of Shaving": See tinyurl.com/cb92ae

252 Write-up on MSNBC: See tinyurl.com/48evm

253 Mantic59 shaving videos: See youtube.com/user/mantic59

254 Geofatboy shaving videos: See youtube.com/user/geofatboy

255 Michael Freedberg has a series of four instructive video tutorials. Scroll down at youtube.com/user/mfreedberg.

256 If you use Reddit, install the Reddit Enhancements Suite (free), which greatly improves the experience. See redditenhancementsuite.com

257 For details on the banning incident, see tinyurl.com/ot72nfz

For insight into the mindset, see tinyurl.com/ys2j6o

258 A comprehensive list: See tinyurl.com/2gwu8c